Discovering the Narrow Path

Also by N. Graham Standish
From Westminster John Knox Press

Paradoxes for Living: Cultivating Faith in Confusing Times

Discovering the Narrow Path

A Guide to Spiritual Balance

N. Graham Standish

Westminster John Knox Press
LOUISVILLE • LONDON

Scripture quotations, unless otherwise indicated, are from the New Revised Standard Version of the Bible, copyright © 1989 by the Division of Christian Education of the National Council of the Churches of Christ in the U.S.A. and are used by permission.

Book design by Sharon Adams
Cover design by Mark Abrams
Cover photograph courtesy of Cameron Davidson/Getty Images

First edition
Published by Westminster John Knox Press
Louisville, Kentucky

This book is printed on acid-free paper that meets the American National Standards Institute Z39.48 standard. ♾

PRINTED IN THE UNITED STATES OF AMERICA

02 03 04 05 06 07 08 09 10 11 — 10 9 8 7 6 5 4 3 2 1

Library of Congress Cataloging-in-Publication Data
Standish, N. Graham, date
    Discovering the narrow path : a guide to spiritual balance / by N. Graham Standish.
        p. cm.
    Includes bibliographical references (p.).
    ISBN 0-664-22451-2 (alk. paper)
    1. Spiritual life—Christianity. I. Title.

    BV4501.3 .S73 2002
    248.4—dc21   2002023000

To my wife, Diane,
who has guided me along my narrow path

Contents

Introduction

We live in times of imbalance. I don't know if the human race has ever lived in balanced times. In fact, I'm pretty sure that we never have. Throughout human history, we have shown a remarkable ability to swing one way or the other on the scales of living. Sometimes the imbalance threatens to break down civilization, as it did during the Dark Ages and World War II; at other times, the imbalance is much milder. The fact remains, though, that humans have never lived in balanced times.

The question we must ask is whether God wants us to live this way. Does God want our lives to lack balance? Each age and culture has its own form of imbalance. In today's North American culture, our imbalance has to do with excess. If you look at the typical complaints people have about their lives, they reveal how Americans do "too much."

For example, stress may be the number one problem in American life today. In medical studies, psychological reports, newspapers, magazines, and television, we constantly hear that stress is ripping people's lives apart. Stress is a result of trying to do and have "too much." People work too many hours. They spend too much time shuttling their kids back and forth to this activity and that. They do too much in their leisure time, going to the movies, sporting events, parties, and all sorts of other activities. They spend too much money on too many things.

The ironic side of stress is that instead of seeing the problem as arising out of excess, we think it arises out of doing or having "too little" and "not enough." Marriages rip apart because couples spend too little time together. People all over the country complain that they don't have enough time.

The experts recommend that we spend more time meditating, exercising, and participating in leisure activities. The problem is that our lives are still not balanced because the experts are suggesting that we *do more* to reduce the stress that comes from *doing too much.*

Jeremy Rifkin, a radio commentator, hit the nail on the head when he said,

> Fact: We are creating every kind of efficient technology imaginable to secure more valuable time for ourselves in this new e-commerce society. Fact: It's not working. We feel like we have far less time available to us than any other humans in history. That's because the great proliferation of labor and time-saving technologies and services only increases the diversity, pace, and flow of activity all around us. No wonder we're all increasingly time deprived.[1]

We are time deprived because, although we keep developing new technologies that give us more time, we also create more activities that rob us of time. The problem isn't so much that we need to teach people to meditate and exercise, although these are good things and can help tremendously. The problem is that even these things can be overdone. For example, the spirituality movement of today suggests that people deal with stress and imbalance by spending more time in contemplation and meditation. Unfortunately, not everyone has the inclination or temperament for such introverted activities. As a practitioner of contemplative prayer, I am intimate with the benefits it can bring, yet it is still not the answer to all our troubles. The problem is not just that we are not spending enough of our limited time in spiritual activities; it is more basic than that.

Christians today need to question how they are living their lives. What are they serving: God or something else? Is the problem really that we do not have enough time, that we don't devote enough time to spiritual matters, or is it deeper than this? Is it that we are living lives that have diverged from the narrow path God has set for us?

The Christian faith calls on us to live a radically different kind of life: a life of balance with Christ as the balancing fulcrum. It calls on us to question and reject the Western kind of life that is rooted in stimulation and activity, and instead to live a life that is rooted in God and God's will for us. This is the life lived on the narrow path.

This book is an exploration of that different kind of life God seeks for us. It explores a way of life that is practical, pragmatic, and effective, but that is so because it is rooted in the values of God's world—God's kingdom—and not those of the world. It explores the narrow path all Christians are called to walk, but that so many ignore in their pursuit of the world's paths. It explores the Christian life that calls us to make choices, prioritize, and put at the center those things that should be at our center. This book is, ultimately, an exploration of the kind of life that leads to a commitment to Christ, compassion for others and ourselves, and communion with God.

In the following pages, we will look at how we can resist the siren calls of our culture, our desires, and our need for easy answers that seduce us to live unbalanced lives, so that we can resist the lure of the promises that the extremes make. We will look at how to resist the lure of those who would tell us that their way is *the* right way. While it is impossible to look at all the ways we become unbalanced in modern life, there are certain topics that Christians need to consider. These are topics such as what the narrow path is that leads to greater balance. What we can learn from the spiritual masters and mystics of the past who understood how to live more balanced lives. How to balance our lives more in the present. How forming a Trinitarian faith and spirituality can lead us to a better understanding of what God wants for us. How we can can become more whole, holy, and healthy in our faith and spirituality. How we can serve God better on the narrow path. How we can make sense of the competing beliefs that pull us in different directions.

As you read this book, it will help guide you on your journey to find God's path. You will not find easy answers in this book because easy answers give us a false clarity about life, and therefore a false security. The path of easy answers is the path that the many false prophets of our culture will gladly lead you on. Instead, this book will give you an invitation to walk the narrow path that is difficult but that leads to God's love and grace. It will help guide you as you walk the confusing and conflicting path that Christ sets for us.

Finally, what you will find as we look at this path is that it is a path of integration. It is a path that attempts to wade through and integrate in a meaningful way the many different and competing perspectives and beliefs that are held by Christians. The way we will do this is by looking at the teachings of the Christian mystics and spiritual masters. These are the people who did more than just speculate about what the Christian life is all about. They lived their lives in a way that transformed the world, or more accurately, that allowed God to transform the world through them. Although you will have a better understanding of who they were after reading chapter 2, for now suffice it to say there have been mystics in every denomination and movement of Christianity since the beginning. The mystics are people who simply love God, and because they do, God's love and grace flow through them. These people have taken the teachings of Christ and lived them practically and pragmatically in their lives. They are people we too often forget today in our zeal to gain clearer theological and biblical understanding.

I invite you to read this book spiritually in a way that allows God to speak to you through the readings. Spiritual reading is a way of reading that is prayerful and more meditative. If you would like guidance on how to do this, I invite you to turn to Appendix A, where you will find a guide to reading the book spiritually. Also, you will find reflection questions at the end of each chapter to help you prayerfully consider what you have read. If you are interested in using this book as part of a study group, in Appendix B you will find a study guide. This guide will give you suggestions on how to start a study group, as well as weekly exercises, prayers, and discussion questions to be used in the group. I hope you will find these aids helpful as you explore the narrow path.

Chapter 1

Discovering the Narrow Path

*D*espite the way many Christians portray it, Christianity is a very difficult faith to live on a daily level. How can it not be? In the world there are over two billion Christians, all adhering to different traditions, being raised in different contexts, and bringing different perspectives to their spiritual quest. How do we tell which tradition and approach is the one that truly leads to God?

As one moves throughout the world, one encounters all kinds of approaches and practices of faith. Among those of us who have been raised in North American Christian culture, there is a tendency to see Christians as being one of two kinds: Protestant or Roman Catholic. While we tend to see Protestants as being cut from the same basic cloth, we also tend to see them as expressing this Protestant faith in a variety of forms: Presbyterian, Episcopalian, Methodist, Baptist, Reformed, Disciples of Christ, United Church of Christ, Assemblies of God, Mennonite, nondenominational, and so forth. Right or wrong, the tendency is to see them as all being shoots off the same Protestant branch.

In fact, Christianity has much more breadth than this. As we move throughout the world, we discover the ranks of those who call themselves Christian grow much greater. These include Eastern Orthodox, Armenian, Coptic, Mar Thoma, and so many other expressions of the Christian faith. All bring their own unique perspectives to the practice of Christian faith, and in many ways each believes that they hold and share the true approach, practice, and perspective toward Christian faith. Which one is right? Which ones are wrong?

It is precisely this depth and breadth of Christian practice and belief that makes Christian faith difficult. A new wrinkle added to the struggle of faith in recent years is an increasing emphasis on individual perspectives and growth that have arisen due to the nondenominational, charismatic, and pentecostal movements. In effect, throughout Christianity there is a growing, rather than shrinking, sense of confusion among Christians as to what is right and what is wrong when it comes to the essentials of Christian belief, faith, practice, and action.

The effect of all this is that it leaves Christians wondering what is the true way to God. It leaves us constantly feeling as though *other* Christians have it all worked out so well. These Christians are absolutely certain that they know what path leads to God, they are absolutely certain that they are on that path, and they are absolutely certain that all others are on the wrong one. How many times have we listened to someone from a different Christian perspective tell us—blatantly or subtly—that he or she is among the true Christians while we are not?

I remember a very passionate discussion with a man quite a few years ago (a man who has since gone on to be ordained as a Roman Catholic priest) who insisted that the Roman Catholic tradition was the only legitimate path to God. We were sitting in the stands watching a sporting event, and our topic changed from sports to religion. We discussed abortion, Communion, baptism, belief, faith, and prayer. In the midst of our conversation, the man insisted that if a person did not follow the Roman Catholic tradition, then he or she was not following the true path to God. I don't remember the exact words he used, but the gist of his argument was that other Christian traditions were really just shadows of the Roman Catholic faith. How could he be so certain? How could he be so confident? Do only Roman Catholics get to heaven?

Years later, I sat at a dinner table with a group of Pentecostals who exchanged stories of how they were "saved." Each told how his world had been spiraling downward until he gave his life to Christ and felt immediately saved by the Holy Spirit. Then one man began to describe how he had once considered himself a good Catholic, going to confession regularly and taking the sacraments weekly. Still, he'd struggled, feeling that what he was doing was hollow, that his faith lacked the power and vibrancy he sought. Everything changed when he attended a pentecostal worship service with a friend and gave his life to Christ. Almost instantly, he felt forgiven and loved. He knew that he had been following the wrong path. Now this man prays for the conversion of all Roman Catholics, who he says are misguided and missing the true presence of Christ. How can he be so certain? How can he be so confident? Is being "saved" the only experience that counts?

My mother also had an experience that reflected the same kind of confusion over which path is the right one. She met a woman at a party who described herself as a born-again Christian. My mother, an Episcopalian, began to discuss religion with the woman. The woman confidently proclaimed that my mother wasn't "saved." My mother, never one to back down from a challenge, immediately shot back that she was a Christian and that she attended church every Sunday. The woman said, "Going to church has nothing to do with it. You aren't saved." The discussion went on for a few more minutes, and the woman became increasingly agitated as she repeatedly proclaimed that my mother wasn't saved. Finally, my mother said, "But I try to love everyone. Isn't that what Jesus said, to love others as ourselves?" Almost shouting, the woman exclaimed, "Love has nothing to do with it!" "What do you mean love has nothing to do with it? How can you say that?" asked my mother. The woman insisted, "Love has nothing to do with it! It all has to do with whether you have been saved or not." How could she be so certain? How could she be so confident? How could she have a faith that didn't include love if God is love?

So, out of all these people, who is right and who is wrong? Are Roman Catholics the only ones to reach God? Are only those who have been "saved" able to experience God? Are Episcopalians and other mainstream Protestants who go to church every Sunday on the right path or the wrong one? How do we tell?

The Narrow Path of Jesus

The basic problem in the cases cited above is not that one group is right and the other wrong. The basic problem is that one group of Christians grabs an incomplete piece of the Christian whole, and tries to make it into *the* whole. This is a reality not only in Christian religion, but among all people. For instance, in the realm of science there is a tendency among researchers in a certain field, who hold to certain scientific perspectives, to believe that they are doing research in the "true" science. This is a constant problem in the scientific realm. Those adhering to one approach tend to denigrate the work of those using other approaches. Biologists are critical of psychologists for being too subjective and speculative, while psychologists accuse biologists both of failing to notice their own subjectivity and of failing to see the world with more depth. Chemists criticize physicists, who criticize cosmologists, who criticize theologians, who criticize philosophers, who criticize sociologists, who criticize psychologists, who criticize biologists, who criticize chemists. Worse, people who integrate ideas and findings from different fields are often criticized the most.

This problem extends beyond the field of science. Americans think that their way of life is best, as do the British, the French, the Russians, the Chinese, the Brazilians, and so forth. Pittsburghers think they are better than Philadelphians, who think they are better than New Yorkers, who think they are better than Californians.

What is the problem here? Why are we so competitive with our perspectives and beliefs? The problem lies in the fact that we human beings are always seeking the clear and certain view. We desire clarity about life. We want to know what is the right way and what is the wrong way because we are extremely uncomfortable living the ambiguous, uncertain, and cloudy lives we all live. We want to find the right perspective, belief, and practice that will make our lives seem more tolerable. When we discover a perspective or approach that fills our empty spaces, we pridefully want to make it *the* approach or perspective.

When it comes to Christian faith, though, this is a severe problem because the Christian way does not necessarily lead to clarity and certainty. The Christian journey is one that leads along a very *narrow path* in which the course and destination remain constantly obscured. When we are walking along the narrow path of Christ, we often do not know which way is right and which way is wrong. All we can do is to continue to walk forward.

What is the narrow path? It is the path that Jesus walked. It is the path that lies between all the extremes to which all Christians and all people seem to be attracted. Jesus lived in a time that was very similar to ours. We live in post-modern times, an age characterized by many different and competing ideas and beliefs about what leads to a healthy and happy life. For example, we hear that if we just follow this diet, we will be happy. If we just buy this book, we will be happy. If we just follow this program, we will be happy. So many ideas and programs exist that it is difficult to know what to follow. The same was true in Jesus' time. The Roman Empire was awash in competing beliefs and religion. Among the myriad beliefs were emperor worship, belief in the Greek gods, mystery religions, Gnosticism, Zoroastrianism, a multitude of pagan religions, and Judaism. In Judaism, a plethora of beliefs existed. There were the Sadducees, the Pharisees, the Essenes, the Levites, the Zealots, and more. The chief competition, though, was between the tradition of the Sadducees and that of the Pharisees.

The Sadducees were the conservatives of the day.[1] They believed in a strict and literal adherence to the law that did not allow for much interpretation at all. They were mostly holders of high priestly offices and came from influential Jewish families. They did not believe in angels, demons, resurrection, or anything else that was not strictly written in the law. As a result, their belief and practice centered around a rigid and meticulous adherence to law.

On the other hand, the Pharisees were the liberals of the day. While they believed in strict adherence to the law, they were a little more free with their interpretation of it. They were primarily laypeople, craftspeople, farmers, and merchants who lived in the country and the city.[2] They did believe in angels, demons, and resurrection. They also were concerned with making the law more practical for everyone and their circumstances.

Jesus was neither a Pharisee nor a Sadducee, but he did not reject completely the views of either sect. Instead, he walked the narrow path between them. He held them in tension. At the same time he was very critical of their rigidity and inflexibility. The narrow path that Jesus walked was not a path that obliterated either point of view. Instead, it was a path that integrated the beliefs and perspectives of both points of view, along with many others. The narrow path that Jesus walked, then, was one that traversed the twilight between these extremes to discover God's path. It was a path that was not clear, but instead was sensed through faith in the Father and Creator more than it was known. It was a path that did not intend to abolish the law that the Pharisees and Sadducees cherished so much:

> Do not think that I have come to abolish the law or the prophets; I have come not to abolish but to fulfill. . . . For I tell you, unless your righteousness exceeds that of the scribes and Pharisees, you will never enter the kingdom of heaven. (Matt. 5:17, 20)

Ultimately, Jesus walked this narrow path that led him to journey into places others feared. It led him to live a righteous life that was also accessible and approachable by the common man and woman. The problem was that in walking this path, he lived as common people live, yet he did things that were uncommon. He was a walking paradox. As a result of walking this path, he was criticized by the Pharisees and Sadducees for being a drunkard, a follower of Satan, a lawbreaker, and a blasphemer. He lived, spoke, and acted in ways that veered away from every conventional and familiar path set by the religious icons of the times. What was Jesus' response to their criticism?

> You are those who justify yourselves in the sight of others; but God knows your hearts; for what is prized by human beings is an abomination in the sight of God. (Luke 16:15)

The Narrow Path in the Bible

Jesus calls on us to walk the same narrow path he did. Jesus warns us that it is not an easy path because it leads us to make choices that will not always make life comfortable. For example, he points to this path when a rich young man asks him what he must do to inherit eternal life (Matt. 19:16–26). Jesus responds in a way that chills the blood of the young man, who has scrupulously kept all the commandments: "If you wish to be perfect, go, sell your posses-sions, and give the money to the poor, and you will have treasure in heaven; then come, follow me" (v. 21). Jesus goes on to tell his disciples:

> "Truly I tell you, it will be hard for a rich person to enter the kingdom of heaven. Again I tell you, it is easier for a camel to go through the eye of a needle than for someone who is rich to enter the kingdom of God." When the disciples heard this, they were astounded and said, "Then who can be saved?" But Jesus looked at them and said, "For mortals it is impossible, but for God all things are possible." (Matt. 19:23–26)

Jesus was not saying that everyone who has wealth has to give it all away. That would not be walking along the narrow path. Nor was he saying that all people with wealth are shut out of the kingdom of heaven. Again, that would mean that wealthy people can never walk the narrow path. Instead, Jesus invited the rich young man to walk the narrow path of God that was set out *specifically for him.* The rich young man declined, choosing to conform to the religious tradition of the time. He chose the path that wealth provided—a path of security and comfort. The rich young man also declined because he pre-ferred to walk the path of the law, not of faith. He had trusted in the law, but now Jesus was asking him to trust in God and become one of his followers. Instead, the rich young man chose to trust in the illusory path of false clarity: "If I just do this and avoid that, I will enter God's kingdom." It was a path that avoided true sacrifice and trust in God, one that led him to trust in wealth and the law.

Jesus also mentioned this narrow path when he was asked who would be saved. Jesus said, "Strive to enter through the narrow door; for many, I tell you, will try to enter and will not be able" (Luke 13:24). True salvation lies not in merely knowing about Jesus, in rituals and practices, or in having the "right" theology or belief. It lies in making a commitment to walk the narrow path that Jesus sets out before us. This is a path of decision. It is a path of com-mitting our lives to God—to love God with all our mind, heart, soul, and strength. This path is difficult because it requires winding through the confu-sion of life while holding on tightly to God and only God. Many people are much more attracted to worldly and even religious beliefs and ideas that bring a sense of clarity, certainty, and comfort. But this is the well-trod path. It is the path that leads away from the narrow door.

What dissuades many people from walking the narrow path is that they believe walking with God should lead to a constant sense of peace and joy. In their conviction that God's way is the way of peace and joy, they choose the path of least resistance and easy answers, convincing themselves that this is the narrow path. Again, the path of comfort, security, and peace is not necessarily the path Jesus points toward in Scripture. He says,

> Do you think that I have come to bring peace to the earth? No, I tell you, but rather division! From now on five in one household will be divided, three against two and two against three; they will be divided: father against son and son against father, mother against daughter and daughter against mother, mother-in-law against her daughter-in-law and daughter-in-law against mother-in-law. (Luke 12:51–53)

The division comes because people have to choose between walking the path Christ has set before them and walking the path of convention and conformity—often theological and religious conformity—that is followed by most of society.

The narrow path Jesus points us toward in Scripture is one that challenges every easy platitude and routine ritual. It requires that we make a decision, and that decision is to follow Christ regardless of the course our path takes. It is a path that can lead to struggle, pain, suffering, and division. It is a path many Christians ignore.

The Narrow Path for Us

Ultimately, the narrow path we are invited to walk is both an individual and a communal one. It is a path that is uniquely ours, but at the same time it must be shared with others. We need others to help us stay on our path, but at the same time ours is a path that requires us to struggle with our own particular demons and desires. We need the wisdom and support of others who are also walking their narrow paths, but at the same time our particular path winds in different directions. What does the narrow path really entail?

First, *it is a path of commitment to God to follow wherever God leads us.* This is not necessarily the way we want to go. We want to walk a path either of our own choosing or of others' choosing, depending on how strong our egos and will are. For instance, we want to choose our own careers, our own interests, our own spouses, our own circumstances, and our own surroundings. Or we want to do what everyone else is doing and avoid anything controversial. We do not necessarily want to go where God leads us. What if God wants us to become a missionary in Africa? What if God wants us to give up all of our possessions? What if God wants us to sacrifice family, like Abraham when he was called to sacrifice his son, Isaac? So many fears arise when it comes to making that commitment to follow God.

Hannah Hurnard, in her wonderful allegory of the spiritual journey, *Hinds' Feet on High Places*, identifies these fears. The main character of the book is a woman called Much-Afraid, for she is very much afraid of everything in life. Much-Afraid makes a commitment to follow the Good Shepherd (the Christ figure) wherever the Shepherd may lead. The Shepherd has offered to lead her to the High Places in the mountains (which represent the kingdom of God). When she begins her journey, the path blissfully leads upward toward the mountains. Suddenly, it veers off into a vast desert. Much-Afraid stops in horror. This is not what she agreed to. She agreed to follow the path to the High Places. This can't be where the path leads.

Much-Afraid calls on the Shepherd and says,

> "Shepherd, . . . I can't understand this. The guides you gave me say that we must go down there into that desert, turning right away from the High Places altogether. You don't mean that, do you? You can't contradict yourself. Tell them we are not to go there, and show us another way. Make a way for us, Shepherd, as you promised."
>
> He looked at her and answered very gently, "That is the path, Much-Afraid, and you are to go down there."
>
> "Oh, no," she cried. "You can't mean it. You said if I would trust you, you would bring me to the High Places, and that path leads right away from them. It contradicts all that you promised."
>
> "No," said the Shepherd, "it is not contradiction, only postponement for the best to become possible."[3]

Much-Afraid expresses perfectly our struggle with making the commitment to walk the narrow path. We are willing to make a commitment to walk it as long as it goes in the direction we want it to go. But as soon as it veers God-ward—as soon as it veers in a direction we do not understand or want—our commitment wavers. This is the point at which we will decide whether we will be guided by our fears or our faith. If we are guided by faith, it means that we will follow God, even though God may lead us in directions that are obscure and uncertain, directions in which our sense of security falls away and we have to walk by faith.

The second thing that walking the narrow path requires is *a willingness to be transformed*. This is perhaps the hardest part about walking the narrow path. Most of us would be relatively happy to walk God's path as long as it leaves us untouched. We want to walk God's way as long as it doesn't call on us to change who we are. You can see this in the way we pray. Most of the time when we pray, we ask God to change others, to change the world, to change our situations, and to change our plight. We neither expect nor appreciate it when God turns around and says, "All right, but first I must change you."

There's an old story about a man who, while admiring the beautiful view off the edge of a cliff, stumbles and falls. Hurtling downward into the abyss, he flails his arms, trying to grab at anything that might protect him from his certain death. With the ground rushing upward to meet him in a violent end, he manages to grab hold of a branch sticking out of the cliff wall. There he hangs, unable to save himself. The top is 100 feet up, while the bottom is 100 feet down.

He had never been a religious man, but with no one else to help him he begins to shout out into the canyon: "God! Are you out there? Help me! If you help me, I'll do anything you ask!" He hears only the sound of the wind swirling along the cliff wall. "God! You are the only one who can help me. Save me, and I'll do whatever you want." Again, he hears nothing but silence. Just as he's about to give up all hope, he hears a booming, thundering voice echo through the canyon, "Sure, sure, that's what they all say." "God? Is that you? I mean it, I'll do anything you ask!" "Are you sure you want me to save you?" asks God. "Yes, I'll do anything." "Anything?" "Anything!"

Again, the man hears nothing but silence. Then he hears God say, "Okay, I'll save you, but you must do exactly what I say." "Of course. You know I'll do it. I'll become a Christian. I'll help the poor. I'll go to church every Sunday." God says, "Here's what I want you to do. Let go of the branch. If you let go of the branch, I'll save you."

The man thinks for a while. Then he looks up and shouts, "Is anybody else out there?"

This is the way we are when it comes to walking the narrow path. We will walk it as long as it doesn't require us to change ourselves. For this man, the challenge was to change himself from being an agnostic who was skeptical of God to being a man who trusted God with his life and his very being. He was unwilling to make that change.

Henry Blackaby, a writer on faith, emphasizes this point. He says that if we are to follow God, the process entails profound change because it will lead to a crisis: a crisis of faith and action. He offers seven realities that come with the experience of God.[4] Among them, two stand out when it comes to walking the narrow path:

> God's invitation for you to work with God always leads you to a crisis of belief that requires faith and action.
> You must make major adjustments in your life to join God in what God is doing.

Blackaby is saying that if we walk the narrow path that God sets before us, it will require, first, that we grapple with our faith and with making it concrete in our lives. We will have doubts. We will be unsure. We will feel lost, and we will not be certain if what we are doing is truly what God wants. Our only option will be to keep going and to trust God. We will be tempted to give up, lose faith, and not act. To keep going means not to know what we are doing or where we are going, but simply to trust. At its foundation, this is what faith is all about anyway.

At the same time, walking the narrow path requires that we adjust our whole way of seeing, thinking, acting, and perceiving. We have to change who we are. We become partners in our own transformation, for when we decide to change ourselves by becoming the clay with whom God can work, we create the conditions for God to transform us. When we walk the narrow path, we become transformed not only by God's grace, but also by our own decisions. We have to make the decision to give up our cherished desires, ambitions, beliefs, and securities so that we can aspire to what God seeks for us. We have to walk into the unknown, not always knowing who we are anymore, because God is changing us in the process. We are making new decisions based on a completely different agenda. We adjust who we are, and in the process trust that God will transform us into the people we were created to be.

If we are making decisions that require faith in the midst of not knowing and changing who we are, then how do we know we are actually on the right path? Generally, the only way we ever know that we are on the right path comes much later, often in reflection, as we look back and see how God was working through our faith. That is why it is a walk of *faith*. Faith means surrendering ourselves to and trusting in God, especially in the face of the unknown.

A woman I know named Joan truly demonstrated how we often only know we are on the right path by looking through the rearview mirrors of our lives. I met Joan on a retreat and was inspired by her story. She was not what she seemed on the surface. She had lived a very tough life, and in many ways her body showed it. But inside that body was the spirit of a transformed person who had been walking the narrow path of God, and because she had, she was a new creation.

Joan had lived a life that should have led to anything but transformation. Her father had been an alcoholic who was verbally abusive, when he paid attention to her at all. As a child, she was molested for three years by a man who lived next door. By the time she was thirteen, she was pregnant with her first child. By fourteen, she was married to the father of her baby, which served the purpose of getting her out of her house. Unfortunately, her husband was also an alcoholic who was never around. By the age of sixteen, she had her second child; by eighteen, she was divorced; by nineteen, she was in prison for possession of drugs.

After several months in jail Joan was released, where she returned to living a rough life on the streets. Over the next several years she twice entered thirty-day rehabilitation programs for drug addiction. The first time, she managed to stay clean for five months, but soon returned to the same old lifestyle. The next time, she managed to stay clean only for a short time after her release. Within five hours of being released from jail, she was as high as she could be on marijuana. Eventually, as she entered her late twenties, she realized that her life was a mess and that she needed to clean herself up. She gave up her drugs, but ironically (or providentially) was caught in possession of someone else's drugs, which she was holding. She was sentenced to ten years in prison for possession with intent to distribute.

For the first few years of prison, she was bitter and angry about her situation. Then she began to take responsibility for it and realized that she had made the bad choices herself. Eventually, she took part in a prison Bible study that was run by Nellie, whom she described as "a little old lady with a big smile." Joan participated in the Bible study for two years, and it changed her life. She began to see God throughout her life. This was the beginning of her walk on the narrow path. She knew that God was calling on her to trust in God, and that she had to be willing to change. She had to be willing to change herself and to be transformed by God. At first the changes were small, as were the crises of faith. In prison, not as many events take place that cause one to act in faith in the midst of crisis as in the wider world. For Joan, those crises came after she was released.

The "little old lady" had invited Joan to come to her church upon release from prison, but Joan felt uncomfortable. It was one thing to go to church in prison where everyone was flawed and everyone knew it. It was another to go to church with upstanding citizens. For the first year after her release, Joan returned to living on the streets, struggling to get by. Finally, she realized that if she didn't do something, she would end up back in the life she had been living before her arrest. So, she got up one Sunday and decided to go to the little old lady's church.

She arrived too late for worship, but as she entered the fellowship hall of the church, she saw what she described as "a sea of gray hair from all the other little old ladies there." Joan felt extremely uncomfortable, and she could not find Nellie anywhere. She was about to leave, but decided to ask someone if Nellie was around. She walked over to a woman and said, "Hi, I'm looking for . . ." Before she could finish the sentence, the woman finished it for her: "Nellie! You must be Joan." Joan was flabbergasted. "How did you know?" "We've been praying for you for the past two years, ever since Nellie told us about you. We knew God would lead you here eventually." It was at that point that Joan knew she was walking on the right path—the narrow path.

It has not been an easy walk for her, but it has led her back into the prison system—this time to serve as the director of a halfway house for women who have been released from prison. She tries her best to bring her faith into everything she does as a director. She will be the first to admit that she doesn't always know the right thing to do, but she is walking the narrow path that echoes the words of the book of Proverbs: "Trust in the LORD with all your heart, and do not rely on your own insight. In all your ways acknowledge him, and he will make straight your paths" (3:5–6). This is what it means to walk the narrow path. It means trusting in God, not our own insights, and trusting that whatever way we walk, God will not only make it the right one, but the straight one.

The Path between Extremes

Why is it so hard to see the narrow path? Because the narrow path is most often the path that winds between extremes. It is much like walking through a narrow valley, shrouded in mist, lying between two ridges. It can be uncomfortable and unnerving because the way is obscured by the uncertainties and ambiguities of real life. When we are in the valley, we can't see exactly where God is leading us. We see neither where we are going nor our ultimate destination. We follow God through ravines, hollows, swamps, mud, bogs, mists, and streams, not knowing how long it will take, how many miles lie ahead, nor even whether we will ever get out. All that we can do is trust in God to guide us. The narrow path is difficult, and the temptation is always to climb up one of the ridges either on our right or on our left—to give ourselves over to ideological, philosophical, theological, religious, or spiritual extremes— because they offer much clearer views. What entices us about these ridges— these extremes—is that when we stand on them they give us the illusion that we can see where we are going and how far we have to travel. They give us the illusion that we can know with certainty where God is leading us by giving us a sense of clarity that really doesn't exist. They tempt us to rely more on our own philosophies, theologies, and beliefs than on God in faith.

The truth is that so many Christians don't like to journey along the narrow path precisely because it is the way of faith in God—the way of trust and surrender. We would rather walk the path of false certainty and clarity that comes through surrender to a simplistic ideology, theology, or practice that becomes a substitute for God. So we are constantly tempted to leave the narrow path for a false path on a ridge that seems clearer and more comfortable. The problem is that when we leave the narrow path and climb up a ridge, we can miss it when the narrow path we are actually called to walk cuts through a gap or a pass to emerge in another valley of God's choosing. Instead of walking where God has called us to walk, we remain stuck on the ridge, thrilled with our visions, but no longer following God's course. We think we are going the right way because the view is so grand, and we feel so sure that this way is the "right" way, but the reality is that God's path has taken another course. We are convinced that we are on the "right" path, but we are only on the selfish, ego-led path. These false paths lie all around us. They are the paths that atheists, people in cults, and so many who warp the Christian faith walk.

At the same time, those who walk along the ridges aren't just those on the fringe. Many more people walk false paths that lie closer to the narrow one that God sets for us. What makes these false paths dangerous is that in many ways they can intersect and follow a course similar to the narrow path, making it hard to distinguish between God's path and the one that leads us astray. Those who walk these paths speak a similar spiritual language to ours and emphasize some of the things we hold dear. Unfortunately, they veer from the narrow path by ignoring the fullness of the gospel. They may emphasize God's judgment, but not God's love. They may emphasize God's love, but not God's judgment. They may emphasize God's salvation, but not God's desire that everyone be saved. They may emphasize God's desire that everyone be saved, but not God's right to choose who will be saved. They may emphasize justice, but not prayer. They may emphasize prayer, but not justice. Even the greatest spiritual people end up walking down these false paths at times, only to realize later that they have been walking away from God. What makes these people great is that they have the humility to recognize where they have been led astray, and they are willing to admit their failures in order to return to God's path. So many others commit themselves to a false path and never admit that they have been wrong.

God may still be with us as we walk these false paths, but we aren't with God. This doesn't mean that the insights and beliefs found on these ridges are completely wrong. What makes them powerfully alluring is that they hold certain fundamental truths. The problem is that these truths are not sufficient in and of themselves. They must be balanced by the insights and perspectives held by those on the other surrounding ridges. In fact, when we are walking the narrow path, streams of living water flow down from all of these surrounding ridges—from these extremes—to nourish us in the valleys. These ridges contribute to our growth by exposing us to specific insights and inspirations from God that the other ridges may be missing. For example, fundamentalists walk along an extreme ridge, but what makes their ridge enticing is that they hold certain truths that we must pay attention to because they are also part of the narrow path. Fundamentalists emphasize the centrality of Scripture and the need to commit our lives to Christ. It is just that they take these truths to the extreme and fail to temper them with the complementary truths held on other ridges: truths that emphasize the need to love all others, create space for the Holy Spirit, and focus our efforts on the disadvantaged and marginalized. Fundamentalists, like those on the other extremes, fail to realize that their truths are not the *only* truths. The same can be said of those on the other ridges, who emphasize love, openness to the Holy Spirit, and focusing on the disadvantaged and marginalized, but who ignore Scripture or the need to commit our lives to Christ.

Unfortunately, the streams flowing from these ridges are mere trickles of truth. No one stream is adequate to fill the valley of God's narrow path with the living spiritual water of Christ. The wonder of the narrow path is that waters from all these ridges flow down to us, bringing their nutrients and minerals—their truths—and create a nourishing stream of faith that fills us with God's truth and grace. Together they form the living streams of water that Christ asks us to drink as we walk along the narrow path with him. No one ridge's stream is completely adequate, just as no one ridge provides a full view of all that God has to show us. So, we cannot ignore the beliefs and truths of those on the extremes. We just have to hold their truths in tension with those from other ridges. In many ways, this is the aim of this book: to help you hold these various beliefs in a tension that will draw you closer to God by helping you discern what your narrow path is. Each chapter offers a way to hold in balance different spiritual perspectives and practices related to a particular topic.

It is hard for us to walk the narrow path because the only way to do so is by surrendering ourselves to God as we grapple with the paradoxes and seeming contradictions that are part of forming a strong and vibrant faith. True faith means following Christ through darkness, uncertainty, difficulty, and suffering, while resisting the temptation to leave Christ's path for another that seems so much easier and clearer. I don't know about you, but I crave clarity and certainty. I don't like the ambiguity required by the narrow path, and I constantly pray for God to show me the way. At the same time, I know that the only way to truly discover and serve God in my life is to walk where God tells me to walk, even if it is a way avoided and ignored by those Christians who have chosen the ridges.

We can see how powerful the incomplete truths of these ridges are just by looking at the lack of balance that exists throughout our twenty-first-century North American culture. Almost all of our problems relate to our struggle with extremes—with our giving ourselves over to the extremes. How many people in our society struggle with overuse, abuse, or addiction to alcohol, drugs, food, gambling, sex, exercise, work, sports, shopping, tobacco, caffeine, the Internet, television, pornography, self-analysis, and even religion? Too many people destroy their lives in the belief that living in the extremes will make us happy, but the reality is that it won't. If you watch television, read magazines or newspapers, or browse the aisles of a bookstore, you constantly see these extremes. Diet books have always offered extreme programs for weight loss and health. Exercise books and programs offer ways to develop an extremely fit body. Books on spirituality offer programs teaching this or that belief, practice, form of prayer, or way of living as the secret to spiritual happiness. All suggest that if you just give yourself over to a particular program, the secret path to happiness will be yours. Unfortunately, it doesn't take many years before other books come out that offer exactly the opposite approach as the way to happiness.

For example, when I was in my early twenties, medical doctors confidently proclaimed that what people ate had no bearing on their susceptibility to cancer. Suddenly, a few years later, we were advised that diet does have an impact on our cancer rates, so we were advised to eat more vegetables and pasta. Soon, the high-carbohydrate, low-fat, and low-protein diets became the rage. Recently, we have been told that eating high levels of carbohydrates has led to obesity, and that the answer now lies in eating a high-protein, high-fat diet. The interesting thing is that no matter what diet is offered, the creators always say, "Eat all you want and lose weight!" Very few suggest that eating everything in moderation (the narrow path of eating) will lead to greater health.

Another example of how extremes fail to bring peace and light is given by Robert Lane. Lane, a former Yale professor, wrote a book titled *The Loss of Happiness in Market Democracies,* in which he examined the relationship between happiness and wealth.[5] What he found flies in the face of what most Americans think. In study after study, he found that the wealthier people become, the less happy they are. As our wealth grows so does our level of unhappiness. In fact, the United States, which is the wealthiest country in the world, ranks near the bottom of the list of developed countries in terms of overall happiness. In other words, we have more money and less happiness than other first-world countries. In another oddity, Lane found that as our income *decreases*, our level of happiness tends to *increase*. The one exception to this is people in poverty. A certain level of financial well-being exists above the poverty line that is required to be happy. What explains this inverse correlation between income and happiness? He suggests that we become happiest when we are engaged in close and caring relationships. The wealthier we become, the more isolated and alone we feel. Just look at how the wealthiest of the wealthy must surround their estates with gates and security, and you can see what he is saying. Close relationships, rather than wealth, are the key to happiness. We keep thinking it is the other way around, but that's because we Americans are attracted to extremes.

The same problem of extremes also exists in the religious realm. As a matter of fact, extremes can dominate the religious realm. People are always trying to climb the religious, theological, and spiritual ridges on either side of the narrow path, proclaiming them to be the "right" path because they offer so much clarity. The people of one religious movement proclaim their way as the only way, while those of another criticize them and then proclaim their way as the best. To see an example of what I mean, consider the arguments related to how we read and interpret the Bible. As Christians, it is imperative that we place Scripture at the center of our lives. The question, though, is how can we do this?

Some Christians teach that the only way to read the Bible is in a literalistic way that leaves no room for the Holy Spirit's guidance. Other Christians mainly ignore the Bible, saying that it is an archaic piece of literature written by ignorant people from a different age and place. In both cases these Christians miss the power of Scripture. They miss how essential it is to walk the narrow path, but even more how essential it is to be on the narrow path if we are to read Scripture in a way that reveals God.

What makes reading and placing Scripture at the center of our lives difficult is that Scripture has a deep meaning that requires spiritual depth to discover. The more we read Scripture, the more it deepens us spiritually. At the same time, the more spiritually deep we become, the more we discover even greater depths of meaning. Ignoring Scripture completely or treating it only in a literalistic way keeps us shallow. The only way to experience the power of Scripture is to read it along the narrow path where we are forced to grapple with it, ponder it, question it, reflect on it, and grow from it. Despite what many may think, there is no way to know Scripture. There is no such thing as a true biblical expert, only those who are experts on certain facets of Scripture. Scripture's power comes not from our knowing it, but from letting it form us. The extreme approaches to Scripture tend either to treat it as objective knowledge that we can know with certainty or to ignore it as archaic knowledge that we should dismiss with certainty. The narrow path treats Scripture as something alive that seeks to nurture our relationship with God so that our lives can be formed according to God's will. So, as we walk the narrow path, we need to pay attention to all perspectives but be captured by none insofar as they threaten to become false idols. We need to recognize that

Scripture is truth and history and literature and myth, but that it is also so much more than any of these. To walk the narrow path means to keep these insights in tension so that we can move ever deeper into Scripture and discover ever deeper truths.

Extreme religious perspectives of every kind eventually kill us spiritually because they offer an illusion of clarity in an unclear world. This was the problem with the Sadducees and the Pharisees. They sought clarity rather than God. They tried to turn the law into a false God. It is much easier to create a rigid, black-and-white system that pretends to lead us to God than it is to follow the living God who goes beyond systems.

Extreme religious perspectives don't allow for the true doubt, questioning, critical thought, yearning, seeking, and reflection that we must work through if we are to grow spiritually. As a matter of fact, if we doubt too much, ask too many questions, or form insights and receive inspirations that lie beyond the pale of these extreme religious beliefs, then we are branded heretics, hypocrites, or heathens. The reality is that walking the narrow path means becoming comfortable with the doubts and questions that often are our constant companions, and then using these doubts and questions to spark us to go further as we seek vistas of God that we had never even considered possible before. When we truly walk the narrow path, we become unwilling to accept a particular religious perspective just because it claims orthodoxy. Instead, we seek God's guidance to lead us beyond orthodoxy.

At the same time, our doubts and questioning can lead us far astray if they become false gods in and of themselves. We can turn our doubts and questions into extreme ridges where we create our own answers to our questions, and thus create our own religions where only our beliefs are right. Our pride and ego can become so strong that they tempt us to create and embrace a religious extreme of our own creation. We don't recognize the authority of Scripture at all, and instead create our own truths. Walking the narrow path means resisting the narcissistic, ego-driven need to create our own religion, a problem that afflicts so many who reject the traditions and teachings of Christianity.

If we are truly open to God and the journey along the narrow path, then we willingly walk the narrow path so that we can discover those truths that lie beyond our logical, rational grasp. As Soren Kierkegaard says, "If I am capable of grasping God objectively, I do not believe, but precisely because I cannot do this I must believe."[6] In other words, the narrow path lies not in knowing all the answers, but in *not knowing* and therefore surrendering ourselves to God in the midst of this void. The narrow path is a journey spurred on by our doubts and questions. We eventually trust in God because we are at the end of our mental tether. Life no longer makes clear sense, and so we give ourselves over to God and the unknown way. Real faith comes not through objective human logic. It comes from a deeper, mystical logic that entails giving of ourselves to God in complete trust and surrender, even as people tell us we are crazy to do so. God then reveals the path that leads to the true life lying beyond all logical and rational systems. In essence, this is what this book is designed to do: help you integrate in a meaningful and Spirit-filled way the many seeming contradictory truths and paradoxes that lie on the path of life that God calls us to walk.

Ultimately, when we decide to make a commitment to walk the narrow path, we also willingly give up the need to have clarity and certainty as central themes in our spiritual walk. When we walk the narrow path, we are truly walking the walk of faith. We don't know where we are going, and we don't know where we will end up. Still, we trust that God will take us there.

Seeking the Narrow Path

What, then, is the narrow path? It is the path that always lies in the tension between extremes. When we walk the narrow path, we are able to hold different ideas, beliefs, and perspectives in tension, even if it seems they are mutually exclusive of each other. At the same time, it is not merely striking the middle ground between these extremes. It is deeper than that. The narrow path is a path of integrating different ideas, beliefs, and perspectives because we recognize that God is not limited to a particular theology or approach. God can speak through different belief patterns and structures, even when they seem incompatible. For example, is God a conservative, a liberal, a traditionalist, a progressive, a Pentecostal, a Protestant, a Roman Catholic, an Eastern Orthodox, a scientist, or a rationalist? God is all of them and none of them. God is the "I AM WHO I AM" (Exod. 3:14). Walking the narrow path means seeking this God who integrates and transcends all human understanding and thought.

The narrow path is not only the walk between extremes; it is the path that maintains balance. In many ways, walking the narrow path involves walking a spiritual tightrope through life. This is why it is so uncomfortable. When walking a tightrope, we constantly lurch to the right or to the left as we try to maintain balance. It is difficult and tiring. It would be so much easier to simply let ourselves fall to the right or the left and to land comfortably in the net that lies below. The problem is that the net is just an illusion. As we lie in the net, we are unable to progress and move forward. We may feel as though we are safely in God's hands because we have given ourselves over to an extreme, but we aren't. We are lying in the hands of a false god, an idol we have created. We have chosen a stagnant pool instead of the living streams of God's water.

As Christians, we are called to constantly walk forward on the tightrope set before us by God the Creator, while holding onto Christ as our balancing pole. As we walk, we are to follow the light of the Holy Spirit as the Spirit leads us foward. When we find ourselves lurching one way or the other, we need to let God in Christ be our center of gravity, keeping us on the rope. Just because we are holding onto Christ doesn't mean we will stop lurching. Occasionally we will find ourselves gravitating toward an extreme. This can be a good thing as we balance ourselves against a lurch we have made in the opposite direction. The problem comes only when we try to make that lurch permanent. We can become frozen in our fear of what may happen if we keep walking forward on this path. Then we lose all sense of balance and let go of Christ. We lose the dynamic tension, and we fall into the net. Once there, the temptation to stay increases. We are no longer willing to grow because the net feels so comfortable and safe. The net holds no risks or stress. We lie in a web of comfort that placates all our fears, but that also keeps us from truly walking God's path.

Walking the narrow path, then, is like walking a tightrope; we must struggle to keep balance in our lives. We have to trust in God to keep us up, especially when we are about to fall. We have to trust that the rope will lead toward God, just as it came from God. We also have to trust that as we continue our walk and gain experience, we will form a natural ability to keep our balance, especially in the midst of the storms and winds of life that threaten to blow us off the line. Walking the narrow path is a walk of faith into the unknown, trusting in the great "I AM WHO I AM" to guide us, lead us, hold us, protect us, and walk with us.

Questions for Reflection

1. Reflect on your own beliefs. What have you considered to be the "right" way to God, and how is this different from the beliefs of other Christians you know?
2. To what extent do you think your beliefs may be tainted by the need to be "right" or to feel secure in your faith?
3. If the narrow path is a path of decision and commitment, what things get in the way of your making a commitment to God? What can you do to overcome them?

4. How has God transformed you over the years, and how have you resisted or allowed these transformations to occur?
5. How have you struggled with extremes recently and in the past, and how have these extremes kept you from God?

Key Learnings

- The Christian path is not one of clarity and certainty, but a narrow path of trusting God wherever God may lead.
- The narrow path is one that rejects extremes and seeks instead to discern God's truth by living in the balance and tension between extremes.
- The narrow path is one in which God's truth for us is revealed slowly as we continually give our lives more and more to God in faith.

Chapter 2

Walking the Mystical Path

*I*f we are going to chart the course of our personal narrow paths, a great place to look for direction is to the lives of the Christian mystics. Mystics of every age have been among the most misunderstood Christians of all precisely because they walked the narrow path. This is especially true today, for so many people misunderstand what a mystic is. Today, we think a mystic is someone who walks, talks, and dresses in a "mystical" way—in a way that seems "spiritual." While some of these people may indeed be mystics, being a Christian mystic involves more than this. The Christian mystics were and are the people who have lived unique lives spent walking Christ's narrow path. Their paths always veered in novel directions that seemed so different from the conventional. They were misunderstood because the world demands conformity, consistency, rules, programs, and systems. Unique visions and practices generally break free of these demands.

Unfortunately, many people in today's culture confuse uniqueness with "being different." Many of today's musicians, artists, and actors try to intentionally walk "different" paths, but they set out on those paths for rebellious and narcissistic reasons. They are merely serving themselves, not God. Mystics walk their paths for more selfless reasons: to love and serve God. Mystics have always lived in ways that are radically open and responsive to God, and because they have, they provide practical guidance on how to find the narrow path and stay on it.

When we talk about "mystics," the response among many Christians is often a blank stare. "Mystic? What's a mystic?" Most Christians are unfamiliar with the mystics because they are rarely mentioned by Christian pastors and professors. Perhaps they are not mentioned because their lives seemed so radical. Perhaps it is because they are seen as being impractical models to emulate. I believe the answer is simpler than that. Mystics aren't mentioned much because their lives were so divinely illogical and irrational that they didn't fit into the systematic and humanly logical way modern Christians try to make their religion. To Christians who demand a black-and-white system of faith, the mystics can be mystifying. Mystics deeply love God, and they break the rules of traditional Christian religion. This was true of Jesus, who is the model for all mystics, and it has been true of all the other great mystics, including Francis of Assisi, Martin Luther, John Wesley, John of the Cross, Dorothy Day, Henri Nouwen, and so many more.

The mystics of Christian history are wonderful models and guides precisely because they broke free of the religious traps that seem to snare the people of every age. These are the traps the Sadducees and Pharisees succumbed to, as have many of today's theologians and religious leaders. The Pharisees and Sadducees tried to turn religion into a logical system of righteousness instead of letting it be an experience grounded in a relationship with God. Mystics, both those of the past and those of today, are different because they do not think theologically so much as they live spiritually. They live in a way that makes theology come alive in daily life through their spirituality. Theological speculation for them has no value unless it is integrated, embodied, and incarnated in daily life. They don't want to know what is right theologically, doctrinally, or dogmatically. They want to know how to form a deeper relationship with God. They don't ask what is ethical and moral in a particular situation. All they ask is "God, what is your will?" They don't necessarily want to figure out who God is and what exactly it is that God is doing. They want to unite their will with God's will so that God can use them to do whatever God wants. They want their will to be God's will, their doing to be God's doing.

I never learned much about the mystics while I was in seminary because at that time, modern seminary education was so focused on studying the teachings of more rational, systematic thinkers. I discovered the mystics first on my own, and then later in more depth as I did graduate work in spirituality. It was then that I discovered a whole new way of seeing, relating to, and being with God. I discovered the narrow path of the mystics.

Who Were the Mystics?

Traditionally, Christian mystics have not been part of any one movement in Christianity, although many mystics began their own movements in the hope of reforming the Christian faith, or at least a particular facet of it. Mysticism is not a movement so much as it is an experience grounded in a profound relationship with God. Most of the greatest writings handed down through the ages in the church have come from mystics. Their writings remain popular today precisely because their insights are ageless. So many more have passed away from memory because they did not leave a written legacy, but their spiritual legacy had an impact on so many during their lives.

Who are the mystics? Ultimately, mystics are people of every age who have had a transforming passion for God. Today there are humble mystics residing in almost every church of every denomination. They are the deeply spiritual people who live humble lives of prayer and seem to inherently know how to live deeper lives. Often, they are not even leaders in their churches, at least not in tangible ways, but their lives inspire others to seek God.

Simply put, mystics are people who have a passion for God, but not in a zealous, fanatical way. Their passion is grounded in love. Perhaps the best definition of the *mystics* comes from one herself. The Anglican mystic, Evelyn Underhill, says

> So the beginning of an answer to the question, "What is mysticism?" must be this: Mysticism is the passionate longing of the soul for God, the Unseen Reality, loved, sought and adored in Himself for Himself alone. It is, to use a favourite phrase of Baron von Hügel, a "metaphysical thirst." A mystic is not a person who practices unusual forms of prayer, but a person whose life is ruled by this thirst. He feels and responds to the overwhelming attraction of God, is sensitive to that attraction; perhaps a little in the same way as the artist is sensitive to the mysterious attraction of visible beauty, and the musician to the mysterious attraction of harmonized sound.[1]

Mystics are people who are in love with God, and because they are they refuse to let themselves be defined by the values of the world. Instead, they want to live life the way God the Creator meant it to be lived, the way God in Christ taught it should be lived, and the way God in the Holy Spirit reveals it to be lived. It is due to their passion for God that they have experiences that go beyond the normal. They don't just experience God secondhand through others—through biblical figures or wizened preachers speculating on how things should be. As Underhill says, "The typical mystic, then, is the person who has a certain first-hand experience and knowledge of God through love. . . ."[2] Mystics experience God firsthand because they are willing to follow their passion and seek God in every relationship, event, experience, and thing.

This does not mean that your typical mystic is otherworldly. In fact, while mystics may have their spirits firmly planted in God's realm, they have their feet firmly planted in this realm. Not all mystics have been monks or nuns, although it may seem this way because many of the greatest mystical writers were. Mystics have also been husbands, wives, parents, children, business-people, and individuals from every other walk of life. The only thing that makes them seem different is that they have fallen in love with God, and so God's grace seems to flow through their lives.

A mystic is not the same as a saint. If we use the definition of "saint" from the Roman Catholic or Anglican traditions, we see that many saints were mystics but that many more mystics have never been designated saints. Typically, the familiar use of the term "saint" is an ecclesiastical designation. Saints are people the church sets aside as remarkable exemplars of the Christian life, and who have had a healing or miraculous impact on others. They have gone through an official church process of beatification and sanctification. In contrast, mystics belong to all denominations, including those that don't have official saints and those that see every member as a saint. They are the people in every denomination who have broken through the dogmas and doctrines of the church to discover and fall in love with the living God about whom those dogmas and doctrines try to teach.

Mystical Foundations

While the mystics were often seen as eccentric, impractical, and beyond our ability to emulate, the truth is that they were extremely rooted, practical, and imitable. You have probably met a mystic, although you might not have known it because she or he did not seem very outstanding and extraordinary by worldly standards. Instead, what you did notice was that, in a strange way, that person seemed so ordinary that it made her or him special. Mystics have a natural humility that is engaging. They laugh at themselves and see themselves as imperfect. In fact, while others around them may praise them for possessing a quality that makes them so naturally spiritual, often they see themselves as weak and inconsequential.

The closer they get to God, the more they see their own imperfections. This does not mean they spend their lives trying to fix themselves in the way so many in our modern self-help society do. Instead, they give themselves over to God and ask God to transform and mold them in God's image. They have a natural trust in God that allows them to grow in God's grace. The thing that makes them special is that they live out the Gospel of Christ in a foundational way that is both practical and natural. They are often plain by the world's standards. They are not necessarily great organizers, orators, or orchestrators (although on occasion they can be). Instead, they are people we know are special, even if we cannot explain why.

There are at least three aspects of their lives that all mystics share in common. First, *mystics are deeply in touch with the center of all Christian life: love of God and others*. In all cases, the true mystics embody in their lives the great command: "You shall love the Lord your God with all your heart, and with all your soul, and with all your strength, and with all your mind; and your neighbor as yourself" (Luke 10:27). As stated previously, they love God above everything else, and because they do, God's love flows through them.

They also incarnate and embody John's description of love: "God is love, and those who abide in love abide in God, and God abides in them" (1 John 4:16). Because they let their love of God be the primary motivation for their lives, they are alive in God and God is alive in them. They love God, and because they are always seeking ways to deepen their love for God, love more naturally flows through them into their relationships. This does not mean that their relationships are perfect. In fact, sometimes the opposite is true. Their love of God can actually put a strain on their relationships.

An example is the Italian mystic Catherine of Genoa. Catherine lived between 1447 and 1510.[3] She was born into an aristocratic family, and was forced by her older brother to enter into an arranged marriage with a man named Guiliano Adorno for strictly financial and political reasons. This marked the beginning of ten years of loneliness, neglect, and what we would consider today to be clinical depression. Her husband was an adulterer who led the couple into bankruptcy. She was so despondent about her life that when she took part in the sacrament of confession on March 22, 1473, she could not even manage to confess. All she could do was ask for a simple blessing from God.

This request for a simple blessing led to a dramatic conversion. She had an overwhelming experience of God's love, and an absolute awareness of her sin, yet this awareness was not a self-demeaning awareness. It made her all the more aware of God's love for her, and how it is beyond anything that we can ever imagine. This led Catherine to say to herself, "No more world for me! No more sin." All she wanted to do was to live in God's love and find a way to serve God in everything. She was not going to let her husband's marital, moral, and financial shortcomings rule her life. Instead, she decided to love, follow, and serve God. Her decision exacerbated the problems of an already strained marriage, but Catherine would not be dissuaded from her convictions.

She served God by tenderly caring for the sick in the Pammatone Hospital. She spent her life caring for people suffering from the ravages of the bubonic plague in Genoa, Italy. No matter what the person's condition, Catherine was willing to care tenderly for him or her. When others recoiled in fear at the large sores on the plague-infected patients, Catherine drew even closer. Whenever she felt repulsed, she forced herself to touch the sores so that she could grow accustomed to them. Catherine was so filled with God's love, and so forgiving, that she was even willing to love and raise as her own the child born of one of Giuliano's affairs, a small boy named Thobia. Catherine's faith and love began to have an effect on the guilt-ridden Giuliano. Eventually, he also had a dramatic experience of God's love, and this led him to serve God by caring for the sick and the poor at Catherine's side for the rest of his life.

Catherine lived the command to love God with everything we have, and because she did, God's love abided in her just as she abided in God. She was an ordinary woman who allowed God's love to flow through her, and it had a profound and transforming effect on the people around her: her husband, the staff of the hospital, the sick, and the poor. She was an ordinary person who had a passion for God—who was in love with God. In fact, Catherine possessed no special talents other than her love. She had been mired in depression, but God's love evaporated that depression the way the morning sun evaporates even the thickest fog. God used her weakness and ordinariness to bring healing and love into her small part of the world. Through her, God's kingdom broke into the world's kingdom.

A second characteristic or quality that all mystics share in common is that *they are scripturally grounded.* They may not have known Scripture particularly well, but they embodied Scripture in the way they lived their lives. Looking at the great passages of Scripture, we can find a mystic who exemplified almost every one. In fact, most mystics seemed to have taken, intentionally or not, one particular passage of Scripture as their model for life, and because they did they integrated all of Scripture into their lives.

For example, the Desert Fathers tried to embody Jesus' transforming desert experience of forty days and nights (Matt. 4:1–11). The Desert Fathers were a group of men who tried to emulate Christ by living for months and years in the deserts of Egypt to wrestle with their demons, be purged of their sin, and be transformed by God. The best known of these was Antony, whose life was chronicled by Athanasius.[4] Antony was a simple man who decided to follow Christ by living deep in the loneliness of the desert in order to depend on God for everything. It was a hard life, but it transformed him into a man of radical faith and grace.

The Hesychasts, Brother Lawrence, and Frank Laubach were all people who tried to live by the scriptural message of "pray without ceasing" (1 Thess. 5:17). The Hesychasts were Eastern Orthodox Christians in the eleventh century who tried to radically embody this passage by making prayer part of their breathing. As they breathed inward they would pray silently, "Lord Jesus

Christ," and as they breathed outward they would silently pray, "Have mercy on me, a sinner." In this way, they made prayer a constant part of their lives. Brother Lawrence, a sixteenth-century French monk, attempted a similar thing by simply carrying on conversations with God throughout his day, and he discovered that as he did God became a real and tangible presence in his life. Frank Laubach was a missionary in the Philippines during the early and middle part of the twentieth century. By forming a constant awareness of God, and by committing his life to God on a moment-by-moment basis, Laubach found that God acted in amazing ways throughout his life.

Julian (sometimes also referred to as Juliana) of Norwich, a fourteenth-century nun, experienced Christ by emulating Christ's suffering on the cross. Witnessing the suffering going on in the world around her as a result of an outbreak of the bubonic plague, she began to see suffering as an avenue to discover Christ. Thus, she prayed constantly that she would suffer as Christ did so that she could experience and be united with Christ in his suffering. When she was thirty, she contracted a terrible illness that left her at the point of death. For three days and nights, she lay teetering on the edge of death, and even received the last rites. It was during this illness that she had a profound vision of Christ dying on the cross and discovered in it the power of God's love. She recovered from her illness, but she was now a changed person. She was an ordinary person willing to suffer, and because she was, she discovered God in a transforming way most of us only rarely do.

George Fox, the founder of the Quaker movement, attempted to live the Pentecost experience found in the second chapter of Acts and to form a radical openness to the Spirit in daily life. He was a simple shoemaker's apprentice who looked at the Christians of the day and decided that they were not authentically living the gospel in their lives. For him, true faith meant letting the Holy Spirit fill his life by creating room in his heart for the Spirit to enter. His writings and teachings not only began the Society of Friends, or Quakers, but became the pillars upon which so many later mystics, such as John Woolman, Hannah Whitall Smith, and Thomas Kelly, built their own experiences of God.

The twelfth-century mystic, Francis of Assisi, was a man of very little talent other than his passion for God. Francis seemed to excel at only one thing: going to parties and carousing with his friend. His father had hoped he would him follow into the family textile business, but Francis showed little aptitude for that. Then his father hoped Francis could distinguish himself as a soldier, but Francis was quickly captured and almost died from his imprisonment. Something happened during his imprisonment, though. He experienced God, and was impressed by Christ's command to the rich young man to sell all his possessions and follow him (Mark 10:17–22). Francis decided to follow that command, and in the process he incarnated the beatitudes throughout his life, especially the focus on the poor, mourning, meek, hungry, thirsty, and pure in heart (Matt. 5:1–11). He renounced all of his possessions to follow God as God would lead him. Today, Francis remains one of the best-known and most cherished of all Christian mystics.

So many other mystics throughout Christian history embodied Scripture in their lives. There is no way to name all the mystics—there have been so many, and most remain unknown to all except God—yet many have left a legacy of faith. Among them are Augustine of Hippo, Benedict of Nursia, Dorotheos of Gaza, Bonaventure, Gregory Palamas, Clare of Assisi, Hildegaard of Bingen, Meister Eckhart, Martin Luther, John Calvin, Teresa of Avila, John of the Cross, Ignatius Loyola, Horace Bushnell, Jean-Pierre de Caussade, William Law, John Wesley, Corrie ten Boom, C. S. Lewis, Hannah Hurnard, Agnes Sanford, Henri Nouwen, Catherine Marshall, Mother Teresa, and so many others. All were ordinary people who felt a conflict between the world and God's kingdom. They chose to live in God's kingdom while planting themselves firmly in the world. They did not live in conformity and obedience to Scripture so much as they embodied it creatively, naturally, and pragmatically in their lives.

A third characteristic all mystics have held in common is that *they have all seen their lives as their mission field.* In the modern church, we often consider mission to be ministry somewhere else. We send missionaries to Africa, South America, Asia, Eastern Europe, Appalachia, Native American reservations, and elsewhere. Sometimes mystics became missionaries, but more often they saw their mission as serving wherever they were. Their mission was to share God's love at home, at work, in the monastery, and anywhere else that people felt an absence of God's love. They saw a need to share God everywhere, for they saw God everywhere.

Their own experiences often determined what their mission field would be. As we've seen many mystics experienced God in the midst of illness, imprisonment, rejection, or failure. Often, they either shared their experience with others, or turned around and cared for people in the same condition as they were. For example, Corrie ten Boom served God during the German occupation of Holland in World War II by hiding Jews. Catherine Marshall used her own miraculous recovery from tuberculosis and the death of her husband to reach out to others feeling God's absence in their lives. Agnes Sanford used her struggle to be healed from her depression as a springboard to bring God's healing to others. Thomas Kelly discovered God through a traumatic failure to achieve his life's goal, and he used this failure to teach others deep truths about what God really wants for us in life. Mystics use their experiences to discover their own unique mission fields.

Basic Lessons of the Mystics

It would be difficult to place in one book all the lessons the mystics have to teach us, but we can glean specific lessons that can help us as we walk our own narrow paths. Most mystics have taught and lived these basic lessons in one form or another. They are lessons that show how the narrow path is a shared path, even as it is a unique one; a practical and pragmatic path, even if it is a creative, difficult, and unusual one. The following are some of the basic lessons we can learn from the mystics of Christian history.

Love of God above All Else

We discussed this earlier, but it bears repeating: If nothing else, the mystics taught and demonstrated that the narrow path is a path originating in loving God above and beyond all else. As Catherine de Hueck Doherty says, "It isn't hard to be a mystic. All we have to do is fall in love with God; the rest will follow."[5] Too often people who study the mystics forget this foundational message. They focus on the mystic's mystical experiences, methods of prayer, ways of living, and how they inspired others. They forget that God calls all of us to the mystical life.

This is especially a problem in the modern spirituality movement. Many contemporary teachers in this field seem to think that spirituality is all about methods of prayer and having certain types of spiritual experiences. Even before it can be about those things, mysticism is about loving God with all our hearts, minds, souls, and strength. All the prayer, disciplines, and experiences are nothing without love of God. It is as Paul says:

> If I speak in the tongues of mortals and of angels, but do not have love, I am a noisy gong or a clanging cymbal. And if I have prophetic powers, and understand all mysteries and all knowledge, and if I have all faith, so as to remove mountains, but do not have love, I am nothing. If I give away all my possessions, and if I hand over my body so that I may boast, but do not have love, I gain nothing. (1 Cor. 13:1–3)

The message from so many mystics is similar to this. It is said, for instance, that late in her life Teresa of Avila would become so ecstatic in prayer that she would levitate. The other nuns praying with her would have to tug on her robe to bring her back down. Instead of being proud that she was so spiritually advanced, Teresa felt embarrassed by these experiences. She thought they distracted others and herself from loving God because the attention was on her levitating, not on God. It is for this reason that most mystics taught that we should not seek signs, marvels, and miracles—what they called "consolations." They believed we would turn them into false gods, which would diminish our love for God. They appreciated signs and miracles as gifts from God, but remained focused on loving God.

Humility

Another thread running through the lives of mystics is that they were incredibly humble people, and they believed that humility was one of the foundations of a deeply spiritual life. They did not understand humility in the way many people today see it. Nowadays people think that being humble means lacking in self-esteem, being overly self-critical, and having no will of our own. In fact, the opposite is true. Truly humble people often become humble only after having strong egos and spiritual pride.

Many of the mystics were strong-willed and stubborn people who had ego-stripping experiences. They got into some sort of trouble because of their egos—their pride—and, in the midst of their turmoil, they discovered God. These experiences often entailed illnesses, failures, imprisonment, poverty, emptiness, and/or some sort of weakness that humbled them and led them to discover how mortal, fragile, and dependent they truly were. They realized, because of their experiences, that they had no true power in life. Only God does.

Humility resembles the process of constructing a brick building. Before the bricks can be laid, scaffolding must be erected. The scaffold supports the building as it begins to take shape. No matter how important the scaffolding is, eventually it must be taken down so the beauty of the building can be revealed. Our egos are very much like the scaffolding. They function to build us up and enable us to become strong, but over time they can get in the way. We need strong egos and a sense of pride to build ourselves up, but there comes a time when we need to be stripped down by God through the events of life to allow our own natural beauty to show. People who have not let go of their egos are constantly consumed with the need to receive acclaim from others: "Look at me! Look at what I can do! Look at how great I am!" In our sports- and entertainment-driven culture, large egos and pride dominate.

In almost all cases, mystics wrote about humility with the understanding that they were writing to people with a tremendous spiritual pride. Mystics emphasized that, to truly be open to God, we must diminish our egos and pride. (I've discussed this in more detail in my book *Forming Faith in a Hurricane.*[6]) The point of humility is not to become nothing; it is to allow ourselves to be open to God. To do this we have to let go of our need to be in control.

Humility is the foundation of all spiritual growth. As we become humbler, we recognize that we are nothing without God. The humbler we get, the more we recognize our weakness and frailty, while simultaneously recognizing God's greatness and power. Humility is never a process of denigrating ourselves as much as it is a process of preparing ourselves to discover God in every facet of our lives.

Almost all of the mystics offered guidance on how to become more humble. Thomas à Kempis told us that the way to begin humbling our hearts is to look at ourselves not through our own eyes, but through God's. In doing this, we begin to see others in a higher, purer light. As we see ourselves more from God's perspective, it not only makes us more aware of our own sins and faults, but it also allows us to recognize the importance of treating others well, for they are fragile just as we are. Humility increases our compassion.

Dorotheos of Gaza took this one step further and said that we should not only think highly of others, but in times of conflict we must accuse ourselves instead of others. This not only leads us to continually recognize our own faults, thus opening us more fully to God, but it heals relationships. As we become humbler, we take a life stance in which we build others up. This does not mean that we tear *ourselves* down, only our egos and pride. The truly humble person is still engaged in life, still serves God, still speaks and acts out against injustices, and still takes on leadership roles. The difference is that the humble person is willing to do all of this for God. She trusts in God, and she trusts that God will take care of everything in the end. If things don't work out her way, she lets God take care of the results.

In addition, the humble person is always aware of how easy it is to turn humility into arrogance. As many of the mystics would remind us, the demonic loves to use our humility against us by making us proud of our humility. "Yes, even pride in our own humility is one of the devil's own tricks,"[7] Thomas Kelly said.

It would be a mistake to think that the mystic is ever perfectly humble. No one is. In fact, the idea of perfect humility is an oxymoron. Instead, the mystic is the one who seeks humility, for he knows that it is part of the process of walking the narrow path. To become humble is a very tricky balancing act, for the humble person is always feeling the tension between the ego and harsh reality. The ego seduces us to be overly self-aggrandizing, yet seeing ourselves in too harsh a reality can lead us to become destructively self-critical. Keeping the two in balance is crucial so that we can be realistic about our faults and yet recognize our potential.

In essence, humility is very simple. It means to be part of life, but not to vie for control of it. As Jesus says:

> When you are invited by someone to a wedding banquet, do not sit down at the place of honor, in case someone more distinguished than you has been invited by your host; and the host who invited both of you may come and say to you, "Give this person your place," and then in disgrace you would start to take the lowest place. But when you are invited, go and sit down at the lowest place, so that when your host comes, he may say to you, "Friend, move up higher"; then you will be honored in the presence of all who sit at the table with you. (Luke 14:8–10)

From a practical standpoint, becoming humble means engaging in relationships with others in a different way. Instead of needing to be in control, it means letting go. It means pointing fingers back at ourselves when we are in a disagreement and accepting blame when things go wrong. It means finding ways not to assert ourselves, but to let God's grace flow through us.

Detachment

Anthony de Mello tells a story about the power of detachment to center us in God.[8] In a small village, there was a young single girl who became pregnant, much to the embarrassment of her family. "Who did this to you?" the father demanded. The young girl, fearful that her family would harm her young lover, said, "It was the old man who lives on the edge of town." She implicated a very religious man who had devoted his life to prayer.

The father, family, and others broke into the man's house, saying, "You despicable man! Look what you've done to this innocent girl, the shame you've brought to us!" Looking up from his prayers, he said nothing more than, "Very well, very well." With that he made arrangements for the girl to have her own house, paid for the midwife, and put away money to pay for the raising of the child.

Months passed, and the girl finally had her child. Overcome with loneliness and guilt over what she had done to the old man, she finally confessed to her family, "It wasn't the old man who made me pregnant. It was the young boy who lived next door. We love each other and want to be married." Aghast at how they had treated the old man, the family rushed over and begged his forgiveness. Looking up from his prayers, all he said was, "Very well, very well."

People in modern life do not understand this kind of reaction. We live in a land of justice and litigation, where everyone tries to assign blame for everything. Why was the old man so untroubled by the injustice done to him? He was untroubled because he had detached himself from the vicissitudes of life in order to be centered in God. I'm not sure the extent to which we should be that untroubled, but the story does emphasize that when we detach and decide to trust God, God takes care of things in the end.

We are not a culture that understands mystical detachment. The closest thing we moderns have to the practice of detachment is the practice of objectivity, but objectivity and detachment are very different. True objectivity is an illusion, and thanks to postmodern thought and quantum physics, more and more people are realizing this.

Researchers in the field of quantum physics, for example, are discovering that even in the objective sciences observers influence what is observed. They have observed that certain electrons behave in particular ways *only* when observed. Prior to being observed and measured, these electrons move in two different directions at the same time (which seems impossible), yet when their movement is measured, they appear to move only in one particular direction. How can this be? The researchers' answer is that the observer influences the study, even when it is as objective as can possibly be. The observer always influences the object of study. When a biologist conducts experiments to test a theory, simply by constructing the test she adds a subjective element. A chemist, by creating a lab to run tests, influences the outcomes in unintentional ways. This is why science, despite what we may think, never really *proves* anything. Each experiment, test, or correlational study merely tests the probability that something is true. No matter how objective scientists try to be, they cannot rid human understanding of subjective elements.

The mystics inherently understood the impossibility of being objective. They never suggested that objectivity was the path toward greater depth in life. Instead, they taught us the practice of *detachment*. To detach means to follow Jesus' guidance to give up worries, concerns, and needs: "Therefore I tell you, do not worry about your life" (Matt. 6:25).

The point is not just to detach and give up worries for detachment's sake. That would be following the false path of objectivity. Nor is the point to be subjective from God's point of view. The point is to develop a kind of spiritual awareness that transcends rational and emotional thought. The point is to give up attachments so that we can "strive first for the kingdom of God and his righteousness" (Matt. 6:33). When we detach, we are trying to discern what really matters at the depths of everything. We are trying to align our wills, our minds, and our hearts with God and seek what God wants. Thomas

Merton says that everything "you love for its own sake, outside God alone, blinds your intellect and destroys your judgment of moral values. It vitiates your choices so that you cannot clearly distinguish good from evil and you do not truly know God's will."[9] Detachment seeks to let go of the passions, the pains, the desires, and the drives that lead us away from God so that we can live more in attunement with God.

The problem many Christians have with the idea of detachment is that they think becoming detached means becoming unemotional and robotic. In fact, the opposite is true. Becoming detached means loving another without needing to control her because we have given up control to God. It means caring for another genuinely and deeply without having to be crushed by his burdens, because we have given these burdens to God. It means being engaged in projects and tasks without worrying about their outcome because we have given God the responsibility for the outcome.

The mystics were not spiritual zombies, walking about in a spiritual bliss. They were people who struggled, cried, laughed, suffered, celebrated, and rejoiced. Their detachment allowed them to actually experience their emotions more deeply. It allowed them to love more deeply because they were able to love people for who they were. For instance, with spouses and children, many were able to love more deeply because they were not obsessed with trying to fix their spouses and children—to create them in their own image. The story of Catherine of Genoa I mentioned earlier is an example. Many of the mystics were known for their deep love and laughter. Often those who knew them said that they had a simple humor that allowed them to laugh from the heart.

Detachment is a practice that allows us to be engaged in the world from a different perspective. It is practical. For instance, being detached at work means doing the best we can by trying to do the best quality work possible, but at the same time realizing that whatever our project is, it is not as important as we think it is. Whatever happens, success or failure, God will still be with us, we will still be with God, and God will care for us. Detachment is detachment from the world so that we can have engagement with God.

Surrender to God

In general, mystics did not have the miraculous powers ascribed to them, yet miracles did seem to occur in their presence. They were not necessarily miracles of the biblical variety—miracles in which mountains are moved, water is walked on, seas are parted, or prison walls fall down. The miracles that took place in the lives of mystics tended to be much simpler. For example, Catherine of Genoa lost all taste for food every Lent and could not eat even though she wanted to, yet she was never hungry and never suffered. It was as though God gave her the gift of fasting as a natural disposition. Once the forty days of Lent were over, her appetite always returned. Francis of Assisi is said to have been able to communicate with animals. The body of Betsie ten Boom, Corrie ten Boom's sister, upon her death from the ravages of a German concentration camp was transformed into a youthful, healed body. Agnes Sanford was able to heal others through her touch and prayers. What accounted for these miracles? Mystics might say that these were all gifts from God that came about through their *surrender to God*.

One of the most important characteristics that all mystics exhibited was the willingness to completely abandon their lives to God. They gave all their concerns about their welfare, future, and destiny to God in utter surrender. They said to God, in effect, "Everything is yours anyway. You created and hold the universe in the palm of your hand. You decide life and death. There is nothing I can do on my own that makes any difference or has any power. But I can give you my life, O Lord, and so I do. Take my life and do with it what you will."

This is a step that most of us are unwilling to take because we want to control our lives. We do not want to give God our lives, even though God already has them. We think that by trying so hard to determine our own outcomes, we can control our journey. The narrow path is a path of surrender. To truly stay on the path, we have to let God have everything. As Jean-Pierre de Caussade says:

> For obedience to God's undefiled will depends entirely on our passive surrender to it. We put nothing of ourselves into it apart from a general willingness that is prepared to do anything or nothing, like a tool that, though it has no power in itself, when in the hands of a craftsman, can be used by him for any purpose within the range of its capacity and design.[10]

Absolute surrender to God is one of the most difficult things for us to do because it requires that we go against all our other gods. We are only vaguely aware of how many false gods we serve in life. We don't call them gods, but they are: money, power, the clock, sports, alcohol, drugs, gambling, sex, entertainment, television, tradition, opinion, innovation, the Internet, our collections and hobbies, and so much more. A false god is anything to which we give the power to completely run our lives. For instance, how often have you given up a commitment or an opportunity in order to watch a favorite television show or sporting event? How often do you find your life being controlled by the clock or an appointment book? Notice how much the pursuit of money and power lie at the center of American life. Not only do we Americans pursue money and power, but we read magazine articles and books about those pursuing money and power.

The mystics did not live life in pursuit of these things. They did not surrender their lives to these false gods. That does not mean that a mystic would not have watched a favorite television show, worn a watch, read articles about celebrities, or accepted a position of power and influence. The difference is that a mystic would do such things only as secondary acts to surrendering himself to God. Mystics lived normal lives, and so in every age they engaged in "normal" activities. The difference is that mystics knew what the center of their life was. That center was and is God.

The true mystic accepts whatever life gives her, and finds a way to surrender her life in the midst of it. One of the mystics who has inspired me tremendously is Corrie ten Boom. Corrie and her family lived in Haarlem in the Netherlands during the German occupation of World War II. Their family had a clock-making and repair business. When the Jews were being rounded up to be sent to concentration camps, Corrie and her family gave themselves to God and asked what God wanted them to do. They sensed God calling them to hide Jews, and so they did. Over the course of the war they became known as leaders of the Dutch resistance movement, although the ten Booms thought of themselves merely as people helping God's children who were being persecuted.

When they were finally caught and sent to a concentration camp, Corrie and her sister Betsie surrendered themselves to God and asked what God wanted from them. They became spiritual leaders in the camp, holding large worship services and prayer meetings to instill hope in the other prisoners.

After the war, Corrie again surrendered to God and asked what God wanted her to do. She sensed that God once again had an important ministry for her, a ministry of forgiveness. So, Corrie traveled all around Europe, especially Germany, spreading the good news of God's forgiveness, even for the evil that had been committed. No matter what her situation, Corrie ten Boom surrendered to God, and discovered God continually guiding her to become a healing and caring steward of God's grace.

Living in the Present Moment

What point in time do most of us inhabit? Would it surprise you to find out that most of us do not really live in the point of time in which we exist? We may live in the present physically, but spiritually, mentally, and emotionally most of us tend to live in the past, the future, or both. It is rare to find someone who truly lives in the present.

The counseling profession is testimony to the power the past has over us. Millions of counselors are paid every day to explore people's pasts. All of us have been shaped by our past, but many of us also have been scarred by it. Whether that scarring came as a result of poor decisions we have made, accidents that have occurred, or the evil others have inflicted upon us, the reality is that many of us live in the past as we analyze over and over again these past experiences.

At the same time, many of us live in the future. We are constantly focusing on events that are coming down the road. Sometimes anticipating the future comes as a result of our work. We constantly have to look to the future in order to meet production schedules, develop products, and organize our efforts. Our personal lives also require a fair amount of thinking about the future. We have to sign up our children for activities, plan for future events, and organize our lives to engage in upcoming activities. Do we have to live in the future in order to plan for it? We not only plan for the future, but because of our fears we can be obsessed with what it may bring. We fear death, possible rejection, potential changes in our lives, and ordinary events that may impinge upon us. We fear what might happen if we admit to others that we have made a mistake. If we get cancer, we immediately become afraid of the worst-case scenario. If we are to speak in public, we become anxious about how we will do. So much of our time is spent focusing on the future.

Mystics live in the present moment. This does not mean that they do not think about the past or let the past influence them, nor does it mean that they do not think about the future. What it means is that they try to live in the moment without letting fear, concern, or anxiety over the past and future control their lives. They understand that it is by living in the present moment that we most deeply discover and are most deeply guided by God's presence. In his classic work *The Screwtape Letters,* C. S. Lewis emphasizes the importance of living in the present moment by speaking through the demons who do not want us to live in the present moment. The demon Screwtape says,

> The humans live in time, but our Enemy [God] destines them to eternity. He therefore, I believe, wants them to attend chiefly to two things, to eternity itself and to that point in time which they call the Present. For the Present is the point at which time touches eternity.[11]

When we live in the present moment, we live in eternity. We live in God's timeless kingdom that is filled with grace and wisdom. We live in a way that gives to God our future and destiny, while also putting into God's hands the task of healing our past. By living in the present moment, we are living in ultimate openness to God. All we ask is that God lead us moment by moment. In our culture, which is so focused on preparing for the future, it is hard to grasp what living in the present moment means. The question inevitably comes, "But if I do this, how can I make a living? What about the projects I have to complete? Doesn't this mean withdrawing from the real, practical world we live in?" The answer to all of these questions is that living in the present moment does not mean ignoring the demands of the future. It simply means not letting ourselves be ruled by the future. By living in the present, we allow God to be part of our work and planning. We do the work we have to in the moment, and share it with God. We do the best we can, and then we let God take care of the results. Instead of worrying about the future—about what may or may not happen—we enjoy the tasks at hand and let them become part of the simple steps we need to take as we walk our narrow paths.

Ultimately, living in the present moment means living according to Scripture. Jesus says, "So do not worry about tomorrow, for tomorrow will bring worries of its own. Today's trouble is enough for today" (Matt. 6:34). We give God our worries and our anxieties, and share the present with God. You have done this in your life, even though you may not realize it. Have you ever stopped to gaze at a flower, to look at a sunset or sunrise, or to be immersed in a piece of music? These moments are special because we spend them *in the present*. They transcend time, and so we do not sense the passage of time while we give ourselves over to them. The mystics live life much in this way, appreciating each passing moment. Yet they take one more step. They intentionally share these moments with God.

Solitude to Action

A crucial element of the narrow, mystical path is the practice of solitude. The mystics of Christian history continually emphasized the need for solitude. Perhaps this is why so many mystics became monastics. They recognized the importance of disengaging from life from time to time, not only to recharge spent batteries, but to re-center themselves upon God.

We live in such busy times. We are constantly pulled by this commitment, that demand, or those activities. No wonder we have such confused and difficult lives. We rarely allow ourselves to regenerate spiritually, mentally, or physically by spending time in intentional solitude. In fact, many people fear solitude because of what solitude exposes. It exposes us to our deepest selves. When we spend time alone, we have no choice but to discover ourselves, and what we find is often not pleasant. This is the time when our anxieties and concerns about the future are most likely to crop up, when anger about past events is most likely to capture our thoughts, and when self-criticism is most likely to dominate us.

So, we complain to others about how we have no time to ourselves, and relegate the need for solitude as a luxury we cannot afford in our busy lives. The mystics saw the need for solitude and silence as crucial for our lives. They believed solitude was as important as air, water, and food. Solitude is not merely a practice meant to reconnect us with God. It is not merely an activity for monks. Solitude is especially important for us if we are going to be actively engaged in the world. Indeed, the mystics believed spending time in solitude and silence was an important factor in serving God.

Why is solitude so important? Thomas Merton tells us, "The solitary life, being silent, clears away the smoke-screens of words that man has laid down between his mind and things."[12] Solitude helps us to determine what is and what isn't important according to God's perspectives. In fact, solitude and silence are critical components of living in the present moment, surrendering ourselves to God, detaching from the world, humbling ourselves, and falling in love with God. Through solitude, we take time to reintegrate.

One problem, though, is the present fascination among many in the modern Christian spirituality movement with solitude, silence, meditation, and contemplative prayer. All of these are important parts of rooting us more deeply in God, but they can quickly turn into false gods. Spending time in solitude and constant prayer can become an extreme act itself. I remember a story told about Mother Teresa. A man proudly told her that he was able to spend three hours a day in prayer and meditation. Mother Teresa's response was that he needed to cut down his prayer by two-and-a-half hours, and go out and work with the poor. In essence, she was saying that praying in solitude is good, but that it must only be for the purpose of serving God more effectively and faithfully in life. Contemplation, meditation, and solitude are practices meant to open us to God so that we can live with God more deeply in our actions.

Without the practice of solitude, we slowly lose our center and become defined by our activities. Time spent in solitude reconnects us with God and with our souls. It allows us to prioritize and to more effectively live life as God means for us to live it.

The Mystical Narrow Path

The narrow path of the mystics is not a path meant for a few, select, special Christians. It is the path set for all Christians. We are all called to be mystics, for we are all called to love God with all our minds, hearts, souls, and strength. What the mystics have shown us is that this path, although seemingly out of sync with the paths set for us by the world, is a practical path. The problem for so many is that it is a path that places God at the center, not power, money, achievement, accumulation, security, or acclaim. It is a path that we walk with intentionality. It is a path that we walk in trust.

The narrow, mystical path is a path in which we are involved in the world, but not ruled by the world. Perhaps the best way to describe it is to say that the mystical path is a path that connects God's kingdom with the world's kingdoms. Many Christians make the mistake of thinking that God's kingdom refers to heaven—to the place we go when we die. God's kingdom is more than this. God's kingdom is present now, and all those who humbly and lovingly live with God in the present moment surrender themselves to God, and make the kingdom real to the world.

Dallas Willard speaks eloquently about this by saying,

> Jesus' good news about the kingdom can be an effective guide for our lives only if we share his view of the world in which we live. To his eyes this is a God-bathed and God-permeated world. It is a world filled with a glorious reality, where every component is within the range of God's direct knowledge and control—though he obviously permits some of it, for good reasons, to be for a while otherwise than as he wishes. It is a world that is inconceivably beautiful and good because of God and because God is always in it. It is a world in which God is continually at play and over which he constantly rejoices.[13]

In effect, Willard is saying that the mystical path is meant to be our path, but we will never realize it until we let our paths originate in God's kingdom.

When we accept the reality that this world is filled with God's presence, and that God wants us to live in it in a way that goes beyond the world's vision, we discover an incredible life—the life lived by the mystics. We discover the narrow path that God sets for each of us.

Questions for Reflection

1. To what extent do you think you are a mystic?
2. How much do you hold love of God and of others at the core of your faith? What gets in the way of placing this love at the core of your faith?
3. What practical things can you do to humble yourself?
4. What things, events, or people are you attached to, and how can you detach more from them?
5. What can you do to surrender more to God?
6. What would you need to do to live more in the present moment?

Key Learnings

- Mystics are people who have fallen deeply in love with God, and so live deep lives that flow from God's grace because they are profoundly grounded in God.
- Mystics are centered in God's love, embody Scripture in a way that brings it to life, and see their whole lives as mission.
- Mystics love God above all else, are humble, detach themselves from the world's ways, surrender themselves to God, live in the present moment, and steep their work in prayer.
- All of us are called to be mystics.

Chapter 3

Walking the Balanced Path

*Y*ou may not recognize Millard Fuller's name, but you probably know about his gift to the world. Fuller has influenced the lives of millions of people through his direct work on behalf of the poor; through his organization, which enlists others to help the poor; and by inspiring others to serve God on behalf of the poor. How he ended up serving God by serving the poor is itself an inspiring story.[1]

Earlier in his life, Fuller was a man who loved money, and he had a gift for making money. His gift first surfaced when he was six years old. After seeing pigs traded at a farm show, he begged his father to buy him one. So, his father bought him a pig, built a little pen in the back yard, and taught his son how to set up a bookkeeping system to understand cost and profits. Fuller scrupulously kept a record of everything it cost to feed and keep the pig, and after he had fattened the pig up a bit, he sold it for a profit. Fuller was hooked. He loved making that profit. He moved on to raising and selling chickens, and he made a profit from them, too. As his profits increased, so did his appetite for larger projects. He bought and sold rabbits, and made a profit there. He and his father bought and sold cattle, and they made a profit in that business, too.

By high school, Fuller was a burgeoning entrepreneur. He was a member of Junior Achievement and had his own little company that manufactured mops and house-number signs. By college, Millard was beginning to bring in larger and larger profits. While studying law at the University of Alabama, he and his roommate, Morris Dees (whose story is equally inspiring—he is the head of the Southern Poverty Law Center, an organization that fights racism), sold and delivered birthday cakes to parents to have delivered to their college-aged children. They also sold doormats, trash-can holders, and lamps made out of cypress. They invested their profits in real estate and owned half a city block and a small trailer park. By the early 1960s, they were making $50,000 a year. By age twenty-eight, Fuller was a millionaire. Who wouldn't be happy to be in his shoes? He was living the American dream. He had every-thing we say should make us happy: money, homes, cars, a wife and kids. So why did he feel like his life was falling apart?

Fuller had become so focused on achieving and acquiring that his life had become horribly unbalanced. At a time when he should have been reveling in how great his life was, his wife left him. She left because she had everything most people think they could possibly want, but all she wanted was her hus-band, and he was never there. Facing the possibility that he would lose his family, Fuller realized he had to do something to get his life back in balance. After talking to a pastor in New York, and then engaging in deep discussions about his life with his wife, they decided they should follow Jesus' advice to the rich young man (Matt. 19:16–30). They decided to sell all their belong-ings so that they could follow Christ. They gave all their money away to char-ity and got involved in a Christian ministry called Koinonia Partners.

From that point onward, Fuller's marriage and life began to improve as the couple centered their lives more in God and God's work. In 1973, Fuller, his wife, and their four children moved to Zaire, Africa, to help build modest hous-ing for low-income families. Their project became so successful that they decided they were being called by God to apply this idea worldwide. They moved back to Georgia in 1976 and created the housing ministry Habitat for Humanity. This organization builds affordable, safe, and reliable housing for low-income families. Since its inception, Habitat for Humanity has built homes for over 60,000 families in more than 1,400 American cities and in 57 countries around the world. This is an organization that cuts across denominational, reli-gious, and national boundaries. Among the volunteers are former presidents, senators, members of Congress, executives, and people from every walk of life.

Today, Millard Fuller receives a salary of only $52,000. The focus of his life is on serving God by serving the poor. Fuller originally walked the wide, unbal-anced path that the world had set before him, but today he is walking the nar-row, balanced path, and this makes all the difference in his life. As he says, "I feel that I am close to God, and I think I am pleasing God. I know that my heart's desire is to express love in a way that touches people. Providing a home for people who need a place to live is an incredible way to touch people."[2]

Walking the Unbalanced Path

Millard Fuller's story is not as rare as we might think. In fact, if we pay atten-tion, we hear stories like this from people throughout our culture. Most peo-ple are not called to do the kind of work Fuller has done because they don't possess the same organizational and entrepreneurial skills. God calls us only to the work for which God has gifted us. Books, newspapers, magazines, televisions, radios, e-mail, and so much more flood us with stories about people who were living unbalanced lives, only to burn out and lose their families, their careers, their fortunes, their health, and their lives because of their imbalance. It is often in the midst of these losses that they discover their need for greater balance and for God. In fact, balance and God go hand in hand.

In Fuller's case, it was the potential loss of his wife and family due to his workaholism that caused him to listen to God, center himself in God, and bring balance back to his life. Many suffer from similar addictive problems. We can become slaves to work, alcohol, drugs, sex, food, gambling, shopping, sports, exercise, television, and a myriad of other addictions.

Many more of us suffer from problems that are more mild than addiction, but these problems have the power to make our lives just as unbalanced. For example, many families are overcommitted. Parents rush to this event or that, all in the name of making their children the best they can be. Many teens fill their days with all sorts of activities, in the hope of getting into a better college and having a better career. Many adults overfill their lives with activities. They do as much in their leisure time as they do at work, hoping that all their frenetic leisure activities will somehow take the edge off all their work activities. In all of these cases, stress heightens to a fever pitch, often creating all sorts of sleep and eating disorders, plunging people into depression, and creating health problems, from hypertension to suppressed immune systems.

Americans and much of the Western world live in a culture of imbalance. While we Christians may claim to place Christ at our center, the reality is that we place all sorts of false idols at the center of our lives along with Christ. As a result, we never quite know whether we are serving Christ or other false gods, and we are never aware of this conflict. We constantly feel the need to appease the gods of hurry, acquire, do, gratify, stimulate, accomplish, achieve, be noticed, obtain, and attain. For many of us, slowing down is unimaginable. I remember a medical doctor who came to me for counseling. She suffered from stress-related problems. In the course of our work, she told me that when she watched television she would simultaneously scan through a pile of catalogs. "Why?" I asked her. She replied, "I don't know. I just feel guilty for sitting there indulging myself by watching television. I feel that as long as I am looking through catalogs, I'm doing something productive."

So many people I know take an almost martyr-like pride in how little sleep they get, how little time they have for anything, and how busy they are. If we decide to balance our lives by trying to get eight hours of sleep a night, eat dinner each night with our families, take a half-hour each day for prayer, another half-hour for exercise, and several hours each night to read, play, or relax, others look at us like we are crazy. It is amazing how trying to be balanced can seem so abnormal to a culture that has no sense of balance.

The truth is that this problem of imbalance is not just a recent phenomenon. People of every age have succumbed to the temptation to live unbalanced lives. Many of us, for instance, dream of an earlier time when things were easier and simpler, when the tensions and stresses of life were not so demanding. Thomas Kelly offers us a reminder that the factors that lead to an unbalanced life are mostly internal rather than external. They are a result of our own choice to give in to the demands of the world around us. In 1938, a time we see as much simpler and free, Kelly wrote,

> Let me first suggest that we are giving a false explanation of the complexity of our lives. We blame it upon the complex environment. Our complex living, we say, is due to the complex world we live in, with its radios and autos, which give us more stimulation per square hour than used to be given per square day to our grandmothers. . . . Complexity of our program cannot be blamed upon complexity of our environment, much as we should like to think so. . . .
>
> We Western peoples are apt to think our greatest problems are external, environmental. We are not skilled in the inner life, where the real roots of our problem lie. For I would suggest that the true explanation of the complexity of our program is an inner one, not an outer one. The outer distractions of our interests reflect an inner lack of integration of our own lives. We are trying to be several selves at once, without all ourselves being organized by a single, mastering Life within us. Each of us tends to be, not a single self, but a whole committee of selves.[3]

Kelly nails the problem pretty accurately. We tend to blame our stress on our circumstances, our situations, those around us, and the unfairness of life. We fail to realize that the only people we can truly blame are ourselves. I am not saying that there are no stressful circumstances, situations, or contexts. All of us go through times of extreme difficulty. The stresses from these times can build within us until we feel we are about to explode. Stress can come from working in a job with an oppressive, uncaring, or inappropriate boss, coworker, or employee. It can come from major life changes and transitions, such as the birth of a new child; sending a child or children to college; divorce; the death of our parents, spouses, or children; the loss of a job; retirement; or the onset of a major disease, illness, or trauma. All of these experiences apply pressure to our lives. They are all incredibly stressful, yet the *degree* to which they are stressful has more to do with how we respond to them than the situations themselves.

I have seen people fall apart completely in the face of small disasters that seem relatively inconsequential. I have also witnessed people of faith struggling with cancer, losing their career, or facing death with a sense of faith, hope, and even joy. The storms of life rage all around us, but it is how we respond to these storms that determines the extent to which they can destroy or deform us. In fact, if we respond to these events and experiences with a sense of faith, hope, and love, they have the power to bring a deeper sense of balance to our lives by centering us in God.

Stressful events, situations, and circumstances surround us. We will never be immune to them, but we do face choices. Will we allow them to unbalance our lives, leaving us wheezing and gasping in their wake, or will we face them in a way that allows us to deepen our lives and grow in God's grace?

Balancing Our Lives on the Divine Fulcrum

When we look at Millard Fuller's life, it is easy to see the factors that made his life unbalanced. He had completely given his life over to his career. He was not balancing his work life with his home life, nor was he centered in God. Instead, he was overcommitted to his career, ambitions, and the need to be a success. What changed? What did he do to bring balance back into his life?

Whenever our lives become unbalanced, we have a tendency to do things that can create even more imbalance, even though we think it is making us more balanced. It is almost like our lives are great balancing scales on which we place all of our activities. When we experience a sense of imbalance, often we become guilty of overloading our activity scale while leaving the rest and reflection scale relatively empty. We load all of our responsibilities, commitments, and requirements onto the activity scale. The more we load onto that scale, the faster our lives begin to crash from the sheer weight of it all.

Unfortunately, too many people try to remedy the imbalance by loading a ton of things onto the rest and reflection scale. For example, if I am overcommitted at work, I may try to load more leisure activities onto the complementary scale of my life, hoping that this will relax me more. So, after spending a hard day at work, I go out to a bar with friends. Or I go to a sporting event or the theater, run five miles, take a pottery class, shop, meet with friends, clean the house, or do a myriad of other events intended to relieve my stress and soothe my stressed soul.

The problem with this approach is that while we think that we are bringing more balance to our lives, we are actually creating a greater imbalance. We *think* that we are putting more onto the rest and reflection scale, but really we are just placing more activities on the activity scale. We deceive ourselves into thinking that we are balancing our lives. We work and work and work, and then we do even more during our time away from work. Instead of taking time to discern how God may be calling us to balance our lives, we take it upon ourselves to balance our lives according to the world's commands, and this leads us to live lives that are even more unbalanced.

We are called by God to balance our lives in a way that places God at the fulcrum. Too often we place everything *but* God at the fulcrum. Many of these things are good in and of themselves, but they are not God. For example, we may place political, economic, psychological, philosophical, and even theological beliefs and traditions at our fulcrum. These are belief systems that can inform and guide us to live more balanced lives and lead us to the center, but they are not living guides that can lead us in the midst of confusion. They are general principles, not personal guides. Our center must be alive, vibrant, and able to have an ongoing relationship with us. We can also place work, family, or ourselves at the fulcrum. While it is important to focus on our families, make a commitment to our careers, and nurture our own personal growth, such activities cannot be at the fulcrum either because they are merely parts of a balanced life. Total focus on one makes us slaves to the part. Nothing other than God can be the center because nothing else has the living capacity to be the center. When God is our center, we are able to seek guidance from God that is unique to our lives. God teaches each of us how to uniquely balance our lives. God may teach us by speaking to us through our belief systems and traditions, and by leading us to focus more on our careers, home, or personal lives, but only God can be our center.

Let me give you an example of what I mean by all of this. In my work as a spiritual director, I have worked with quite a few pastors over the years. One of the things that amazes me about so many pastors is how unbalanced their lives are. It is ironic because pastors are entrusted with teaching others how to live balanced lives. Too many pastors live quietly anguished lives as they devote themselves to their churches, often at the expense of their families, their health, and their faith. They work sixty to seventy hours a week, trying their best to make their churches successful. Sometimes they reach their goal, but the price they pay is often an internal emptiness and loneliness that they must keep hidden from the members of their church. Why are these servants of God suffering so much? In many or even most cases it is because they have placed something other than God at their fulcrums.

Is God really asking them to sacrifice their marriages, families, and health all for the sake of God? Some believe this is the case. I remember speaking with a pastor friend of mine. He told me that when he was in seminary, a professor suggested that if he wanted to learn to be a pastor, the best thing he could do would be to read the book *A Man Named Peter*. This is the biography of Peter Marshall, written by his wife, Catherine. Marshall was pastor of National Capital Presbyterian Church in Washington, D.C., during the 1930s and 1940s, and was also chaplain to the U.S. Senate during the late 1940s. He was, by all accounts, a wonderful pastor, but he overworked himself. He was a heavy smoker and worked sixty, seventy, and sometimes eighty hours a week. Even after he suffered a heart attack in his early forties and his doctors advised him to slow down, he wouldn't. Soon afterwards he died, leaving his wife and children without a husband and father, and with no means of support. After reading this book, my friend's reaction was, "If I do what Marshall did, I will be dead in my early forties just like Marshall! This can't be how God wants me to be." I would not presume to say that God wasn't at Peter Marshall's fulcrum (nor at that of my friend's professor), but it is clear that something else shared Marshall's center with God. At his center was a cultural idolization of work and the need to make work the most important thing in our lives, especially work on behalf of God. It is the idolatry of our culture telling us that to be successful we have to get to the top of the heap.

So many of today's pastors feel inadequate because they are pastors of small, seemingly insignificant churches. They want to be seen as stronger and better pastors, but they feel trapped in small churches. It is almost as if their churches are a fiery brand, marking them as failures in the world's eyes. Are they failures? Often the answer is no. God has placed them there for a reason, but because they fail to place God at their center they no longer sense what that reason is. Sometimes being successful in God's eyes means not being successful in the eyes of our culture and of our peers.

As I said earlier, many pastors have come to me complaining that they are burned out, that they dislike their churches, and that they don't like their lives. Often, my work with them is simply helping place God at the fulcrum of their lives again. For example, one pastor I know consistently complained that the members of his church wouldn't do what he asked them to do. They looked to him for leadership, and he would bring all sorts of new ideas, but then they would resist them. He was frustrated. Over and over I heard from him, "What's wrong with these people? If they don't want what I'm bringing to the table, why do they keep asking me to lead them?"

As we worked together, we explored the possibility that something else was at his fulcrum other than God. What became apparent was that he was placing the culture's values at his center. He was responding to the call of the American culture to be a strong leader who casts the only vision, and then was responsible for the minutiae of reeling it in. They did not accept his vision because it was his, not theirs and not God's.

Over time, we talked about replacing the cultural standards at his fulcrum with God, and listening to what God was calling for him as a pastor and then for the church. Was being active, overworked, and burned-out what God really wanted for this man? Was there an alternative vision? Over time, he began to back off his need to control the church and became much more involved in sowing seeds of ideas and then letting the members decide whether or not to nurture them. He began to listen more for what God was calling him to do in his church. Soon, he discovered something unexpected: he was no longer burning out. He felt that he was engaging in more of a partnership with his members, and the result was that he was enjoying their company more. He was spending less time on administrative duties because they were doing more. Finally, he began sleeping better at night, and his weight dropped to a healthier level. All of this happened because he was letting God be his fulcrum, and the result was a rebalancing of his life.

While I am talking about the work of pastors, the truth is that there is no career where God cannot be placed at the fulcrum. No radical difference exists between ministry and the rest of life that results in an inability to place God at the center. In fact, most people would be surprised at the number of pastors leading churches who actually don't place God at their fulcrums. The laity often don't notice it because they themselves have not placed God at their fulcrums. How can they notice it in a pastor if they fail to notice it in themselves?

I remember hearing something remarkable that a pastor whom I respect deeply said to the audience of large, denominational conference. He was talking about the process of finding God in our lives and ministry, and told a story about his own experience as a pastor immediately after discovering that he had multiple sclerosis. He struggled deeply with the onset of this disabling disease. How could God give such a loyal servant a disease like this? How could God treat him in this way? He said that for the next year, he never mentioned God in any of his sermons. Afterwards, he reflected on this and said, "I don't know what bothered me more. That I spent a year as a pastor never mentioning God, or that the members of my church never seemed to notice."

We've become so accustomed to placing anything else but God at our fulcrums that it doesn't seem out of place when others do, too. It is crucial that God be placed at the fulcrum of life no matter who we are or what we do. Whether we are executives, laborers, homemakers, clerks, accountants, lawyers, doctors, teachers, waiters, researchers, mechanics, or cooks, the only way to ultimately balance our lives is by placing God at the fulcrum. We place God there by listening to God as God shows us how to balance our lives.

Sometimes God will call us to balance the activities we have on our activity scales by leading us to engage in *more* stress-reducing activities. More often, God will ask us to *remove* activities from these activity scales. In essence, God asks us to scale back our activities so that we have more room to center our lives in God. This may mean learning to say no: "No, I can't be

on that committee." "No, I can't go to the game." "No, you can't join the soc-
cer team because you are doing too much as it is now." "No, I can't take on
that added responsibility at work." "No, I have to spend more time with my
family." "No, I have to spend more time with God."

The key to all of this is that we have to be clear about what is at our center
so that we can decide how to set boundaries and limits on our activities and
ask, "Is this what God wants?" It is only by placing God at our fulcrums that
we begin to achieve real balance. This whole balancing act is a process. It is
not something we will ever achieve with perfection (only people who are
unbalanced seek perfection). You will never achieve balance immediately or
perfectly. Sometimes, balance comes only after we've struggled through a
long period of imbalance. We may actually have to undergo a time of imbalance in order to bring about balance. For instance, if we decide to scale back
at work, we may have to devote more time to our job for several months to
prepare the way for a life of greater balance. The key is listening to God as
God calls us to balance our lives.

The Balance of Jesus' Life

To truly understand how we are called to live a balanced life, we must pay
attention to how Jesus balanced his own life. Typically, when we Western
Christians reflect on Jesus' life, we see him as a bundle of activity. This is a
man who was constantly surrounded by people clamoring for his help, healing power, teachings, and forgiveness. Everywhere he went he was busily
engaging in some sort of ministry. If there was ever a prototypical Western
male in terms of work ethic and activity, Jesus was it. Or was he?

How many people devote themselves entirely to their ministry for Christ,
all while thinking they have to give up *everything* to do God's work? How
many people believe that to be a disciple of Christ means giving up all concern
for themselves in order to respond to all the needs of the world? It is helpful to
look at how Jesus lived his life. Did he live a life of balance or imbalance?

Several years ago, I went through Matthew's Gospel and charted how balanced or unbalanced Jesus' life was. What I did was very simple. I made two
columns: *Active Ministry* and *Rest and Reflection*. Next, I wrote in Jesus'
activities in the appropriate column. Then, I drew a path down the middle that
reflected Jesus' being active or spending time in rest and reflection. I was surprised by what I found. Jesus lived an incredibly balanced life, at least for the
three years of his ministry. My scale is shown in figure 1.

Some explanation of figure 1 is needed. If you look at the beginning of
Jesus' ministry (right after John baptized him), Jesus' first act was not typical

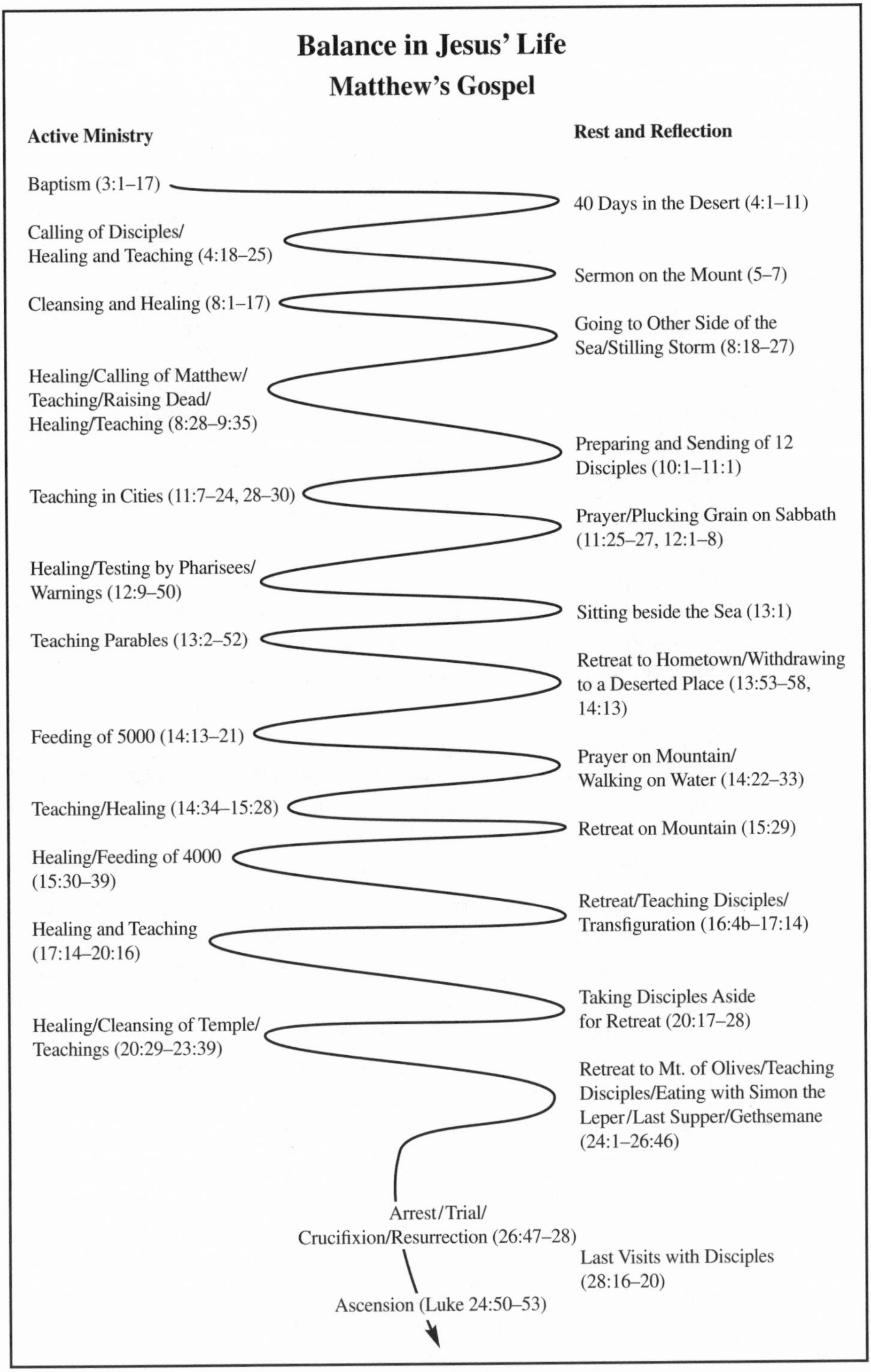

Balance in Jesus' Life
Matthew's Gospel

Active Ministry

Baptism (3:1–17)

Calling of Disciples/
Healing and Teaching (4:18–25)

Cleansing and Healing (8:1–17)

Healing/Calling of Matthew/
Teaching/Raising Dead/
Healing/Teaching (8:28–9:35)

Teaching in Cities (11:7–24, 28–30)

Healing/Testing by Pharisees/
Warnings (12:9–50)

Teaching Parables (13:2–52)

Feeding of 5000 (14:13–21)

Teaching/Healing (14:34–15:28)

Healing/Feeding of 4000
(15:30–39)

Healing and Teaching
(17:14–20:16)

Healing/Cleansing of Temple/
Teachings (20:29–23:39)

Rest and Reflection

40 Days in the Desert (4:1–11)

Sermon on the Mount (5–7)

Going to Other Side of the
Sea/Stilling Storm (8:18–27)

Preparing and Sending of 12
Disciples (10:1–11:1)

Prayer/Plucking Grain on Sabbath
(11:25–27, 12:1–8)

Sitting beside the Sea (13:1)

Retreat to Hometown/Withdrawing
to a Deserted Place (13:53–58,
14:13)

Prayer on Mountain/
Walking on Water (14:22–33)

Retreat on Mountain (15:29)

Retreat/Teaching Disciples/
Transfiguration (16:4b–17:14)

Taking Disciples Aside
for Retreat (20:17–28)

Retreat to Mt. of Olives/Teaching
Disciples/Eating with Simon the
Leper/Last Supper/Gethsemane
(24:1–26:46)

Arrest/Trial/
Crucifixion/Resurrection (26:47–28)

Last Visits with Disciples
(28:16–20)

Ascension (Luke 24:50–53)

FIGURE 1

of what we might have done. If we had what we thought was a legitimate inspiration from the Holy Spirit, calling us to serve God in a ministry of teaching and healing, we probably would be in a rush to get started. Oddly, Jesus began his ministry with a retreat into the desert for forty days. The purpose of this retreat was to prepare him so that he would remain focused on the Father's will, not his own human will. He wanted to be sure that he was open to the Holy Spirit, and not just following his own desires for power and control.

At the end of his time of fasting and prayer, a time of weakness and suffering, Jesus was put to the test. Satan tempted him. The test was whether or not he was truly grounded in the will of the Creator. If he wasn't, Satan's offers of self-sufficiency, security, and supremacy were sure to expose his weakness and destroy his ministry. Jesus needed that time in the desert to truly surrender himself and his will to the Father, so that he could withstand the temptations of life.

From there, Jesus immediately set out to call his disciples, his new family, and to begin teaching and healing. Now, it might seem odd to place the Sermon on the Mount in the "Rest and Reflection" column. It is until you realize that Jesus was climbing the mountain (as he often did) for his own personal retreat. The Sermon on the Mount came about because crowds of people followed him. They wanted more of his healing and teaching. So, he turned around and taught them.

Jesus then embarked on a series of cleansings and healings, and afterwards went to the other side of the sea to get away from the crowds for time alone with the Father. He stilled the storm only because the disciples were in a panic while Jesus slept calmly in the bow of the boat. He then performed a series of healings and teachings, and even raised a person from the dead. Then Jesus took the disciples aside, prepared them for their mission, and sent them out to teach and heal. Knowing the way Jesus was, we can conclude that he spent time with the Creator alone afterwards.

Next, Jesus taught in the cities and then spent time in prayer. It was during his time of resting and walking that the Pharisees criticized him for plucking grain on the Sabbath. From there he went on to perform some healings, at which point the Pharisees tested him. Jesus then withdrew from them to sit alone beside the sea. Unfortunately he found it difficult to be alone, for crowds followed him everywhere. Jesus responded to them by teaching them in parables. He later retreated to his hometown, where he spent time with his disciples and his family, although he also did some teaching and was rejected.

He ended up teaching the crowds again, and afterwards had compassion for them and fed them by dividing five loaves and two fish into enough food for everyone. He withdrew to pray on a mountain, which led to the circumstances of his walking on water. Do you know why Jesus walked on water? It was because while he was off praying, his disciples had gone on without him by boat, and Jesus was walking on the water to catch up with them after he had spent time praying.

Then he devoted more time to teaching and healing, and again took a retreat on a mountain. More healings followed, along with the feeding of the four thousand. Then he took time for retreat with his disciples and by himself, which is where the transfiguration occurred. Jesus had taken Peter, James, and John onto a high mountain for retreat, where he was made dazzling white. Again, Jesus went from there to teach and heal some more, and he took the disciples aside for a retreat to teach them.

Note that I have interpreted time spent teaching the disciples privately as retreat or "family" time. The disciples had become Jesus' family, and similar to our time spent with our families, much of his time was spent teaching, too. This time with family is still a time of rest and reflection because it is time spent with loved ones, and the disciples were Jesus' loved ones. They had become his family.

From there, Jesus went to Jerusalem, healed and taught, and cleansed the Temple. Then he withdrew to the Mount of Olives to be with his disciples. He taught them, ate dinner with Simon the Leper, spent Passover supper with his disciples (the Last Supper), and took time alone in the Garden of Gethsemane to pray. Finally, he was arrested, tried, crucified, and resurrected. For the remaining days after his resurrection, he spent time with his disciples, preparing them for their ministry and mission to come. Then he ascended into heaven.

You can see from all of this that Jesus lived a surprisingly balanced life. Even though people constantly crowded him, demanding more and more, Jesus knew he had to reserve hours for prayer, reflection, and rest. At times he had no choice but to teach and heal. The people crowded into his privacy, but he responded with love and compassion, and waited patiently for his next time of prayer. Jesus never went too long without prayer and re-centering himself in the Father.

Perhaps this constant centering explains why Jesus called the Creator "Abba." We translate the word "Abba" to mean "Father," but the term is more intimate than that—more like "Dad" than "Father." Jesus was intimate with the Father, and because he was, the will of the Father flowed through him. They had become as one. Jesus says as much to his disciples: "If you know me, you will know my Father also" (John 14:7).

So, what does all of this say? It says that if we are to truly imitate Christ and live the Christian life, we need to balance our lives as Jesus did his. The call to be a Christian is not one of constant activity. It is one of ministry and mission that is rooted in prayer, rest, and reflection. We cannot serve Christ if we let ourselves constantly get off center—if we let ourselves get off God.

Even When We Try to Be Balanced, We're Unbalanced

So, how did we get so unbalanced? Perhaps the obvious answer is one that is used so often in our present culture. We have gotten so off center because we do not keep the mind, body, and spirit in balance. While this answer is true, people can mean different things when they talk about keeping the mind, body, and spirit in balance.

Several years ago, I went to a conference on the connection between healing and spirituality, sponsored by an organization devoted to the mind, body, and spirit connection. Throughout the conference, I was fascinated by what the speakers were telling us. They were describing things I already knew in general about faith and healing (we will talk more about this topic in chapter 5), but they were putting flesh on the bones, offering us dramatic and inspiring examples of the connection between the two. Among the presenters were a well-known author and medical doctor, a nurse who had been practicing therapeutic touch, a shaman from Hawaii, a local medical doctor who had been praying with patients, and a band that played Hindu music on handcrafted and hand-carved instruments. What seemed odd was that the conference included no Christian presenters. Now, you have to understand that I am not one of those Christians who believes Christianity should be at the forefront of everything, nor do I reject things because they aren't Christian. It surprised me, though, that there were no Christian speakers because of the fact that the connection between faith and healing has been a part of the Christian faith since Christ. One-fourth of the Gospels is devoted to healing, and even though mainstream Christianity has tended to diminish the importance of the connection between faith and healing, there are still many, many Christian denominations, groups, and individuals for whom healing prayer is central to their faith.

Afterwards, I introduced myself to the wife of the man responsible for the conference and told her that I was the regional coordinator for an association of spiritual directors. I explained that spiritual direction and the whole field of spiritual formation was devoted to integrating the spirit with the mind and body, and that the spiritual healing that led to physical healing was a part of it. She was excited and suggested that I talk to her organization's coordinator.

When I called the coordinator the following week, however, she was less than enthusiastic. It quickly became apparent that she had two problems with my offering to create a dialogue between her organization and our group of spiritual directors. The first problem was one that was endemic of the whole conference, and that continues to be a problem with all the conferences the organization has offered in the years since I first spoke with this woman. While they were interested in the connection between spirituality and heal-ing, they also seemed to have what I would call an "ABC" mentality. In other words, they were interested in exploring the connection between healing and spirituality as long as it was "anything but Christianity." This is a problem in many of the medical and psychological fields that are exploring the connec-tion between spirituality and healing. I suppose that it is our own fault. For far too long Christians have been a judgmental lot, and so many in the heal-ing fields have left Christianity because of scars they bear from what they con-sider to have been the oppressive, regimented, and judging nature of their churches. At the same time, this attitude completely ignores the one faith tra-dition that has had healing as a part of it since the beginning.

The other reason, I suspect, she was not so receptive to my offers of a dia-logue was that while the fields of medicine, psychology, and health talk about balancing our mind, bodies, and spirit, they really are not referring to balanc-ing the three. Medicine, psychology, and the other related fields of health are so rooted in the nonspiritual, tangible world that they don't understand the realm of the spirit. For many of them, what they would call "spirituality" is simply a heightened form of psychological awareness and consciousness. For instance, they may teach meditation techniques, but the focus of their medi-tation is on becoming more aware of themselves, their bodies, and their sur-roundings, or on integrating the connection between their minds and their bodies. They will not talk about God, God's Spirit, or even the Divine for fear of turning off the people they are teaching. The question is, can you have spir-ituality—which is focused on matters of the human spirit and of God's Spirit—without the Spirit? Without God, there is no spirituality, because spir-ituality is by its very nature an openness to the Spirit.

A lack of balance exists among those trying to bring a greater sense of bal-ance. While they may talk about bringing into balance our minds, bodies, and spirits, what they are trying to do is balance the mind and the body. This is typical of our culture. We don't know what to do with spirituality, even among the religious. Some suspect that if you are a Christian and claim you are inter-ested in spirituality, then you are guilty of being a New Ager or of not being Christ-centered. It places everyone in a conundrum: those outside of Chris-tianity are skeptical of Christian spirituality, and those inside of Christianity are skeptical of Christian spirituality. It is no wonder that even as we try to be balanced, we remain unbalanced.

A Lack of Integration

The basic problem, when it comes to bringing more balance to our lives, is that there is too often a complete lack of integration between the spiritual, mental, physical, and relational dimensions of our lives.[4] As human beings, we are spiritual, mental, physical, and relational beings, as figure 2 illustrates. All of these dimensions are given to us as gifts from God, and they are meant to be integrated within us in a way that is relatively harmonious. The problem is that they rarely are. Unfortunately, we tend to overdevelop certain dimensions of our lives, while ignoring other dimensions.

The *spiritual dimension* is the dimension of our lives that is most focused on matters of transcendence. The human spirit always aspires to transcend normal human restraints in order to embrace the Divine and let it flow through the rest of our lives. It is at the level of the spiritual that we commune most with God and receive inspirations from God (although communing with and being inspired by God also involve the other dimensions). It is through and due to the spiritual dimension that we *aspire* to live the lives God seeks for us. It is also through this dimension that we receive guiding and sustaining *inspirations* from God's Spirit.

The *mental dimension* is most concerned with functioning, organizing, and implementing ideas, objectives, and plans. In other words, our minds are always working to figure out how to "do." This is true whether we are talking about organizing a corporation, figuring out how to write a paper, planning a

---

The Four Dimensions of Human Life

Spiritual
Aspiring toward and Being Inspired by God

Mental
Functioning, Organizing, and Achieving Ambitions

Physical
Satisfying and Gratifying Urges, Drives, and Desires

Relational
Relating to Others in the Present, Past, and Future

FIGURE 2

party, deciding what to have for dinner, or scanning the television guide to decide what we will watch on television. Our minds are always planning, organizing, and executing. The level of the mind is always most focused on function. At this level, *achieving our ambitions* in an efficient and effective way is the most important goal.

The *physical dimension* is most concerned with feeling, sensing, and doing. It is at this level that we feel and respond to urges, impulses, drives, and instincts. It is also at this level that we act on and do what our spirits and minds guide us to do. Our bodies are amazing creations. They are able to embody and make tangible what otherwise remain urges, drives, thoughts, and aspirations. At the same time, the bodily dimension is often in conflict. Do we follow our urges and drives, or our thoughts and inspirations? Do we act on our impulses, our ambitions, or our aspirations?

The final dimension is the *relational dimension*. Despite what some people may think, human beings were created for relationships. Look around and you'll see all the evidence you need. Families, schools, churches, political organizations, clubs, companies, stores, roads, parks, telephones, televisions, and the Internet are all reflections of our need for relationships. The relational dimension is always concerned with maintaining, facilitating, and deepening our relationships. These are not only the relationships we have with those around us today, but with those who came before us and come after us. For instance, one of the foundations of Christianity is that we are not only the present-day body of Christ (1 Cor. 12:4–31) in the sense that we are meant to have loving relationships with those living today. We are also part of the past and future body of Christ, and thus we are to build our faith and love on the teachings of those who came before us, and for the benefit of those who will live tomorrow. We are to learn from the traditions of our faith in order to care for everyone in the present and the future. Ultimately, this relational dimension connects us in an ever-deepening relationship with God, who *is* love (1 John 4:7–21).

Human beings were created as embodied spirits (Gen. 2:7) with a mission. We are to live in relationship with God, with others, and with the world (Gen. 2:4–25). We are to integrate our spirits, minds, bodies, and relationships, as shown in figure 3. Ultimately, the spiritual dimension needs to guide and flow through the mental dimension, which must guide and flow through the physical dimension, which must guide and flow through our relationships. There also needs to be a reciprocal flow so that feedback from the relational dimension radiates back through the physical dimension, the physical through the mental, and the mental through the spiritual. When our lives are balanced in this way, we experience a kind of harmony of the soul in which our lives seem to be in sync.

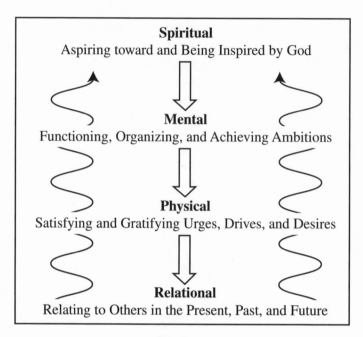

FIGURE 3

You have experienced this harmony before. Think of a time in which every-thing you did just seemed "right." You made a decision or did something that you just "knew" was what God wanted. You were able to make a plan that seemed right, you were able to act in just the right way, and your actions enhanced one relationship or many. For instance, I remember this feeling when I decided to become pastor of Calvin Presbyterian Church. It followed a period during which a lack of integration had been growing between my dif-ferent dimensions.

I had been involved in trying to start a new church-development project that seemed right for a while, but that began to fall apart as more and more people got involved. The vision had been to create a church that would seek to nurture people spiritually, and help them to listen to God in their daily lives. It would target people who had been disaffected by the traditional church, and had become attracted to Eastern or New Age practices.

When I first began work on the new church project, it was a project rooted in prayer. I had been praying, asking God what God wanted me to do, and in the midst of this I received an inspiration to start a new kind of church. For several days, I continued to listen, trying to discern whether or not this was just my ego talking, or if it was really God's Spirit speaking to me.

The idea grew over time, and so I decided to test it. I began to make my plans. I mentally organized the inspiration and put a plan to paper. I met with a denominational executive, who got very excited about the project because he had just read about a new, different kind of church in Seattle, Washington. He had been wondering why our denomination couldn't do something similar in our area. The two of us began working on the project. You can see here that we were taking the inspirations of the spiritual dimension, letting them flow through the mental dimension as we organized and made our plans. These inspirations and plans flowed through the physical dimensions as we did the actual physical work—writing, meetings, speaking, listening—needed to make the project go. Also, we formed a relationship, and in the process formed even more relationships with others as they joined us. For a while, a growing sense of integration and harmony ensued as more people caught the vision and joined us in our efforts.

The disintegration and disharmony began as fear took over. The fears of two pastors, afraid they would lose members to this new church, began to infect the project. More of us became fearful, including me. It became harder to listen for God because more egos were involved—theirs and mine. The functional plans became more important than the overall inspiration. Sides were chosen as some opposed the project and others supported it. The spiritual dimension was gradually cut out of our work. I realized this during a committee meeting when we began discussing how to change the project to address everyone's concerns. In the midst of it, I began to cry (which I very rarely do). I realized in that moment that both the project and I were in the midst of disintegration. Nothing was working in harmony. I no longer felt integrated enough to truly sense God through my spiritual dimension, and the same was true for the others, both those supporting the project and those opposed to it. The spiritual had been effectively cut off from our work as mental dueling took over and our relationships eroded.

As the process dragged on, I began to tangibly feel this disintegration within me. When the members of the local denominational group voted to postpone a vote on the project, it was as if I had been freed from the dissonance. In that moment I knew that there were other possibilities and that God was calling me to let go and move onward. God may (or may not) have been calling me to start a new church, but because of our lack of faith both in God and one another, the project was no longer a possibility. I heard God calling me to something else—to become pastor of Calvin Presbyterian Church, my present church—and I followed. I have felt a relative sense of harmony, integration, and consonance ever since as Calvin lives out much of the original vision I had for the new church project.

The demise of this new church project reflects a problem that plagues our culture, and not just our churches. Our culture does not know what to do with the spiritual, and this often includes the church. We can become guilty of creating spiritually vacant, mentally rigid, physically subdued, and relationally constricted churches because we do not try to integrate the spiritual into everything else. In our churches and in the rest of our culture, we can become dominated by the need to function, the need to placate our desires, or the need to conform. So, we cut off the spiritual dimension, as illustrated in figure 4.

When the spiritual dimension is cut off, the remaining dimensions do not integrate very well. They begin to conflict with each other. One of the other dimensions always ends up dominating our lives, enslaving us to a life in pursuit of money, power, or control (when the functionality of the mental dimension dominates); physical perfection, gratification of desires, or addiction (when the urges of the physical dimension dominate); or blind conformity to the will of others and the culture (when the conforming commands of the relational dimension dominate).

We can see how the lack of integration affects lives when these other dimensions dominate. For instance, look at how being dominated by the men-

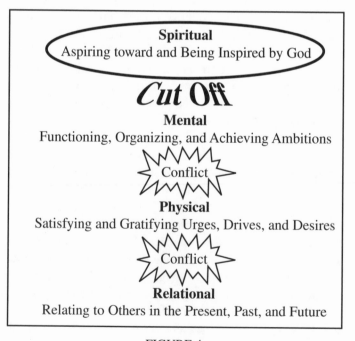

FIGURE 4

tal dimension can harm us. How many executives, entrepreneurs, politicians, or managers ruin their health and relationships all in the pursuit of more money and power? They become slaves to the functionality of the mental dimension. All that matters is achieving their plans and ambitions. The same is true when the physical dimension dominates. How many people have lost their ability to function and destroyed relationships because of their physical addictions, their pursuit of eternal youth, and their need to gratify their immediate urges? Again, the same kind of destruction can occur when the relational dimension dominates. How many people have let their spiritual, mental, and physical health diminish by remaining in destructive relationships, binding themselves to destructive cults, or blindly and uncritically following people and ideologies that slowly poison their lives? Cutting out the spiritual dimension slowly destroys the rest of our lives because we live in a constant battle zone as the different dimensions try to control our lives.

When I tried to start a new church, this disintegration took place in all of us. We stopped letting the spiritual dimension and God guide us. We allowed functional, mental concerns to dominate us. On my part, I worried about what would happen to me as my plans slowly crumbled. The others wondered what would happen to their churches and their plans. We also allowed physical urges and desires to dominate us. All of us became slaves to fear at different points, and placating those fears was most important. Finally, we allowed relational concerns to dominate us. I began to worry more and more how others would see me, especially if this project failed. Would I be considered a failure? I had cried in a meeting. Would I be seen as weak? The relational dimension dominated others involved in the project. Some supporting the project lost the vision because they worried about accommodating everyone's concerns instead of listening to the Spirit. Others opposed to the project complained that it didn't conform to the traditions and beliefs they held dear. They were so focused on "this is the way our tradition says a church should be" that it began to stifle the possibility of creating a new and different kind of church.

The key in all of this is that we are called to integrate the spiritual, mental, physical, and relational dimensions of our lives in a way that allows the spiritual to guide the mental; the spiritual and mental to guide the physical; and the spiritual, mental, and physical to guide our relationships with others. As part of this integration, all the dimensions must to work together.

I would like to offer one word of caution. While I have been describing a model for harmony and consonance among the different dimensions, we can make the mistake of thinking we can achieve perfect harmony. Perfect harmony among all the dimensions is not truly possible. The dimensions ebb and flow in their strength and ability to integrate. There is no one point of perfect harmony. The belief that such a life is possible comes from people who try (without success) to live their lives almost completely in the spiritual dimension, while attempting to cut off all the other dimensions. In other words, they try to "bliss out." They seek to eliminate their functional, physical, and relational needs in order to live in some sort of perfect bliss with God. We have to remember that Christian spirituality is an embodied spirituality. If we cut it off from the other dimensions, it becomes a fantasy spirituality that is no longer in touch with reality or with God. True Christian spirituality engages the realities of life and is embodied in all the dimensions, which means that perfect harmony will never be possible because we live in an imperfect world.

True spirituality is never perfect. There are times in which a particular dimension will be stronger than the other dimensions relative to our situation, context, and task. In prayer and worship, the spiritual dimension will be stronger. When we're doing our taxes, the mental dimension will be stronger. When we're planting a tree, our physical dimension will be stronger. When we're going out on a date, our relational dimension will be stronger. The key is not in achieving a perfect harmony, but in allowing God to guide and touch us through each dimension, and this happens by keeping the spiritual dimension strong and allowing it to integrate all the others.

Living a Balanced Life in an Unbalanced World

Walking the narrow path means achieving a sense of personal balance in the midst of a world that wants us to live unbalanced lives. We live in a culture that prizes and praises the pursuit of money and power. How do we live lives that are not dominated by this pursuit? We live in a culture that praises and prizes physical perfection and instant gratification. How do we live in the midst of this culture so that we do not become dominated by these temporary and diminishing pursuits? We live in a culture that demands conformity, especially to fads and fashions that pretend they are not conformist when they really are. How do we live in community with others without having to conform completely to what others want us to do? What does it mean for us to live balanced lives in an unbalanced world?

A model for this kind of balance was Millard Fuller, whom we discussed earlier. Fuller had been living a life dominated by the functionality of the mental dimension. He had been living his life in pursuit of money, possessions, prestige, and achievement. The main goal in his life was achieving his ambitions. It wasn't until he realized he was on the verge of losing his wife and children that he sensed the call to rebalance. He rebalanced his life by becoming more open to the spiritual dimension—to following his deeper aspirations to serve God, as well as the inspirations he received from God's Spirit. This led him to eventually form Habitat for Humanity. The question is, are we all called to be like him? This could be a problem because if all of us were called to start charitable organizations, who would be left to run our businesses, staff our hospitals, take care of our children, and build our houses?

We are called to be like Millard Fuller in rebalancing our lives, but we are not called to do exactly what he did. Balance is always going to be different in different people's lives because each of us is called by God to do different things and live in unique ways. What matters is that we allow our spiritual aspirations and inspirations to guide (not dominate) the rest of our dimensions. In essence, balance requires that we live in openness to how God is calling us to live. So, if we work in business, we may still be called to that work, but the key is that we constantly ask how God wants us to be involved in it. Are our decisions only going to be decided by the norms and values of a functional society, or are we going to seek something deeper? How will we deal with the conflicts that will arise between the two? Will we trust in God, even if taking a stance imperils our career? Are we willing to change jobs and/or careers if that is what we sense God is calling us to do? The same kinds of questions are critical in all other careers and vocations as well.

For example, as pastors, are we willing to make our aspirations and the inspirations of the Spirit more important even than having a seemingly successful church? What if our churches want to remain functional, conformist churches? Am I willing to listen to how God is guiding me to lead the church to pay more attention to the spiritual dimension? Will I have the courage to do so in a gentle, loving, but committed way? Will I faithfully and gently encourage and teach others to do so?

As a parent, am I willing to make listening to God more important than trying to raise my children in my own image? In other words, am I so committed to shaping the future of my children with my ambitions that they will become doctors, lawyers, or captains of industry that I fail to listen to how God is calling me to nurture the spiritual dimensions of their lives? Am I willing to nurture them spiritually, even if it leads them to make decisions that I find troubling, such as moving to Africa or Haiti to work with the poor; becoming nuns or monks; choosing fulfilling but impoverishing careers; or taking risks because they are doing what they believe God is calling them to do? These are important questions to ask, for they reflect how well we allow our spiritual dimensions to guide our lives.

Ultimately, we are called to balance our lives like Jesus. He not only lived in a balance between activity and reflection, but he lived in balance so that his spiritual dimension was central. He did so much mentally, physically, and relationally, but all of it was guided by his aspirations to serve the Father and his openness to the guidance of the Spirit. This is what made Jesus' life so rare, and what made it such a tremendous model for us. He showed us how to live in radical balance, and through this balance how to incarnate God's presence throughout our lives.

Questions for Reflection

1. To what extent have the demands of your life caused it to become unbalanced?
2. What specific things do you think you can do to place God more squarely at your fulcrum?
3. How can you imitate Christ and live a more balanced life?
4. Which dimension(s) of the human life is (are) strongest in you? How can you rebalance them so that the spiritual dimension guides all the others?
5. How are you being called by God to rebalance your life?

Key Learnings

- Too many of us live unbalanced lives because we place everything but God at our center.
- We are called to balance our lives by placing God at the fulcrum of our lives.
- To achieve greater balance, we need to be more intentional about integrating the spiritual, mental, physical, and relational dimensions of our lives.
- When we allow the different dimensions of our lives to be integrated, it enhances God's ability to work in and through us.
- We are called to balance our lives in ways that are unique to us and our situations.

Chapter 4

Walking the Trinitarian Path

When we walk the narrow path, there is one obstacle that most Christians stumble across. This rough patch traps many Christians and makes it hard for them to walk further without taking a major detour. Some Christians try to walk across it, but they become befuddled by its seeming complexity, and so they walk another way, trying to create their own alternative. What is this patch that impedes the progress of so many Christians? It is the doctrine of the Trinity.

Why is the Trinity such a difficult concept for so many Christians? Probably the key problem is that over time it has been reduced to a mere doctrine and concept. It is no longer rooted in an experience of God that arises out of a personal relationship with the Trinitarian God. People who talk about the Trinity tend to talk about it in theological language, not practical, experiential, and relational language. They discuss the nature of the Trinity, the substance of the Trinity, and the persons of the Trinity in such complex and technical language that it actually becomes an impediment to forming a relationship with and experiencing the Trinitarian God—with the Creator, Christ, and Holy Spirit. In fact, because theological discussions about the Trinity have always been so complicated, most Christians, while nominally saying they are Trinitarian, are anything but. Most pastors will not preach on the Trinity, not because they are not Trinitarian, but because they are intimidated by the theology of it. Most laity will freely admit that they believe specifically in God, in the Father, in Christ, or in the Holy Spirit, but have no idea what to do with the Trinity—with how there can be three persons but only one God. In fact, many will admit that the Trinity confuses them. I saw an example of this years ago when Johnny Carson interviewed Kareem Abdul-Jabbar, the legendary basketball player, on *The Tonight Show*. Carson asked him why he became a Muslim. Abdul-Jabbar, whose name prior to becoming a Muslim was Lew Alcindor, explained that he became Muslim because he didn't know what to do with the Trinity. It made no sense to him, and Allah, or God, did make sense to him. In Islam there is one God and one God only, and we are to worship that one God. Many Christians struggle with the Trinity just as Abdul-Jabbar did.

What too many Christians do not understand is that before the Trinity was ever a doctrine or a theology about God, it was an experience of God rooted in a relationship with God. The problem today is that because we have lost our Trinitarian grounding, we don't know what to do with Trinitarian experiences. In fact, we can be afraid of the full range of Trinitarian spiritual experiences, and so we end up in a limited relationship with God. What is a Trinitarian spiritual experience? It is an experience of God that is open to God as God fully is, not necessarily as we want God to be.

Before we move any further, it is important for you to understand that the following exploration of the Trinity is a spiritual, relational, and experiential exploration, and not a purely theological one. It is an attempt to recapture something of the Trinitarian spirituality that existed among the early Christians, and that has been lost among later Christians. It is an exploration of how the narrow path that God calls on us to walk must weave its way through the Trinity so that we can form a balanced, Trinitarian spirituality and faith. The place to begin this discussion is by exploring how the doctrine of the Trinity came to be.

Biblical Foundations of the Trinitarian Path

When people gather to discuss the Trinity, many inaccurately claim that the doctrine of the Trinity cannot be found explicitly in the Bible. This statement is true to the extent that none of the writers of the Gospels or the epistles ever use the word "Trinity," but the New Testament flourishes with experiences of the Trinity. The writers of the New Testament continually experienced God as Father and Creator, as Son and Messiah, and as Spirit, Advocate, and Guide. For example, Paul was clearly speaking of the triune God when he said that there is "one God and Father of all, who is above all and through all and in all" (Eph. 4:6). This is a deeply Trinitarian statement about God being Creator, Spirit, and Christ.

Prior to Christ's coming, the primary Jewish experience of God was of God the Creator, Father, and Master of the Universe. The Jews experienced God as an all-knowing, all-powerful, mostly distant (but not always) Father and Creator who was and is responsible for everything's existence. They also saw the Creator as providing basic laws for living, which were given to them through

Moses. While they experienced the Creator as intimate at times, and even built the Temple in Jerusalem as a home for God (with the Ark of the Covenant as God's throne), the primary experience of God was of a distant, loving, but judging God. They yearned for the day when the Messiah would come and make God the intimate presence God was in Genesis, when God walked with Adam and Eve in the garden during the evening breeze (Gen. 3:8).

While this experience of God as distant and transcendent was fairly standard among the Jews (with variations according to what sect or movement of Judaism one belonged to), Jesus brought with him a whole new experience of God. Jesus opened the door to experiencing God as a tangible, real, and embodied presence. God wasn't just a distant, far-off God residing in heaven. God was real, tangible, and able to be experienced in Jesus. It was this experience that led Peter, James, and John to discover during the transfiguration that Jesus was the Son of God (Matt. 17:1–13). Peter said of his experience,

> For he received honor and glory from God the Father when that voice was conveyed to him by the Majestic Glory, saying, "This is my Son, my Beloved, with whom I am well pleased." We ourselves heard this voice come from heaven, while we were with [Jesus] on the holy mountain. (2 Peter 1:17–18)

The experience of God in Jesus led Thomas, upon seeing Jesus after the resurrection, to recognize that Jesus was God incarnate. He had his doubts, but eventually he shouted out to Jesus, "My Lord and my God!" Thomas experienced God in Jesus, and all the apostles, through Jesus, experienced God as a close, intimate presence who loved, healed, taught, guided, and tenderly cared for them. Along with Jesus' other followers, they had an experience of God that was fundamentally different from the typical Jewish experience of the time. Suddenly, God was close, involved, and embodied in this man, Jesus. To the Jews, the idea that God would be incarnate in a common man was blasphemous, but for those with Jesus it was a revelation of how close God could be.

The writer of John understood the nature of this experience of God in Jesus probably better than any of the other Gospel writers, and it accounts for why he included material about Jesus' divinity that the other Gospel writers did not. Only in John's Gospel do we find Jesus explaining how God, who has been experienced as Creator and Father, is incarnated in the world in him: "If you know me, you will know my Father also. From now on you do know him and have seen him. . . . Whoever has seen me has seen the Father" (John 14:7, 9). Jesus was saying that he is God incarnate, for he and the Creator are one, and a relationship with him is a relationship with God the Creator.

John emphasized the tangible, embodied nature of God in Jesus Christ at an even more profound level. He shows that we can experience God through Christ not only when we read the biblical account of Jesus, but also when we experience God in nature, for nature is the ongoing creation of the world. When we experience God's power and grace tangibly in a sunset, a flower, the stars, or the ocean, we are experiencing God in Christ. John tells us in the beginning of his Gospel that Jesus *is* creation. The Father may be the Creator, the source, of all that is, but the ongoing creation that continues to this day is Jesus active in the universe:

All things came into being through [Jesus], and without him not one thing came into being. What has come into being in him was life, and the life was the light of all people. (John 1:3–4)

The apostle Paul affirmed this by saying, "For in [Jesus] all things in heaven and on earth were created, things visible and invisible, whether thrones or dominions or rulers or powers—all things have been created through him and for him (Col. 1:16). Jesus is still involved in creation, and as we experience the energy of life, we are experiencing the incarnated, tangible, embodied power of God that courses through creation. We still experience God in Christ today anytime we experience an incarnated presence of God in nature, each other, music, art, drama, literature, and especially in the Scriptures. It is for this reason that John calls Jesus "the Word." Jesus is the articulation, the sound of God, as it resonates throughout the universe.

The early Christians experienced God in Jesus not only when he was alive, but in their relationships with the world and one another. It is for this reason that Paul talks about the fact that, together, we are all the "body of Christ" (1 Cor. 12:12–31). Together we continue to incarnate and embody Christ to and for one another and the world. Again, this isn't just biblical theology. It is experience. All of these are experiences of God in Christ.

The New Testament also expresses a third experience of God in the Holy Spirit. This experience is much more difficult for many mainstream Christians because it is not as defined as the first two. The Holy Spirit is the experience of God as wild, uncontrolled, transforming, and making the impossible possible. We read about the experience of the Holy Spirit all throughout the book of Acts, but especially in the beginning:

When the day of Pentecost had come, they were all together in one place. And suddenly from heaven there came a sound like the rush of a violent wind, and it filled the entire house where they were sitting. Divided tongues, as of fire, appeared among them, and a tongue rested on each of them. All of them were filled with the Holy Spirit and began to speak in other languages, as the Spirit gave them ability. (Acts 2:1–4)

This was not the only time the apostles and followers of Jesus would experience the Holy Spirit. God in the Holy Spirit was experienced by the earliest of Christians throughout their lives. The Spirit guided them so they could discover what God wanted for and from them. The Spirit infused them with the power to heal, teach, and preach. The power of the Holy Spirit followed Paul as he spread the gospel. The Holy Spirit filled the early Christians with the power to see and understand things that were obscured and unavailable to those not open to the power of the Spirit. Jesus promised that the power of the Holy Spirit would come after his ascent to heaven:

But the Advocate, the Holy Spirit, whom the Father will send in my name, will teach you everything, and remind you of all that I have said to you. (John 14:26)

The Holy Spirit was not just a concept or a mild presence of God the early Christians felt on rare occasions. The Holy Spirit was a vivid experience of God that was radical, powerful, and transforming. It was an experience of God at God's most intimate and present. It wasn't just an experience of knowing that God is our source. It wasn't just an experience of God in nature, Scripture, others, and our own hearts. It was and remains an experience of God that infects our souls and fills us with a power that lies beyond us. Many Christians today fear this kind of experience of God because it is far too intimate, tangible, and real. Most mainstream Christians would rather that God be a distant and less tangible experience, despite what we may say about wanting to have God be active in our lives.

If the biblical descriptions of God are true, then the early church had a profound and comprehensive experience of God that went far beyond what we encounter today. First, they experienced God the Creator as the source of everything there is. This was an experience of the transcendent, all-powerful, mysterious God. Second, they experienced God in the world, in one another, and in their own hearts through God the Son/Word/Messiah. Finally, they experienced God as a wild, transforming, and enveloping, grace-filled power through God the Holy Spirit. It is not only they who have experienced God in these ways, but we are supposed to similarly experience God in all these ways. If we are to walk the true narrow path, then the early church experience of the triune God is meant to be our experience of God, too. The problem is that the path we take too often detours around the Trinity because of our fear and ignorance, and so our experiences of God become limited. As they do, we are enticed to walk away from the narrow path.

Forming the Doctrine of the Trinity

So, how did we get from these relationally raw and unrefined experiences of God in the Creator, Son, and Holy Spirit to where we are now, which is a dry doctrine and theology of the Trinity that often inhibits Trinitarian experience? The problem began to arise as the early Christians of the second and third centuries stopped yearning for an *experience of God* rooted in a relationship with God, and sought instead an *understanding of God* rooted in rational speculation. As the early church became more sophisticated, theologically oriented thinkers wanted a greater intellectual understanding of their experiences: What causes these experiences? Who is the God that underlies them? What is God's nature? Over time, a fascination with understanding dominated the pursuit of experience, and so disagreements arose as to what the true explanation of Christian experience was. Different theologians offered different ideas, and debates raged about the true nature of God underlying all of these experiences.

While theological understanding is meant to be a crucial component of spiritual experience, it can also become a pursuit in and of itself. At its best, theology is an attempt to discern the true nature of God, the cosmos, and life, but it can also become disconnected from spiritual experience as theological speculation becomes more intellectual. The best theologians have always been those who ground their insights in a deep prayer life, trying to see life more from God's perspective. Unfortunately, as theology becomes increasingly intellectual, it can become disconnected from practice, prayer, and experience. As the early church became more sophisticated in its theology, it also became more intellectual in its attempts to explain God who underlies all of those early Christian experiences. Thus, bitter arguments arose about the true nature of the Creator, Christ, and the Holy Spirit.

Over time, all sorts of different ideas on how to explain the experiences of the apostles and early Christians were formed. The primary questions mostly tended to circulate around the issue of "Who was Jesus?" Was Jesus God? Was Jesus a lesser god than God? Was Jesus an equal god to God? Was Jesus merely a man? Did Jesus only appear to be a man? These questions vexed the early Christians as they tried to gain a more rational and logical understanding of the nature of God, Jesus, and the world.

With so many different ideas coming to the forefront, what were Christians to believe? The raw experience of the early Christians was becoming solidified in the religion of Christianity. The leaders of the Christian religion were searching for ways to understand Christian experience, and so they tried all sorts of different explanations. As the theologian Catherine Mowry Lacugna states, "Theologians of the second, third, and fourth centuries tried out many different syntheses of biblical revelation, philosophy, experience, and faith, before arriving at what we now call 'orthodoxy.'"[1] The focus of the early church became "figuring out" who God was and is. While the explanations of the experiences changed, the experiences did not. People might not be able to understand God, but they were still experiencing the triune God.

All of this crystallized into a doctrine, an "orthodoxy," of the Trinity after the Roman emperor Constantine became a Christian and made Christianity the official religion of the empire. At the battle of Milvian Bridge in 312, he saw a vision of the Christian cross in the clouds, and he heard the words "By this you will conquer." So, he interpreted his vision as a sign to make the empire Christian. Over time, Constantine became frustrated by one particular aspect of Christianity. There were so many different beliefs about God, Jesus, and the Holy Spirit that it was hard to know what to believe. So, he decided to end the division and arguing once and for all by calling a church council. In 325 A.D., in the city of Nicaea, Constantine called a council of church leaders to settle all of these questions once and for all.

The Council of Nicaea focused on questions that continue to leave many laity and clergy scratching their heads. The debate was over the substance of the Trinity. Were the Father, Jesus, and the Holy Spirit of the same essential substance, or were they made of different stuff? Were they really one person? Were they three distinct persons, but sharing the same substance? The answer that eventually emerged from this council, and the subsequent ones of Constantinople in 381 and Chalcedon in 451, was that there is one God with whom humans form a relationship through the three persons of the Trinity. These beliefs were articulated in the Nicene Creed, which along with the Apostles' Creed are the grounding creeds for so many denominations. These creeds affirm that we have a relationship with God the Father, Son, and Holy Spirit. Each relationship is distinct in its quality, character, and experience, yet all are experiences of God. To explore how this can be is beyond the scope of this chapter. The major point is that all three are God and with all three we can have experiential relationships that are loving, transforming, saving, and inspiring.

For Christians, the one person of the Trinity who is emphasized the most is Jesus Christ, for the simple reason that Jesus opened the door to these complex, mysterious, and transforming relationships with God. This is why we say that as Christians we are christocentric—centered in Christ. The door to experiencing the triune God has been opened by Christ. By reading Scripture, by hearing the teachings and stories of Jesus, and by discovering God in the world, others, and our hearts, we discover God in a way that was not apparent before Jesus. We discover God who is all-powerful, yet willing to be weak for us; all-knowing, yet willing to sit in human darkness with us; transcendent, yet willing to be involved with us; omnipresent, yet willing to be an intimate, individual presence with us; eternal, yet willing to suffer in the world with us. The problem, as we shall see later, is that over time many Christians have lost their sense of being christocentric, and instead have become *christoencapsulated*—so much so that they believe the *only* valid experience of God is through Christ.

Christoencapsulation is the tendency of Christians to make Christ so central that any experience of God is dismissed unless it fits a christocentric orthodoxy. For example, some Christians attack others if they use the name "God" for God too much. They say that we should talk about Jesus, not God. This christoencapsulation ignores the valid experiences both of the early church and of many people throughout the history of Christianity.

I have experienced this christoencapsulation many times over the years, especially from some evangelical Christians who, in their zeal to be Christ-centered, cross a line and become christoencapsulated. I am not trying to be critical of evangelical beliefs, since often evangelicals are the strongest advocates of maintaining a clear and life-giving emphasis on Jesus and the incarnated God. What they bring to the Christian table is wonderful, except when they lose the Trinity in their zeal to be Christ-centered.

Let me give you an example of what I mean. Not too long ago I was at a meeting with other pastors and church leaders in which we were talking about salvation and what it takes to be saved. I told the group that for years I had struggled with who Jesus was and is. For years I wondered, was Jesus really God, as many Christians believe? Was he just a great human being, as many other Christians and non-Christians believe? Was he another prophet, as the Muslims believe? I didn't know what to think, and I thought that I might have to give up being a Christian. Finally, I told the group that I went to God and said, "God, I can't understand this on my own. I need you to guide me. If Jesus really is you, you need to show me." Over the course of the years, I experienced the Holy Spirit leading me to form a relationship with Christ, and to experience Christ more tangibly in my life. I became more comfortable with Christ, and it was clear to me that the Holy Spirit was leading me there. This makes sense, though, because I have always had much more comfort with the Holy Spirit than with Jesus. Today I have no more questions about this—at least not enough to shake my faith.

After a few more people in the group spoke, an evangelical pastor to my right said, in somewhat strident tones, "The only way it works is that Jesus leads people to the Father, and Jesus leads people to the Holy Spirit. It cannot work the other way around!" This was a man who was christoencapsulated.

The irony is that he said he based his beliefs on Scripture, yet this is not what Scripture teaches. In fact, Scripture teaches something closer to my experience over and over. For example, Paul says that "no on can say 'Jesus is Lord' except by the Holy Spirit" (1 Cor. 12:3). Paul also tells us that when we cry to God the Father, it is the Holy Spirit crying within us (Rom. 8:16; Gal. 4:6). The Holy Spirit leads us to both Christ and the Creator, just as the Creator leads us to Christ and the Holy Spirit, and Christ leads us to the Creator and the Holy Spirit. The Creator, Christ, and Holy Spirit are in perfect communion with one another as one God. This points out the basic problem of the Trinity: most people are much more comfortable with one person of the Trinity than with three, and so they try to simplify and limit their experiences so that they can create a framework of God that makes God easier to understand, and that makes it seem as if God is more under control.

A Split Trinity

The narrow path is a path that leads us to form a relationship with God in all three poles, all three experiences, and all three persons of the Trinity. We are meant to have a foundational and grounding relationship with God the Creator. We are meant to have a real and tangible relationship with God in Jesus Christ. We are meant to have an inspiring and transforming relationship with God the Holy Spirit. If this is what is supposed to happen, why doesn't it?

The problem is that ever since the Councils of Nicaea, Constantinople, and Chalcedon, when the orthodox or "right teachings" about the Trinity were set, the practice of the church has created a split in the Trinity on a practical, experiential level. The theology of the church remained Trinitarian, but its practice separated the persons of the Trinity from one another, as God the Father became emphasized over Jesus, and Jesus became emphasized over the Holy Spirit.

Over time, this split in the Trinity became more pronounced as God was identified mainly with the Father, the church with Christ, and the power of the Holy Spirit with the sacraments. In contrast to the experience of the early church, the church of the Middle Ages and Renaissance became much more hierarchical, and the experience of God in the Trinity became less tangible and more abstract.

As the fifteenth century waned and the sixteenth century waxed, the desire to experience the triune God exploded upon Europe. This was the time of the Reformation, and if the Reformation was anything, it was an exploration of Trinitarian experience. The Roman Catholic Church had squelched a broad experience of the Trinity for so long by controlling access to Scripture, prayer, and the sacraments. The church believed that individual experiences by the laity were dangerous and asserted that only priests and the religious (those belonging to religious orders) were trained adequately to have these experiences. The laity were considered too ignorant and uneducated to understand Scripture and to receive the sacrament regularly. Scripture was to be reserved for clergy and those in religious orders. Since the only translation of Scripture was in Latin, reading of Scripture was reserved for those who could read and understand Latin. Thus, for ages the laity had been prevented from experiencing Jesus directly through Scripture. Despite the church's attempts to control them, experiences of the Trinity began to blossom in people willing to experiment. The Reformation was a sprouting of Christ-centered Trinitarian spiritual experiences.

We can see how experiences of Christ exploded throughout Europe during the Reformation. The desire and need to experience Jesus in Scripture could not be repressed forever, and so the reformers emphasized the need for laity to read the Bible for themselves. In conjunction with this, the Bible was translated into the native languages of the Germans, French, English, Italians, Hungarians, Polish, and many others.

Reformers such as Martin Luther, John Calvin, and Ulrich Zwingli stressed the importance of laity receiving the Word of God in Christ through a personal and regular reading of Scripture. For Calvin and most other early reformers, the person of the Trinity explored most was Jesus Christ, especially as he is revealed through Scripture. They believed that the function of the Holy Spirit was to guide us in the reading of Scripture. Most of the Trinitarian explosion during the early part of the Reformation was experienced as a re-centering on Christ. Experiencing Christ through Scripture was considered key to true faith. It became so strong that today most Protestant traditions emphasize the fact that they are Christ-centered in their Trinitarian faith just as Calvin, Luther, and the other reformers were. This movement also led the Roman Catholic Church to reform itself by allowing the laity to read Scripture and experience Christ more tangibly for themselves. As a result, the Roman Catholic Church today supports individual experiences of God in Christ by the laity in Scripture and sacrament.

As the Reformation and Protestant movements progressed, the lack of direct experience of the Holy Spirit became apparent to some. This is what led George Fox, for instance, to abandon the Anglican Church in order to explore a more immediate experience of God in the Holy Spirit. It is what led John Wesley, the founder of the Methodist movement, to create a method for spiritual growth that attempted to be more balanced by creating room for the Holy Spirit to work.

The creation of different Christian denominations has generally been, at its core, an attempt by different Christians to more fully explore and experience the triune God. The problem is that as each denomination discovers a new experience of God through their Trinitarian explorations, they tend to make their own particular experiences normative for everyone. They tend to think that their way is the "right" way. This has led to battles between denominations that persist today, as each one declares its experience and practice to be *the* most authoritative and filled with God's truth. We will explore this more later.

The Rise of the Holy Spirit

The fastest-growing Christian movement on the planet today is the pentecostal movement. Some researchers have said that the pentecostal movement is growing at a rate of up to 250 percent per year in the United States, and possibly up to 500 percent a year worldwide. They estimate that by the year 2040 or 2050, Pentecostals will make up the majority of the world's two billion Christians, overtaking the Roman Catholic Church. They estimate that pentecostal churches may be growing by up to 20 million members per year. This is in stark contrast to most of the mainstream Christian churches, which continue to lose members at a rate of 5 to 10 percent per year. My own denomination, the Presbyterian Church (U.S.A.), has declined at a rate of almost 30,000 per year since the mid-1960s, to a total membership in 1999 of 2,560,201.[2]

Why have the Pentecostals been able to grow so rapidly over the past twenty-five years while mainstream denominations have all declined? One answer is that pentecostalism has attempted to balance the unbalanced Trinitarian experiences of mainstream Christians. The Pentecostals have done this by jettisoning most of the practices of mainstream Christianity in order to become more open to God in the Holy Spirit. Most of the mainline Protestant denominations have been fairly good at helping people experience God the Father, and sometimes God the Son, but they don't quite know what to do with the Holy Spirit. The Father focus in mainstream Christianity has created a stable, stately form of religious experience rooted in Scripture, traditional worship, and the sacraments, but it can also be overly rigid, dogmatic, and closed to experiencing God in the Holy Spirit.

Profound experiences of the Holy Spirit, especially those that include biblically expressed experiences such as healing, speaking in tongues, prophecy, and divine inspiration, are eyed with suspicion by mainstream Christians. For the most part, they are feared because these Spirit-filled experiences are an aspect of God that cannot be controlled. Suspicion of these kinds of spiritual experiences has even led some theologians to assert that these experiences were limited to the New Testament period because God only dispensed these gifts during that time so that the church could grow. They say that now these experiences are unnecessary for the more sophisticated Christians of today. The pentecostal movement would argue that this is not quite true.

The problem among mainstream Christians is that they don't often expect to experience God in the Holy Spirit. Brad Long and Douglas McMurry say that

> for many of us, our God is too small, and our expectations of the Christian life microscopic. We have limited and tamed God by our fears, worldview and lack of knowledge. We do not really expect anything to happen in church except to meet a few friends, hear a pleasing sermon, sing some familiar hymns, contribute to an offering and go home to a good Sunday dinner. In our lives we expect God to do little, except perhaps bless our homes and our children and get us through the day. Many of us sincerely hope that nothing much else *will* happen! And because we expect little, God does little.[3]

In contrast, this lack of expectation is not evident among Pentecostals. In fact, they expect miracles.

Where did the Pentecostals come from? The pentecostal movement began in earnest in Los Angeles at the beginning of the twentieth century.[4] Though the pentecostal movement had some roots in the writings of George Fox and the Quakers, and in the Plymouth Brethren movement of nineteenth-century England, it was mostly started by a blind, African American man named William Joseph Seymour, who founded the Asuza Street Revival in Los Angeles. He believed that if people persisted in prayer, they would have an experience of the Holy Spirit akin to that of the first Christians on the Day of Pentecost. The people who gathered with him prayed fervently for the Spirit, and suddenly they were overcome by a variety of spiritual experiences. These experiences included speaking in tongues, prophecy, and a giddy excitement over God's presence.

What made this gathering of Christians in 1906 so different was that it was a movement begun among poor and uneducated people of African American, Hispanic, and every other ethnic descent. In contrast, white, educated men dominated the mainstream churches of the time. As the meetings on Asuza Street continued, their popularity grew and spread. Eventually, the movement gained strength as more and more pentecostal preachers felt the call to begin their own churches. There was a flexibility and openness to the Spirit's call that was missing in the more mainstream denominations, and it attracted attention and devotees. Today, pentecostalism is a powerful force in Christianity, even if the mainstream Christian church barely acknowledges it.

The important message to gather from the growth of the pentecostal movement is not that they possess the "right" approach to God. The important message is that they provide a Holy Spirit balancing act to the unbalanced spirituality often expressed by other Christian denominations. Pentecostals are just as unbalanced as mainstream Christians. Their imbalance, however, lies in their overemphasis on the Holy Spirit, while the mainstream and evangelical imbalance is their reliance only on the Creator and Son.

Understanding the Trinitarian Experience

Why are there so many different denominations, sects, and movements in Christianity today, and why do even more seem to appear? The answer is simply that each denomination, sect, or movement is a reaction to the unbalanced Trinitarian spirituality of previous denominations, sects, or movements. The founders of a particular denomination or movement are often frustrated by what they see as the failure of a more dominant denomination or spiritual climate in the church at large to provide the kind of theological grounding, spiritual practice, and/or religious experience that they seek. In other words, the more dominant denomination, sect, or movement from which they are sprouting has prevented them from experiencing and forming a relationship with God in the way they feel called to do so.

If you take gelatin and squeeze it in your hand, what happens to it? Does it just compress and form a nice little ball? No, it squeezes out through your fingers in a way that is uncontrollable. This is what happens whenever a dominant denomination or movement tries to squash down an alternative, yet valid, experience of the triune God.

So, for example, John Wesley, the founder of the Methodist movement, and George Fox, the founder of the Quakers, sought God the Holy Spirit in a way that was not allowed by the more dominant Anglican Church. When they began to experience God in the Holy Spirit, the Anglican Church could not suppress it. In fact, the more the church tried, the stronger the movements became. One way to test the legitimacy of a movement is that if it truly is of the triune God, it will strengthen as the attempts to repress and suppress it grow stronger. Both the Methodist and the Quaker movements were reacting against the tradition and sacramental focus of the Anglican Church.

The Swiss and Scottish reformers, as well as the Lutherans, were reacting against the failure of the Roman Catholic Church to allow for a stronger focus on God incarnated in Holy Scripture. The Anabaptists and Baptists were seeking an alternative experience of God to both the Protestant Reformers and the Roman Catholics. The evangelical awakenings of the nineteenth century were seeking a different experience and relationship with God than the staid and rigid faith the established churches allowed. The same can be said of the pentecostal and evangelical movements of the twentieth century. If you look at any one denomination or movement, you can see that it is generally unbalanced depending on which aspects of the Trinity it emphasizes. Today, this splitting of groups from one another in order to experience the triune God in a unique way has become so rampant that new denominations and sects of Christianity are born every day worldwide.

David B. Barrett, who coauthored the *World Christian Encyclopedia,* estimates that there are now 33,800 different Christian denominations around the world. And "the fastest-growing are the independents, who have no ties whatsoever to historic Christianity."[5] The interesting thing about all of these different denominations is that most of them are sure that their beliefs, practices, theologies, and experiences are better and more complete than those of other Christians. In fact, many of them would assert that other Christians who do not believe the way they do are deficient, misguided, or "unsaved." They think that their particular beliefs and experiences of the triune God are the right ones. Perhaps what this says even more clearly is that there are so many valid experiences of the triune God because we simply cannot proclaim a particular experience as the proper one. God comes to us in such a depth and variety of ways that we cannot possibly experience God in God's completeness. So, we are left seeking God in a way that is compatible with our personalities, backgrounds, ethnicity, socioeconomic situation, nationality, and so forth. The competition among Christians to follow the "right" way may say as much about human sin and pride as it does about God.

So, with all of these different beliefs and approaches to God, how do we know which ones are right and which ones are wrong? How do we know if we are worshiping the triune God, or just one person of the Trinity? How do we know whether we are truly being Trinitarian in our beliefs, practices, and experiences? Perhaps the best way to answer this is to explore the Trinity in more depth, especially in terms of how we experience God. The following is an alternative way of understanding the Trinity in terms of a relational experience rather than just theological explanation or function.

To look at the Trinity from a spiritual perspective, it is important to understand that while we experience God through three primary personal relationships with God as Creator, Son, and Holy Spirit, in reality our experiences of the Trinity are much like the mixture of colors. While there are three primary colors—red, yellow, and blue—they can combine in many ways to create all colors possible. The same is true of Trinitarian spiritual experiences. We can experience God as one of the three primary persons of the Trinity, but the reality is that most people experience God in a unique way that blends their personal beliefs about, experiences of, and relationships with the three persons of God to create certain shades and colors of experience. There is a theological term that emphasizes that inherent connection and interrelationship among the different persons of the Trinity: *perichoresis*. This is the idea that in the Creator we also find the Holy Spirit and Christ; in Christ we find the Creator and the Holy Spirit; and in the Holy Spirit we find the Creator and Christ. Each is inherently infused with the others, so to experience one is to also experience the others. Yet they are distinct, so as with the different colors, we may see a certain color but that color is still a blending of other primary colors in a unique way. When we experience God, we experience the blending of the triune persons in a unique way that is all our own. In other words, God relates to us through the Trinity in a way that is in sync with who we are and who God calls us to be.

It is impossible to describe and explain all the ways the triune God can be experienced in all of God's color. Instead, we will focus on the primary Trinitarian experiences of God: the God of Purpose, Presence, and Power, or, as we know them more commonly, the Creator, Son, and Holy Spirit. In figure 5, I have chosen to use the names *Eternal Purpose*, *Incarnational Presence*, and *Inspiring Power* for these three persons of God to help us look beyond the images of the triune persons that classical and contemporary theology and religion have given to us.

The Eternal Purpose

When we experience and form a relationship with God as Creator, it is primarily an experience of God as *Eternal Purpose*. We experience God not only as our source, but also as God who transcends space and time. The Eternal God is ultimately a mystery. God the Eternal Purpose, whom Jesus called "Abba," goes beyond all our understanding and experience. In many ways, the experience of the Eternal Purpose is an experience rooted in thought, speculation, and intuition. We know the Creator exists, not because we experience the Eternal Purpose directly, but because we look at everything there is and know it must come from a being who is all-powerful, all-wise, and all-knowing. We also know that the Creator has created certain laws of the universe that maintain order in the cosmos—that maintain a certain sense of cosmic purpose. These are laws that physicists and other scientists are discovering, but they also

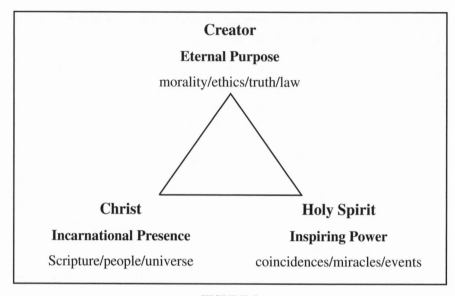

FIGURE 5

include those not discovered and understood. Ultimately, they include the grounding purpose of the universe expressed in the first letter of John:

> Beloved, let us love one another, because love is from God; everyone who loves is born of God and knows God. Whoever does not love does not know God, for God is love. . . . God is love, and those who abide in love abide in God and God abides in them. (1 John 4:7–8, 16)

From a spiritual perspective, love is the binding purpose of the universe, and when we love or are loved, we are living according to the purpose of the Eternal God. We know this because deep in our hearts we feel that we have done something "right"—something that has meaning and purpose.

There is an even deeper experience of the Eternal Purpose, though. It comes when we live our lives in a way that intuitively feels like it is in consonance and harmony with God. It comes when we sense in our guts that our own personal purpose is in sync with God's purpose for the universe. This is very hard to explain except to say that God has created each of us for a purpose, even though we may not always follow that purpose. Each of us has a call that beckons us to live, act, and be in a way that is consonant with God's universal purpose for us, for the world, and for the cosmos. When we are following that call, everything we do becomes an expression of God's eternal purpose, whether it is as a parent, pastor, engineer, doctor, contractor, driver, filmmaker, family, friend, or anything else that might part of how God is calling us to live and serve. When we follow our calling and feel in harmony with God's purpose for us, we are experiencing the Eternal God—the Creator— who is God the Eternal Purpose.

For example, in my work as a pastor, there are awe-inspiring times when I feel in sync with God, and I know that what I am doing "fits" with what God wants. I've had this experience many times, but among the most profound are the times I've been with dying people. In some of those cases, the families and I knew it was time that we prayed for death instead of health. So, we prayed for death. One woman died in the middle of our prayer as her family and I held hands around her bed and prayed. It felt profoundly right that we would pray for her death, and that she would die in the middle of our prayer. Another time, the children of a man dying of severe emphysema and lung cancer gathered with me in the living room as he gasped for air in his bedroom. He was on oxygen, but there was nothing more that the doctors could do. We prayed for his release, and ten minutes later we heard a noise in his bedroom. As we walked in, he stretched his arms out to the side as if he was on a cross. He then let out a final breath and died. It was the day before Easter, and at his death I had a profound sense that his death was part of God's purpose. In both cases, the families and I felt as though we were in sync with God's will and the ways of life. In the midst of all this, we became profoundly aware that death is a part of life. When we focus on God the Eternal Purpose, we seek not only God's will for us, but God's will for all of life. The most deeply spiritual people are those who seek to conform their purpose to the Creator's.

It is from this experience of God as Eternal Purpose that morality and ethics spring. They are part of the eternal laws of God that not only govern life, but also the universe. The law, as it was given to Moses, is an expression of God's purpose, although it is an incomplete expression because it is outside the human heart. Scripture tells us that the law given to Moses was incomplete because it was external and bound human behaviors to God's purpose, but not their hearts. Jesus came to reveal the more intimate and deeper connections of that purpose, which we discover through faith—through our connection with God's eternal purpose: "Do not think that I have come to abolish the law or the prophets," Jesus said. "I have come not to abolish but to fulfill" (Matt. 5:17). Paul continues by telling us that "before faith came, we were imprisoned and guarded under the law until faith would be revealed. Therefore the law was our disciplinarian until Christ came, so that we might be justified by faith" (Gal. 3:23–24). In essence, there is an eternal purpose that brings order to all space and time, and when we live in harmony with it, we experience harmony and consonance with the Eternal Purpose, our Creator.

This experience of the Eternal Purpose is the experience Jesus had on a continual basis. We are called to imitate Christ because he lived in complete, moment-to-moment harmony with the Eternal Purpose. The Creator's purpose was Jesus' purpose, and Jesus' purpose was the Creator's purpose. When he was tempted in the wilderness by Satan, he responded by reminding Satan that there was a deeper order—the Creator's order—that we must abide by. When he faced death upon the cross, he said to the Father, "yet, not my will but yours be done" (Luke 22:42). He was living according to and in harmony with the Eternal Purpose.

Of all the experiences of God that mainstream Christians share, this experience of God the Eternal Purpose is the most common. While it is limited in comparison to a full, Trinitarian experience, experiencing God through the sense of meaning that comes through trying to live a "golden rule" life—by adhering to God's purpose as laid out in the law and commandments—is still a valid experience of God. Christians who relate primarily with this person of God tend to emphasize following the Ten Commandments, living a moral life, living an ethical life, and/or seeking justice in the world. They try to understand the principles of life that give it meaning and purpose, and then try to adjust their lives to it. They experience God most when they feel that they are following God's law and commandments. The main method of discerning God's will for those who primarily relate to the Eternal Purpose is by using their God-created rational mind. They think about God and what God wants, and then try to follow their conclusions.

The apostle Paul has said that while God is one, God is also above all, through all, and in all (Eph. 4:6). If Paul is right, then those who focus on God the Eternal Purpose relate with and experience God mainly as above. They see and experience God primarily as being *above* all, but not so much through all and in all.

The Incarnational Presence

When we experience God in the Son, Jesus Christ, we experience God the *Incarnational Presence*. For many Christians, this is limited to an experience of God in history and in Scripture, but it can be so much more. One of the problems with our treatment of Jesus Christ is that we consistently say that "The Lord is risen" and "Jesus is alive," but then treat Jesus as nothing more than a historical figure. We triumphantly shout that Jesus has died once and for all for our sins, but then leave Jesus behind in Scripture and the first century A.D. Certainly Jesus dying for our sins is crucial, yet what is forgotten is that Jesus also arose from the dead to give us life. Those who treat Jesus as though he is still alive often relegate him to Scripture. The Bible is the living Word, and so that is the extent to which they see Jesus as being alive. They experience God's presence when they read Scripture, but not in very many other places.

While the Bible is the main way we experience God, it is only one incarnational experience of and relationship with God in Christ. The incarnational nature of Christ is much more vast. For example, Christ is incarnated and can be felt as a presence in relationships: "For where two or three are gathered in my name, I am there among them" (Matt. 18:20). Christ is incarnated and can be felt as a presence in our churches when we become the "body of Christ" (1 Cor. 12:12–31). As stated previously, whenever and wherever creation is taking place, there is Christ—there is the Incarnational Presence. We feel God's presence in a sunset, a flower, a bee, the grass, the trees, and so much more.

Christ is also incarnated in our minds. As Paul said, "Examine yourselves to see whether you are living in the faith. Test yourselves. Do you not realize that Jesus Christ is in you?" (2 Cor. 13:5). Christ is not only outside of us, but incarnated in us. Everything in our minds—our beliefs, imaginations, and thoughts—can be touched by Christ's Incarnational Presence. For example, I have spoken to so many people over the years who, during times of trouble, had a vision or experience of Christ in a dream or while awake. I have even spoken to and been with people suffering from mental illness who experienced Christ healing them through their hallucinations. I am unwilling to brand their experiences as false, for the proof is in the fruits of their experiences. Their experiences were spiritually transforming and brought these people closer to God. As Jesus said, when questioned whether he was the messiah, "the blind receive their sight, the lame walk, the lepers are cleansed, the deaf hear, the dead are raised, and the poor have good news brought to them. And blessed is anyone who takes no offense at me" (Matt. 11:5–6). When people experience the presence of God, their experience is healing and transforming, and it brings them closer to God. How can anyone doubt the validity of that experience? Sure, there are experiences that are not valid, but so many people experience God's Incarnational Presence in a healing, saving way that we should be cautious about rushing to judge and criticize their experiences.

Besides experiencing the Incarnational Presence in Scripture, relationships, and our imagination, we can also experience Christ incarnated in our hearts. Whenever we sense a peaceful and calming voice—a Presence—from within guiding us and leading us to live according to God's eternal purpose, this is Christ incarnated within us. As Thomas Kelly says so beautifully,

Deep within us there is an amazing inner sanctuary of the soul, a holy place, a Divine Center, a speaking Voice, to which we may continuously return. Eternity is at our hearts, pressing upon our time-torn lives, warming us with intimations of an astounding destiny, calling us home unto Itself. Yielding to these persuasions, gladly committing ourselves in body and soul, utterly and completely, to the Light Within, is the beginning of true life. It is a dynamic center, a creative Life that presses to birth within us. It is a Light Within which illumines the face of God and casts new shadows and new glories upon the face of men. It is a seed stirring to life if we do not choke it. It is the Shekinah of the soul, the Presence in the midst. Here is the Slumbering Christ, stirred to be awakened, to become the soul we clothe in earthly form and action. And He is within us all.[6]

We experience the Incarnational Presence every time we discover God in Scripture, a sunset, a sonnet, a song, in the words of a friend, or in our hearts. We experience the Incarnational Presence any time we experience God *in* life. This is the God who is experienced *in* all, rather than above all and through all.

Just as Christ is the Incarnational Presence in all of creation, when we are fully open to Christ we become incarnated in Christ. It is a reciprocal relationship. As Jesus said, "Abide in me as I abide in you" (John 15:4). The apostle Paul was fond of saying that when we accept Christ, we become a new creation in Christ: "So if anyone is in Christ, there is a new creation: everything old has passed away; see, everything has become new!" (2 Cor. 5:17). In fact, Paul takes our incarnation in Christ a step further. He says that whenever we become a community of Christians, we become the incarnated body of Christ in the world (1 Cor. 12:12–31). Together we become Christ's Incarnational Presence in the world, making God's kingdom real in the world. In effect, when we form a relationship with God the Incarnational Presence, we not only experience God in Scripture, creation, others, and ourselves, but through our experiences together we incarnate Christ in the world. If you think about it, this is pretty amazing stuff.

The Inspiring Power

Finally, when we experience the Holy Spirit, we experience God the *Inspiring Power*. This is God who is active in life through all sorts of activities, coincidences, miracles, and life events. This is the experience of God that Pentecostals and charismatics emphasize, but most mainstream Christians avoid. When I use the term "power," I do not mean it in a political sense, or in the sense of being strong. I mean it more in the sense of a dynamic energy that gives life to everything we do. Just as God breathed God's Spirit into the first human being and gave that human life (Gen. 2:7), that same Inspiring Power gives us a renewed life every time the Holy Spirit touches us, fills us, and works through us. Openness to the Inspiring Power, to God in the Spirit who has a direct effect on life, can lead to anything from a mild awareness that God is working through us to a dramatic experience, such as being baptized in the Spirit. What is baptism of the Spirit? It is a "threshold across which we may pass into the works of God, just as Jesus did at age thirty. It involves us in a personal and spiritual crisis in which we give up a life based only on rational certainty and surrender our desire for personal control."[7] Baptism in the Spirit is an experience of complete surrender to God in which God's Spirit enters us with power—maybe gently, maybe not. The Holy Spirit becomes a guide, leading us to live that eternal purpose that is rooted in the Creator and to continually experience God's presence in Christ.

This kind of spiritual experience of the Holy Spirit can be, but is not usually, dramatic. Usually it is peaceful and calming. As we align our lives with the Holy Spirit, small coincidences and miracles just begin to happen. Frank Laubach describes it by saying

> I feel simply carried along each hour, doing my part in a plan which is far beyond myself. This sense of cooperation with God in little things is what so astonishes me, for I never have felt it this way before. I need something, and turn round to find it waiting for me. I must work, to be sure, but there is God working along with me. God takes care of all the rest. My part is to live this hour in continuous inner conversation with God and in perfect responsiveness to his will, to make this hour gloriously rich. This seems to be all I need to think about.[8]

This kind of openness to the Holy Spirit comes out of a more contemplative awareness and openness. The contemplative approach to God is one that is as ancient as Christianity. When we practice contemplation, we practice a kind of prayer and prayerfulness in which we empty ourselves of all agendas, thoughts, and expectations so that we can become radically open to God. Those who practice contemplative prayer may sit in silence for an hour or more, being open to everything but attaching their attention to nothing. They simply sit in unified openness to and oneness with God in all of life. The point is not to gain insight, to pray for God to do something, or even to listen for God. It is simply to open ourselves to God and allow a oneness with God to form. Forming a contemplative awareness and openness emerges from our living in the present moment, and from trying to empty ourselves of attachments and desires so that we can simply be open to how God leads us moment by moment. That is the approach practiced by Frank Laubach and by many other mystics throughout Christian history, such as Brother Lawrence of the Resurrection, Jean-Pierre de Caussade, George Fox, and Thomas Kelly. Contemplative awareness is an attempt to become open, moment by moment, to the Inspiring Power of the Holy Spirit as the Spirit fills our emptiness.

Whether it is through the pentecostal and charismatic approach, or through the contemplative approach, the experience of the Inspiring Power in the Holy Spirit is an experience of God who is involved in our lives moment to moment, inspiring us with new insights and possibilities, but also transforming us and the world around us. The more open we are to experiencing the Inspiring Power, the more we discover that Power working in our lives, not only in large events but especially in the smaller events of life. So many Christians think that the only time we can ask for the Spirit's presence is when major traumas and events are unfolding in our lives. Frank Laubach teaches us that God wants to be involved in every part of our lives. No matter is too small or insignificant for God to be involved.

I know a woman who insists that whenever she is in a hurry and cannot find a parking space, she prays for God to help her and immediately a good spot becomes available. Is this too small an event for God? Many Christians are skeptical. The answer, though, comes from Jesus' mouth: "Ask, and it will be given you; search, and you will find; knock, and the door will be opened for you" (Matt. 7:7). Jesus did not say, "Ask, only when it involves something big; search, only for big answers; knock, only when things are mighty desperate." Apparently, Jesus meant for us to bring the Inspiring Power into the nitty-gritty of life. My own experience is that the more open I become to the Inspiring Power in the details of life, the more God seems to make coincidences happen. God, in the Spirit, is always at work around us. Why do we have such a hard time seeing this? Henry Blackaby says,

> Right now God is working all around you and in your life. One of the greatest tragedies among God's people is that while they have a deep longing to experience Him, they are experiencing God day after day but do not know how to recognize Him.[9]

For mainstream Christians, experiencing the work of the Holy Spirit—the Inspiring Power—is the part of the Trinitarian experience most avoided, even as it is the experience most sought by Pentecostals. Mainstream Christians avoid this person and experience of God who can feel just a bit too real for our lives. We don't mind God as long as God remains the God of morals and ethics, with a wee bit of Jesus' teachings thrown in. It's when we experience God as the Inspiring Power, an experience of God that can be far too real and tangible for some, that we step back from God because this God doesn't fit into our box—our conception of how God *should be*. Still, God as Holy Spirit—as Inspiring Power—was the experience many in the early Christian church sought and had of God. What stands in the way of our experiencing God in this way today? What stands in the way of our experiencing God in all three persons of the Trinity?

When we experience the Inspiring Power, we experience God in a peace that blankets our lives as we open ourselves to God; in small coincidences (or providences) that just seem to happen; in miracles that transform us and the world; and in events that transform our hearts and our souls. We experience God who is *through* all, and not just above all and in all.

The Modern Trinitarian Split

The basic problem we all have in forming a truly Trinitarian spirituality is that we belong to denominations or movements that are Trinitarian in creed only. Most Christians say that they are Trinitarian, but in practice they are not. You can do a simple test to tell what person or experience of God your denomination, the Christian movement you identify with, or your church identifies most with by listening to the prayers of the laity. To which person of the Trinity are they most comfortable praying? Whomever they pray to tends to reflect which person of the Trinity they are most comfortable with. For instance, most mainstream Christians, when praying, will tend to begin their prayer by calling on the Creator, Father, Father-God, Mother God, or just God (generally there is confusion between God and Father so that many think the only true God in the Trinity is the Father). Evangelicals will tend to pray to Jesus. Pentecostals and charismatics (Christians who focus on manifesting the gifts of the Spirit such as prophecy, speaking in tongues, and the like) may pray to the Holy Spirit, to Jesus, or to the Father, but their focus is on asking for the Holy Spirit to enter their lives. It is the rare Christian who is balanced among all persons of the Trinity, yet that is exactly where the narrow path leads. The narrow path is Trinitarian and balanced. It allows us to form a relationship with and experience all persons of the Trinity—with God as God is instead of the particular person of the Trinity we want God to be. The problem is that almost all of the denominations, movements, and sects of Christianity are split according to the Trinity. So, they constantly argue with one another over whose experiences and practices are "right."

Today, a tremendous fight over the Trinity is brewing among mainstream Christians, evangelicals, and Pentecostals/charismatics/contemplatives in a way that is dividing all the denominations. For example, most mainline

Protestant Christians of the Lutheran, Presbyterian, Episcopalian, Methodist, Baptist, Congregationalist, Disciples of Christ, Reformed, and other denominations tend to be most comfortable with God as Eternal Purpose. When others criticize them, it is generally for being too dispassionate, not grounding their faith enough in Scripture, and not believing in the power of prayer. Basically, they are criticized for being too focused on God the Eternal Purpose.

Mainstream spirituality tends to emphasize serving our Creator and Source, who is in heaven, through our deeds in this world. We are stewards of a distant God. This approach gained influence during the Enlightenment Age, when it was believed by many Christians that God was in heaven, not on earth, and that our purpose on earth was to serve God to the best of our ability by using our rational minds and bodies. When our spiritual focus is solely on God the Eternal Purpose, we believe that we are to be God's stewards on this earth, and that our rewards will come when we die and reach heaven. To do this, we try to follow the commandments, live moral and ethical lives, and/or try to bring justice to the world.

When it comes to trying to discern the will of God, folks who are centered on God the Eternal Purpose emphasize using their God-given rational minds. They engage in a rational analysis. They do not actively engage in trying to hear God's voice because they don't necessarily believe it can be heard while we are here on earth. So, they may study Scripture, science, philosophy, theology, psychology, sociology, anthropology, and all other fields of thought, and then try to make the best rational decision possible. To them, discerning God's will is a matter of using their own God-given minds.

People who are most comfortable with God as Eternal Purpose are extremely uncomfortable with other Christians who want to experience and relate with God as either Incarnational Presence or Inspiring Power. For them, God is mostly distant, and our purpose is to serve this distant God through our actions on earth. They see evangelicals and Pentecostals either as being Holy Rollers who are overly emotional and irrational in their religious practice, or as being too literal with Scripture and failing to use their rational minds enough.

Personally, I understand the emphasis on God as Eternal Purpose the most because it is the tradition in which I grew up. From childhood on, I saw God as mostly distant. For a long time, I saw prayer mostly in psychological terms. It was something that made us comfortable, calmed our minds, and helped us think the way God created us to think. As a small child I felt God's presence and gentle power, but as I grew the combination of churches I was raised in taught me to see God as more distant. As a result, it has taken me much longer to realize that God's power could flow through and affect my life, and to sense

God as a tangible presence. I had to unlearn some of the Father-centered teachings I had been given in order to become more Christ-centered and Spirit-receptive.

Those who seek God as Inspiring Power mainly focus on receiving, being filled with, and being inspired by the Holy Spirit. As I stated before, they include Pentecostals and charismatics, but also contemplative Christians. They look at mainstream and evangelical Christians with suspicion. For them, both can seem too sedate, cold, and aloof. They complain that there is no passion in these folks' faith, and that they are devoid of the Holy Spirit. Contemplatives would complain that neither mainstreams nor evangelicals are prayerful enough. They are too activity focused, and do not take enough time in serious prayer to become open to the Holy Spirit. Pentecostals and charismatics would complain that mainstreams and evangelicals do not believe strongly enough in the power of the Holy Spirit and in the gifts of the Spirit, such as speaking in tongues and prophecy. They would complain that both mainstream and evangelical Christians are guilty of not being truly open to the power of God, and so really are neither saved nor truly Christian.

The inherent problem with Pentecostals, charismatics, and contemplatives is that they can become so focused on living by the Spirit that they fail to ground themselves in the laws, morals, ethics, reasoned thought, and purposes of the Eternal Purpose. They also fail to ground themselves adequately in Scripture, the guidance of other Christians, and the body of Christ—the church. In other words, they become overly individualistic and self-focused in their spirituality and practice. They follow only the voice of what they hope and believe is the Holy Spirit. This can become a problem. For example, the sexual scandals that have rocked many popular televangelists were caused, in large part, by their failure to realize that their own inner shadows and sins were as powerful as they were. They thought that their desires for other women and their availability must be a gift from the Holy Spirit for all their good work on behalf of God. They confused their own pride and desires with the Holy Spirit because they were not simultaneously grounded in the Eternal Purpose and Incarnational Presence—in law, morality, ethics, Scripture, reason, and the guidance of others. The same kind of problems plague those who started Christian cults—people like Jim Jones, David Koresh, and so many others.

Meanwhile, evangelicals, creation-centered (those whose spiritual focus is on the presence of God in creation), and sacramental Christians tend to emphasize the experience of God's Incarnational Presence. Among evangelicals, the focus is on seeking and experiencing God's presence in Scripture. Among creation-centered Christians, it is on seeking and experiencing God's presence in creation. Creation-centered spirituality is focused on God as Incarnational Presence experienced in nature, others, our own hearts, and the universe. Sacramental Christians include Christians of the Anglican and Roman Catholic traditions. They emphasize seeking and experiencing God in the sacraments. They especially seek a tangible experience of God in the elements of Communion and the water of baptism.

Evangelical, creation-centered, and sacramental Christians seek a tangible experience of God's presence. Often, those who subscribe to each approach are critical of each other for their limitations. Evangelicals will criticize creation-centered and sacramental Christians for not being grounded enough in Scripture. Creation-centered Christians are critical of evangelicals and sacramental Christians for neither being aware of God in nature nor of caring enough for God's creation. Sacramental Christians are critical of all others for not placing the sacraments at the center of their faith. The same criticisms they lob at each other they also use against mainstream and pentecostal Christians.

The biggest problem among all who are focused on incarnational experiences of God's presence is that they are not particularly open to the Holy Spirit. For the most part they try to be open to God the Creator. For instance, since Scripture reveals God's law, morality, ethics, truth, and purpose, it does become part of evangelical spirituality. Their problem is that they may not allow enough room for the Holy Spirit. They may become overly rigid and literal in their reading of Scripture and not accept that reading Scripture requires the enlightening power of the Holy Spirit, nor that the Holy Spirit can lead us to understand Scripture in new, less literal, and less archaic ways. Meanwhile, creation-centered Christians can be wonderfully appreciative of God in nature, but somehow confuse being natural and animal with being pure. For example, they may believe that since sex is natural, it is good to explore our sexuality freely. They don't accept the moral belief that sexuality is a gift to be shared in the context of a monogamous relationship. They confuse the life of the flesh with the life of the spirit, even as some evangelical Christians may try too hard to separate the life of the flesh from that of the spirit. The Holy Spirit can lead us to understand that there needs to be a balance between the two that is grounded in our purpose and our spirit. Finally, sacramental Christians can become so focused on the power of the sacraments to redeem their lives that they seek neither God's purpose nor God's power. For instance, one stereotypical criticism of Roman Catholic laity is that they will party all night, engaging in all sorts of sinful behavior, go to confession and Communion the next day, and then go out and do the same thing. They believe in the power of the sacraments to forgive and redeem them, but they do not necessarily realize how it is important to live by certain moral standards. Nor are they particularly open to how the Holy Spirit may be calling them to live in a more moral way.

The point of all this is not that one or the other spirituality is right while the others are all wrong. It is that all are valid, for all are experiences of God. Unfortunately, over the course of Christian history we have become split in our faith. We tend to seek a relationship and experience of God that only allows for certain kinds of experiences. In many ways, it is like trying to have a successful and loving marriage that only stresses sharing the duties of a household; that only stresses communication and time spent together; or that only stresses sexual activity. A successful and loving marriage integrates all of these aspects of our relationship with the other. If only one is emphasized, the marriage will suffer, and in fact many do. The same is true of our spirituality. We must seek God in all three persons of the Trinity so that we can follow God's purpose, experience God's presence, and receive God's power.

Forming a Trinitarian Spirituality—Walking the Trinitarian Path

So, what does it take to form a truly Trinitarian spirituality that allows us to form a strong relationship with God as Eternal Purpose, Incarnational Presence, and Inspiring Power? What it takes is to be open to integrating the wisdom of all the different relationships with God. The problem in modern Christianity is that everyone argues over which kind of spirituality is right and which is wrong, instead of trying to learn from one another how our different approaches can lead us to a deeper relationship with God.

For instance, we need to respect the approach of those who mainly seek God the Eternal Purpose. How can we respect and incorporate their emphasis on using the rational mind? How can we incorporate their emphasis on morality and ethics? How can we include in our faith their emphasis on bringing love, justice, and peace to a world driven by division and violence?

We also need to be open to experience God the Incarnational Presence in all of life. We need to ground our faith in Scripture, but also be open to God who is more than Scripture. How can we be open to God as God is incarnated in all of creation, in others, and in our own hearts? How can we form a renewed appreciation for God as God is present in the rituals, symbols, and experiences of the sacrament? How can we experience God in all of life?

Finally, we need to be open to God the Inspiring Power. Can we become open to God's power by practicing the disciplines of contemplative prayer? Can we form minds and hearts that are open to God's Spirit as it fills us and guides us to live the life God calls on us to live? How open to the power of God's Spirit are we willing to be? How can we allow the power of the Holy Spirit to fill us so that we can be transformed by this power?

While it is important to work on becoming much more open to God as God truly is, it is a mistake to try to be a Christian who belongs to all Christian movements. If we do, we can end up being a thousand miles wide and two inches deep. What I mean is that we try so hard to understand and experiment with all sorts of different approaches that we end up having no personal depth at all. Each of our own denominational, theological, and spiritual faith traditions has legitimacy. They each offer profound and deep experiences of God. While these experiences may be limited in a Trinitarian sense, they can be powerful in a spiritual sense. Rooting ourselves in our own traditions is the doorway to experiencing God. Our traditions push us to grow deeper in our particular experiences of God.

We need to maintain a sense of tension between the teachings of our own traditions and those of other Christians. If we only emphasize the teachings of our own traditions, we can fall into a spiritual trap where we become too comfortable with one person of God whom we try to create in our own image. True growth in God is always uncomfortable. It always requires being spiritually self-critical and self-appraising, while being aware of how our biases may be misguiding us. To return to the theme of chapter 2, part of the answer may lie in reading the works of the mystics, for they were, if nothing else, profoundly Trinitarian. It also can mean forming a willingness to experiment with the experiences other Christians are having, and to suspend our skepticism in order to share experiences. If nothing else, forming a Trinitarian spirituality means letting go of our criticism of other Christians for their beliefs and experiences, and trying to find out just how God may be legitimately present to them. It means breaking down labels such as conservative, liberal, moderate, pentecostal, evangelical, feminist, liberationist, orthodox, reformed, Protestant, or Catholic in order to explore the experiences and legitimate inspirations that come from each perspective, approach, and practice.

To walk our own individual narrow paths requires walking them with the triune God who leads us to experience God as Creator, Son, and Holy Spirit—as the Eternal Purpose, Incarnational Presence, and Inspiring Power. This is a lifelong journey. We will never come to the point of being perfectly balanced in a Trinitarian way. This is not what God wants. God's aim is merely to lead us to experience God as broadly and deeply as possible so that we can form a deep relationship with God grounded in love. To love God, we need to discover the person of God in all three persons of the Trinity, and the way to do that is to allow God to relate to us through all the persons of the Trinity.

Questions for Reflection

1. To what extent do you think you understand the Trinity, and to what extent has it confused you?
2. To what person of the Trinity do you normally pray, and how comfortable are you with praying to the others?
3. How have you experienced God's purpose in your life, and God as Eternal Purpose?
4. How have you experienced God's presence in your life, and God as Incarnational Presence?
5. How have you experienced God's power in your life, and God as Inspiring Power?
6. If you haven't experienced God as Purpose, Presence, and/or Power, what do you think may be getting in the way?

Key Learnings

- The Trinity is meant to be a deep and profound experience of God.
- From a spiritual perspective, we experience God as we sense God's purpose, presence, and/or power in our lives.
- We experience and form a relationship with God the Eternal Purpose as we discover our purpose in life, and as we seek to live according to God's eternal purpose for us and the cosmos.
- We experience and form a relationship with God the Incarnational Presence when we sense God's presence in Scripture, others, the church, nature, our hearts, and life.
- We experience and form a relationship with God the Inspiring Power as we open our lives to God, allowing God to work through us to transform our hearts, others, and the world.

Chapter 5

Walking the Healing Path

*I*s there any topic in Christianity that generates more doubt and disbelief than the idea of Christian healing? If there is, I'm not sure what it is. Most mainstream Christians don't know what to do with the connection between faith and healing. When we read the stories about Jesus healing others in the Bible, we aren't sure what to think. Did Jesus really cast demons out of a man in the land of the Gerasenes, sending them into a herd of pigs, which then ran into the lake and drowned (Luke 8:26–33)? Did a woman really have her hemorrhages healed just by touching the fringe of Jesus' cloak (Luke 9:42–48)? Did Jesus really raise from the dead the daughter of a leader of the local synagogue (Matt. 9:18–26)? When Jesus sent his disciples out to heal others, were they really able to do so as they reported (Luke 10:17–20)? Were apostles like Peter really able to heal others on behalf of Christ (Acts 3:1–10)? Was James serious when he suggested that the elders of the church should pray over the sick and anoint them with oil (Jas. 5:13–15)?

We confront several problems in trying to ascertain how true or false the Bible is regarding the topic of healing. First, we live in such an ultra-rational age that we feel compelled to come up with modern scientific explanations for these events. For example, many suggest that Jesus, his disciples, Peter, and the others were doing nothing more than healing psychological or psychosomatic (what today are called somatoform) problems. So, they might explain that the Gerasene man just had a problem with schizophrenia, and Jesus helped him by being the master psychologist. They might explain that the woman with hemorrhages merely had some sort of hysteria and was causing her own hemorrhaging. She just willed herself to be healed when she touched Jesus' cloak. The young daughter of the synagogue's leader probably only appeared to be dead. Perhaps she was just in some sort of amnesiac coma brought on by a hysterical reaction to some trauma. Jesus just knew how to bring her out of it. In the same way, they might explain that the disciples did more of the same things that Jesus did. The disciples were doing nothing more than taking care of psychological problems. In fact, these skeptics might explain that the only reason James suggested that the elders pray with those who were sick was to be compassionate and to give the sick hope.

The problem with all of these explanations is that they assume that the people of Jesus' day were merely ignorant peasants who could not tell the difference between real physical problems and psychosomatic ones. This is a glaring mistake, because people back then understood and encountered disease, trauma, and death on a much more regular basis than we do today. They knew the difference, maybe not intellectually, but certainly experientially. Is it possible that we are the ones who are ignorant of things that go much deeper than we suspect?

A second reason we tend to dismiss the connection between Christian faith and healing is that we have seen televangelists who had great healing ministries, only to discover later that they were charlatans bilking money out of innocent, gullible, and desperate people. We have read about their manipulations and so assume that anyone in the religious sphere who offers a healing ministry of prayer must be a charlatan or a fake. We do not consider the possibility that some Christians may actually have some sort of healing power that is connected to the power of the Holy Spirit.

Third, since our mainstream churches rarely have any kind of healing ministry, and since pastors of mainstream churches rarely preach about healing, we just don't think much about the possibility that there is a live-wire connection between faith, prayer, and healing. We aren't steeped in the healing tradition of Christianity, and so we don't think about it all that much.

Finally, many people dismiss the possibility that faith and prayer can be connected to healing because they assume that God would never make faith a precondition for healing, at least not if God was truly a good God. Why wouldn't God heal everyone out of love? Why would God require us first to have faith and to pray? A good God wouldn't work this way. If God was truly good, God would first heal us to demonstrate God's great love and grace. This is the argument I made when I was in seminary. I remember having lengthy discussions both in and out of the classrooms about the connection between faith and healing. I was one of the people saying that a good God wouldn't require us to have faith. I now know that I was wrong.

The problem with all of these arguments is that they are not grounded in real experience or observation. They are grounded in speculation: about how God works, about the motives of anyone offering a healing ministry, and about the intelligence and awareness of people from biblical times. For me, it has been my firsthand experiences with healing and with people who have been miraculously healed that have opened my eyes to so many greater possibilities. Among all the people I have known who have been healed, no person has embodied the mystery of God's healing more than Rita Klaus. Rita is a living testimony to the power of God to heal.

Rita Klaus

I first spoke with Rita on the telephone one morning in 1997 after a healing group that I was leading suggested we have Rita come and talk with us. The members of the group had heard of Rita through an article in the local newspaper. In 1986, Rita had been healed of multiple sclerosis, and now she traveled around the world speaking about her experience. She didn't live too far from us, and was a member of the Roman Catholic Church in our town.

When I called Rita, I had one of those wonderful little coincidences (or providences) that happens to us as we grow more intimate with God. She answered the telephone and I introduced myself. She told me that it was odd that she was answering the phone. She had just returned from a three-week speaking engagement in Australia and New Zealand, and was about to take off for a two-week trip through Canada. She was in town for only three days, and wasn't planning on answering the phone at all because she didn't want to cram any more appearances into her schedule. Rita told me that she answered my call only because something told her to do so.

I asked her whether she would be interested in speaking to my group, and she suggested that she come and speak to our whole church community. It was during her talk—in November of 1997—that I first heard her amazing story.[1]

From the time she was a small child, Rita had wanted to be a sister in a Roman Catholic order. Whenever a teacher in her small Roman Catholic school in Iowa would ask, "Which of you is going to be a priest or a sister when you grow up?" Rita would quickly raise her hand. Every time Rita saw a sister from a different order, she would study her habit, trying to decide if it was one she wanted to wear for the rest of her life. In 1955, at age fifteen, she entered a convent and spent the next thirteen years as a nun, living in community, teaching, and trying her best to live a life of prayer and service.

In 1960, something happened that would dramatically change her life. She woke up one winter morning, shivering in the cold of her attic room. The heat did not quite reach all the way up to her room in the convent. In fact, it was so cold she could see her breath. She hurriedly put on her robe and slippers and darted down the hall toward the bathroom, looking forward to the hot water of a shower. As she stood in shower, letting the hot water cascade over her skin and body, something strange happened. The lights seemed to dim, and she felt a deep chill inside of her. Slowly, all the lights seemed to go out and everything went black. She could feel herself blinking, but she couldn't see anything. It dawned on her that the lights hadn't gone out at all; it was her sight that had faded. Then, just as suddenly as her sight had gone away, it returned. Something was seriously wrong.

After a series of medical tests, the doctors came back with a frightening diagnosis: multiple sclerosis. Over the next several years, the symptoms gradually worsened, so much so that it interfered with her ability to remain a nun. Her legs had deteriorated to the point that she had great difficulty walking, and she constantly struggled with dizziness and imbalance. She left the convent and moved to Mars, Pennsylvania, becoming a teacher in the local public school system. For a while, her symptoms abated and she managed to live a relatively normal life.

In 1971, a few years after she had left the convent, Rita met and married Ron Klaus. This was such a different life from the one she had felt destined to lead as a nun, but she loved it all the same. She had three children, the last one a daughter born when Rita was thirty-nine in 1978. Then the bottom fell out of her life. Her MS came back with a vengeance, and eventually it confined her to leg braces and a wheelchair. As her symptoms increased, so did her bitterness. She became more and more surly with her husband and children as she sunk deeper into her pit of despair. The more her MS crippled her, the higher the wall between her, her family, and her friends rose. As the MS worsened, it also crippled her faith to the point that God no longer mattered to her.

In the midst of her darkness, a light was soon to shine. A friend of hers, Marianne, called one day and said, "Rita? Listen, there's going to be a healing service over at St. Ferdinand's next Wednesday evening—want to come?" Rita scoffed at the idea. "I don't believe in healing. That stuff happened two thousand years ago. It's a bunch of fakes! I've watched them on TV, those televangelists shouting: 'You in the green dress! Come up here and be healed of your arthritis!' And the people who come up, they're all plants. Don't you know anything?" Her friend tried to convince her, but Rita was adamant and resolute: "And when they lay hands on people, and they fall backwards—you don't think they're really 'slain in the Spirit,' do you? They've been pushed—and they're too embarrassed to get up."[2]

But Marianne persisted, and she finally convinced Rita to come. The service was held on a Wednesday evening, and by the time they got there the church was packed. The only seat available was in the front, which is exactly where Rita did not want to sit. She stood there at the back of the church in her leg braces, defiantly digging her crutches into the floor. Suddenly, an usher grabbed her and pulled her down the aisle. He stopped by a pew near the front, asked a man to make room for her, and nudged her into the pew. She sat down, embarrassed by the attention and fuss she had caused.

As the first hymn began, everyone stood up to sing. Rita did too, but the metal of her braces slid on the floor, and she slowly started to slide under the pew in front of her. The people around her grabbed her and held her up. A person next to her held the hymnal in front of her face. She was humiliated. All she had wanted to do was to sit in the back of the service unnoticed and then leave at the end, proving to Marianne that healing didn't work. Instead, she was now the center of attention. The priests processed down the aisle beside her. As the priests passed by, she heard a loud whisper from another priest behind her, saying, "Wait, wait!" The procession stopped, turned around, and looked at her. The priest put his arms around her and prayed. The other priests laid their hands on her and prayed with him. This was Rita's worst nightmare. Then, something incredible happened. Suddenly she felt as though an ocean of peace was inundating her. She says,

> It flowed through me, filling every part of me. . . . It was like being hugged by God.
> I never felt so—*loved*—in all my life! It reminded me of when I'd almost drowned—the only comparison I could think of.
> And I found myself praying the first real prayer I had said in months, years: "Dear God, I don't know what this is. I don't know what You're doing. But whatever it is, it's okay."[3]

This peace lasted for the rest of the evening. She was a transformed person, yet her physical illness remained. She didn't care, though. All the anger, bitterness, and despair had evaporated, and in its place was gratitude, love, and peace. She said to God, "If I had been You, I would have washed my hands of me long ago! How could You possibly still love me? I was so mad at You, I wouldn't speak to You, and—You just picked me up and hugged me! Oh, God, I love You!"[4]

Rita had experienced a spiritual healing. While most of us might have been happy with it, I suspect we would still be disappointed that it didn't also include a physical healing. Why would God heal her spiritually but leave her unhealed physically? Rita didn't ask this question. In fact, this spiritual healing was infinitely more important to her than any physical healing could be. She told me that given the choice between a physical healing and a spiritual one, she would take the spiritual one every time. It allowed her to plunge back into life with faith, hope, love, and purpose. Still, over the next few years her body declined even more. On the inside she felt a great sense of peace and harmony, but on the outside her body was slowly deteriorating. Eventually, she was forced into a wheelchair. She prayed to God, but surprisingly not for healing. Instead, she prayed for God's grace to sustain her.

One night, she had an experience of Christ. She was crying about her illness when she saw Jesus standing in front of her with his back to her. He turned around, and she saw the most loving person she had ever seen. He said to her, "You have not given me everything." She replied, "Lord, I have. I have nothing left to give You. I completely trust in You." He said to her, "Then give me your sins."[5] She did, and in an instant she felt completely free. Her first healing was of her spirit as its spark was rekindled in her. Now, an even deeper healing of the soul had occurred.

Over the next few years, Rita devoted herself to Christ. She immersed herself in a variety of spiritual disciplines and practices, often in the hope that they would lead to physical healing. She tried the Medjugorje fast (a discipline started by devotees of those who had received apparitions of the Virgin Mary in Medjugorje, Yugoslavia). She lost fourteen pounds, but there was no physical healing. She took courses in Scripture and theology at a local college. Still no physical healing.

One night, she went to bed and, as was her custom, spent quiet time with God. She had been doing this for the three years since her spiritual healing. She was praying the rosary when she heard a voice: "Why don't you ask?" She looked around the room but could see no one. The television and radio were off. She knew in her heart that the voice was real. It was a gentle, almost pleading voice. She wondered what it was that she was supposed to ask for, and suddenly it came to her: she was to ask for healing. This was something she had never asked for. She had prayed about many things in the past, but not specifically for her own healing. Suddenly, it was as if the following words formed in her heart and came out of her mouth: "Mary, my mother, Queen of Peace, whom I believe is appearing at Medjugorje, please ask your Son to heal me in any way I need to be healed. I know your Son has said that if you have faith, and say to the mountains, 'Move,' that they will move. I believe. Please help my unbelief."[6]

As she said the last word, it was as though an electric current passed through her body. In her mind, she tried to convince herself that this was not happening. Rita possessed a critical mind that looked for rational answers to life's experiences, and in cases like this it was typical for her to be skeptical of her own non-rational experiences. She quickly fell asleep. The next morning she woke up, forgetting her experience from the night before.

She had to hurry because she had overslept and was late for a class. With help from her husband, she got dressed and drove herself to her class in her specially equipped van. As she entered the classroom, Rita was embarrassed by the noise and commotion she and her wheelchair caused as the professor continued his lecture. Things seemed normal until the class break. During the break something strange happened. It felt as though heat was surging from her feet through her legs, and across her whole body. She felt itchy all over, especially in her legs. Her toes were moving inside her shoes, which is something that hadn't happened in years. She scratched her leg and could feel her fingernails. This was something she hadn't felt so completely in years.

After class, she drove home. As she pulled into her driveway, she felt a sensation she hadn't felt in years—she had to go to the bathroom. She stopped the van and hurriedly dragged her braced body, using her crutches, out of the door and onto the driveway. The braces locked in place, and she scissor-stepped across the driveway to the front door. In the bathroom, she unlocked her brace and looked down at her leg. It was completely normal. For years her one leg had grown progressively shorter than the other as the kneecap moved to the inside of her knee. Suddenly, her leg was normal. She quickly began taking off her braces. As she did she remembered the prayer from the night before. She thought to herself that if she was healed she should be able to walk up the stairs. With that, she launched up the stairs with a bound. She reached the top, let out a yelp of joy, and ran down them, out the front door, and into the driveway. The sky was a crystal blue, and she yelled out, "Thank you, God! Thank you, Blessed Mother!" The dog came and joined her as she ran back and forth across her property. She had been healed.

Since that day in 1986, Rita has never had a recurrence of her MS—even of minor symptoms. She travels the world over to tell others her story and to tell about God's love. She also reminds people of several things. First, healing is a blessing and a gift from God. It is not something we can force God to do, but it is something that God freely gives to so many. There is no way to predict how, when, or if healing will occur. It is all up to God. Second, she reminds them that given a choice between spiritual healing and physical healing, the spiritual healing is ultimately more important. Finally, she reminds them that they must trust God no matter what happens. The only way to receive healing is by trusting completely in God, even if it does not lead to healing.

The Connection between Faith and Healing

In our modern culture, with our rational, skeptical, and scientific perspectives, we don't know what to do with healings like Rita's. As one woman told me after hearing Rita speak, "But people go into spontaneous remissions of MS all the time. What's so special about her story?" What was special was the connection between Rita's faith and her healing. Many people are religious, but not all have a faith that is alive and vibrant, and that provides a live-wire connection with God. The narrow path is one that is reliant on God in faith and that deeply trusts in God for everything. It is this connection with God through faith that opens us to God's healing power. The narrow path is one that opens us to God's healing not only for ourselves, but for other people through us.

Agnes Sanford, one of the great healers and writers about healing of the twentieth century, says about the connection between faith and healing:

> God is both within us and without us. He is the source of all life; the creator of the universe behind universe; and of unimaginable depths of interstellar space and of light-years without end. But He is also the indwelling life of our own little selves. And just as a whole world full of electricity will not light a house unless the house itself is prepared to receive electricity, so the infinite and eternal life of God cannot help us unless we are prepared to receive that life within ourselves. *Only the amount of God that we can get in us will work for us.*[7]

In essence, Sanford is saying that God's healing power surrounds us, but unless we are willing to plug into God through faith and prayer, nothing can happen. In essence, the more faith we have, the more we create the conditions for healing to take place. At the same time, the more skeptical and doubting we are, the more we disconnect from God's power and inhibit healing.

Sanford is not telling us anything that is not scriptural. Throughout the Gospels, Jesus makes the connection between faith and all sorts of miracles, not the least of which is healing. Jesus says,

> "Truly I tell you, if you have faith and do not doubt, not only will you do what has been done to the fig tree, but even if you say to this mountain, 'Be lifted up and thrown into the sea,' it will be done. Whatever you ask for in prayer with faith, you will receive." (Matt. 21:21–22)

Jesus meant this literally, and it applies to the whole issue of healing. If we are to walk the narrow path, it is a path that not only trusts in God's healing, but also allows us to become healing agents for others. This is why Jesus so often said to those he healed, "Your faith saved you; go in peace" (Luke 7:50), or "Daughter, your faith has made you well; go in peace" (8:48).

Would it surprise you to know that almost one-fourth of the Gospels pertain to healing? If we focus only on the narrative portions of the Gospels, that figure jumps even higher. Forty percent of Matthew, 40 percent of Mark,

35 percent of Luke, and 33 percent of John deal with accounts of Jesus' heal-ing.[8] Whenever we talk about Jesus' ministry, we tend to focus on his teach-ing, preaching, crucifixion, and resurrection, but ignore his whole emphasis on healing. When we ignore it, we miss a crucial component of the narrow path that Jesus has set before us, for healing lies at the very core of what Jesus' ministry and mission were all about.

What was Jesus' mission? Many people argue over the answer to this ques-tion, but the answer Scripture gives is that Jesus came to save us. Most Chris-tians would agree with this answer, yet they fail to realize how much healing is a part of the process of salvation. In our modern times we have completely lost the connection between healing and salvation. When we hear the word "salvation," we say that it refers to Jesus' atoning sacrifice on the cross that rescues us from the clutches of sin. Further, we say that Jesus' sacrifice on the cross prepares a place for us in the kingdom of God, even though God would have every right to reject us based on our sinfulness. In effect, we believe that Jesus' saving sacrifice procures for us a ticket to heaven. So, we tend to asso-ciate salvation with our getting into heaven after we die. Unfortunately, when we explain salvation in this way, we fail to understand the *whole* nature of salvation.

The word "salvation" comes from the Latin word *salvus*, which not only means to rescue, but also to heal. It is the same root that the word "salve" comes from. When we place a salve on a wound, it heals the wound. In many ways, Jesus is the salve on the woundedness of our souls. Healing is part of Jesus' saving act: "Those who are well have no need of a physician, but those who are sick; I have come to call not the righteous but sinners" (Mark 2:17).

It is not just the Latin word for "save" that connects salvation with healing. The most common Greek word used in the New Testament for "save" con-nects healing with salvation. This is the Greek word *sozo*. It means both to save and to heal. So, for example, in Matthew's Gospel we read that the angel tells Joseph that Mary "will bear a son, and you are to name him Jesus, for he will save his people from their sins" (Matt. 1:21). If we are to be true to the meaning of this word, it is telling us that Jesus came to both rescue and heal us. Throughout all the Gospels, the connection between salvation and healing is quite apparent.[9]

The same kind of connection exists between health and holiness. The word "holy" comes from the Old English *hal*, which is also the root of other words like it such as "hale," "heal," and "whole." To be holy means to be whole, healthy, and hale. In other words, when we are truly saved by Christ, we undergo a process of holiness in which we are made progressively healthier and whole in body, mind, spirit, and soul.

To bring all of this together, it is important for us to understand fully the connection between salvation and holiness. We are not saved simply so that we can get to heaven when we die. When Christ begins the process of saving us from our sin, the power of sin (which leads to decay) diminishes within us. The walls that divide us from God, that divide us from the holy, are torn down. This is what ultimately makes healing and holiness possible. To put it in Agnes Sanford's terms, Christ plugs us into the power of the Holy Spirit, who heals us. The God within connects us with the God without so that slowly we become united with the purposes and power of God.

We can see the evidence of this connection between salvation, holiness, and healing in Scripture. At one point, a paralyzed man is brought before Jesus. Jesus says to him, "Take heart, son; your sins are forgiven" (Matt. 9:2). This is a somewhat surprising response because we would expect Jesus simply to heal the man, but he doesn't. It isn't until the scribes get upset with Jesus and attack him by saying that he is blaspheming because only God can forgive sins (Luke 5:21) that Jesus makes the connection between healing and salvation:

> "Why do you think evil in your hearts? For which is easier, to say, 'Your sins are forgiven,' or to say, 'Stand up and walk'? But so that you may know that the Son of Man has authority on earth to forgive sins"—he then said to the paralytic—"Stand up, take your bed and go to your home." (Matt. 9:4–6)

There is an intimate connection between salvation—the forgiving of sin—and healing. In effect, any true healing must work from the soul outward. Sometimes Jesus was content to heal the body first. Then he would say to those healed, "Go and sin no more." More often, especially for those whose wounds were more psychological and spiritual in nature, Jesus healed from the soul outward.

You can see how true healing begins in the soul and permeates outward in Rita Klaus's story. Her healing began with a spiritual healing, which she said was the most important one. A year later it deepened as she gave Jesus all of her sins and her soul was cleansed. It wasn't until much later that she was healed physically. Unfortunately, this is not the order we want when we pray to God for healing. We ask God to heal our bodies or our minds, the implication being that we want God to leave our spirits and souls alone. *So many people really don't want spiritual healing because it transforms us to the core.* It changes who we are and what we care about. It makes us dissatisfied with the life we have been living. Who wants that? What so many want when they pray for healing is for God to just heal their bodies and to leave the rest of their being alone.

To walk the narrow path means to seek a healing of the soul first—to want spiritual healing first—and then to seek a healing of the body and mind. This is what it means to have our faith heal us. Remember that Jesus often said to those he had healed, "Go, your faith has made you well." In essence, he was saying that it was not just God who heals us. We are healed by our connection with God, by our openness to God, by our plugging in to God. Not only does God want this connection, but the only way we can truly be made holy and whole is through this connection. It is our relationship with God that makes us whole, that makes us holy, and that saves us. Perhaps a better way of saying it is that while God makes us whole, holy, and saved, it is our connection with God that allows God's saving, holy, and healing power to flow into and through our lives.

The Narrow, Healing Path

How do we form the kind of faith that leads not only to our healing, but also to our becoming a healing presence for others? First, we need to realize that the entire purpose of God's healing is not necessarily for our healing alone. God wants us to share God's healing with others. This is what distinguishes Christian spirituality from much of today's pop spirituality. Much of what our culture embraces as spirituality is self-centered and selfish. It offers techniques and objects intended to procure healing only for ourselves. The whole point of pop spirituality is to make us the best we can be—to be self-actualized. Being the best we can be isn't such a bad thing, and Christian spirituality does emphasize individual growth and transformation, but then it takes us further. In Christianity, *the transformation of the individual is always intended to eventually transform the communal*. In other words, the purpose of our transformation is to help transform others. In a church context, our own healing is ultimately meant to be a healing for the body of Christ—for the church community as a whole. The healthier and more whole we become as individuals, the more we are able to create a healing and holy context for others. The opposite is true, too. The healthier a church becomes, the more it becomes a place of healing for others.

I have witnessed this power of healing in my own church. As Calvin Presbyterian Church itself has become healthier and more whole, healing of past traumas, disease, relationships, and lives has occurred more regularly among many of our members. People have told me that their lives were going downhill, but once they started coming to worship, things began to turn around. Things did not turn 180 degrees overnight, but they did improve slowly and progressively. People have also told me that after making a commitment to their faith and making God central to their lives and church an important part of their focus on God, their lives began to improve dramatically. They could not cite anything specific other than the fact that their lives just seemed more centered and whole. It wasn't just their participation in worship. It was the fact that they were becoming more focused on others and not just on themselves. It was also the fact that the church's faith helped its members deepen their faith and trust more in God and God's grace. The community of faith, when it acts in faith, becomes a healing place.

These observations are not just my own. Research has been done on the subject. David Larson is a medical researcher who has devoted a large part of his life to researching the effect of religious commitment on physical and mental health. He embarked on this course after Duke University Medical School advisors suggested that the only impact religion had on health was to make people weaker and less healthy. He decided that a true scientist and researcher had to test these theories and not just speculate.

Larson and his colleagues did not choose to conduct original research. Instead, they surveyed all the research that had already been done on the connection between religious commitment and health.[10] They were fairly particular in terms of what kind of research they would consider. It had to meet specific scientific requirements regarding validity and reliability. In reviewing all of these studies, they found that the connection between religious commitment and better health was positive and strong. For example, they found that as religious commitment increased, substance abuse decreased. They found that there was also an increase in overall mental health, including improvements in adjustment and coping abilities, as well as reductions in the rates of depression, hostility, general anxiety, death anxiety, and other psychological symptoms. In addition, they found that religious commitment improved general health, reduced rates of hypertension, and improved the quality of life among cancer patients, while also increasing their rates of survival (as well as those of heart patients). Finally, they found that those who had a greater level of religious commitment also reported greater life satisfaction, marital satisfaction, well-being, altruism, and self-esteem.

While religious commitment and faith are not necessarily identical, Larson's studies do suggest that the deeper our faith is, the healthier we become. This is what Christianity has always taught us. It is not only God who makes us well, but our faith—our link to God.

Forming the kind of faith that leads to healing requires several things. First, it requires abandonment, surrender, and a relinquishing of our wounds to God. Most Christians aren't even remotely aware of what this means. Most committed Christians are relatively good at reading the Bible, attending worship, contributing time and money to charities, and caring for the welfare of others. We certainly aren't perfect, and very few Christians are strong in all of these areas, but overall most committed Christians are relatively good at practicing these disciplines and virtues. Where almost all of us fall short is in the area of faith. We think that faith means simply believing that God exists. It is much more than that. True faith means abandoning ourselves to God.[11] To abandon ourselves to God means giving God control over everything in our lives: our desires, plans, and destinies.

Most people do not understand what it means to have this kind of faith. They think that it means becoming spiritual slugs who do nothing and leave everything up to God. To abandon ourselves to God means to do the best we can with what God has given us, and then to entrust God with the rest. We are actively engaged in the world, but we also let God take care of us. We live in the present while giving God the future. We make plans and work on projects to the best of our abilities, but then we let God take care of the results. If we get the results we want, we thank God for making them possible. If we don't, we take it as a possible sign that God either wants us to be patient or to move in another direction. Real faith means being engaged in the world, while giving God the responsibility for our burdens, fears, worries, and results.

This means that we ask God for healing, but at the same time we accept whatever God does. We must walk a fine line here. Some people will take this to mean that we should never ask for healing because we should want only what God wants. They think that to ask for specific healing would be to impose our will on God. Others believe that we should be direct in asking God for healing and suggest that if we are not healed it is because our prayers and our faith have not been strong enough. Both of these perspectives come from people who have stepped off the narrow path in their need to have things clear and defined. They are uncomfortable with the tension we must keep in seeking both healing and God's will.

In contrast, walking the narrow, healing path means praying in a way that is determined and persistent in asking God for what we want, but that is simultaneously open and accepting of the mysterious ways God answers our prayers. We pray, maintaining a balance between clarity and acceptance. We begin by being very precise in asking God for healing, even to the point of creating and communicating a clear image of what it is we want God to do. In doing this, we follow the Scripture that says, "Ask, and it will be given you; search, and you will find; knock, and the door will be opened for you" (Matt. 7:7).

Next, we need to become persistent in our prayers, coming to God over and over again (Luke 11:5–8). As Agnes Sanford says,

How long should we continue praying for healing? Until the healing is accomplished. Sometimes a prayer once or twice a day is sufficient, but sometimes we need to "pray without ceasing," to keep ourselves open to the continuous inflow of God's power. We do this, not by saying over and over again, "Oh please, Lord," for that sounds as though we do not believe He is really working. It is much better to keep the power flowing by continually giving thanks for it. Every time we think of a condition within ourselves that needs healing we can say, "Thank you, Lord, that your power is making me well."[12]

We then need to pray with the expectation that God is going to answer us. In fact, as we pray we need to develop a trust that God has already started to answer our prayers. As Jesus said, "So I tell you, whatever you ask for in prayer, believe that you have received it, and it will be yours" (Mark 11:24).

Finally, we need to accept that in answering our prayers, God may answer them in ways that are deeper and more complete than we expect. We accept the way God heals us, for God does not necessarily answer our prayers as we ask them to be answered. That would turn God into a genie, not God. God answers our prayers by going much deeper, healing us either from the soul outward, or beginning in the area most needed according to God's judgment.

A man I met named Dan taught me the power of praying clearly with persistence, expectation, and acceptance. I met Dan when he and his wife joined a healing group I had been leading. He had lung cancer, for which he was receiving chemotherapy. Over time, we talked about healing prayers, and Dan was very clear about his intention to pray for healing. So, all of us in the group prayed that God would heal his cancer. We were persistent and prayed with expectation. For a while it seemed to work. Dan's tumor was shrinking. Suddenly, complications arose. He had a seizure, and the tests revealed that he had cancerous lesions in his brain. He had to discontinue the chemotherapy so that he could undergo radiation. The radiation treatments were mildly effective, but in the meantime his lung tumor had grown exponentially. It became apparent that he would not be healed of his cancer.

I visited Dan in the hospital and asked him whether he was disappointed that the prayers didn't seem to be working anymore. He smiled and told me that they were still working. He explained that over the past few months he had been able to eke out time that otherwise he wouldn't have had. He believed that his cancer was not God's fault, but his own for smoking for twenty-five years. Dan also said, "You don't realize, after my divorce my family fell apart. I didn't think I'd ever fall in love again, and my one son and I have been estranged ever since. But then when I turned my life over to God, things began to happen. I met Bonnie [his wife], who has been such a blessing to me. She has taught me how to live and to love in a way that I didn't know I could. She has helped me to understand what my priorities in life should be, and God is at the top of that list. My cancer has just made us closer, and it has taught me to love and what it means that God loves me. If I hadn't had these extra months, I never really would have understood and I wouldn't have been ready to die. Also, for the first time in years my son and I talked the other day, and at the end we both said that we loved each other. You don't realize how important that is to me. I would rather die having reconciled with my son than continue to live with us as enemies."

Dan died about a month later, but in the process he taught me a lot about healing. His prayers for physical healing had worked for a while, but God's primary focus was something far deeper. God cared more about healing Dan's spirit, his mind, his relationships, and his soul. Healing of the body was not the main concern, and in the end Dan realized that the body can pass away unhealed, but what's important is the healing of the soul, which is eternal. It was Dan's surrender and abandonment to God that allowed all of this healing to take place. Ultimately, Dan abandoned himself to God, and even though he wanted physical healing, he had surrendered everything to God so that God could heal him in the way God wanted, not necessarily just in the way Dan wanted.

To form the kind of faith that leads to a healing of others and ourselves also requires that we balance the different dimensions of our lives in the ways discussed in chapter 3. It requires a balancing integration of our spiritual, mental, physical, and relational dimensions in a way that allows the spiritual to guide the mental, physical, and relational. Christ's vision was one of spiritual, mental, physical, and relational balance, integration, and wholeness.

We cannot say in every case that our physical, mental, or relational illnesses and ailments are *always* due to a lack of integration with the spiritual. What we can say is that *often* our lack of health is due to a failure to integrate the spiritual, mental, physical, and relational dimensions. In the Larson studies cited earlier, there was an obvious correlation between attention to the spiritual dimension and our psychological, physical, and relational health. This is also attested to in Scripture. For example, we are told in Proverbs, "Do not be wise in your own eyes; fear the LORD, and turn away from evil. It will be a healing for your flesh and a refreshment for your body" (3:7–8). James tells us, "The prayer of faith will save the sick, and the Lord will raise them up; and anyone who has committed sins will be forgiven. Therefore confess your sins to one another, and pray for one another, so that you may be healed. The prayer of the righteous is powerful and effective" (Jas. 5:15–16). In the first passage, humility and openness to God leads to physical health. In the second passage, prayer and faith lead to healing, but since it is done as part of the community of faith it also deepens relationships.

These dimensions feed and support each other. The more spiritually committed we become, the healthier it makes us mentally, physically, and relationally, but the contrary can also be true. The more relationally healthy we become, the more it can make us physically, mentally, and spiritually healthy. Why? Because *healthy* relationships with *healthy* people teach us how to be healthier as individuals. In the same way, the more physically healthy we become, the more it can make the other dimensions healthier. Why? Simply because it is hard to have healthy relationships, minds, and spirits if we neglect our bodies. If we eat poorly, fail to get enough sleep and exercise, and basically mistreat our bodies, it affects our ability to focus on God in prayer, have the energy to use our bodies in God's service, and physically will ourselves to seek God's purpose. Again, the more mentally healthy we become, the more it allows the other dimensions to become whole and holy. The subject of mental health is a delicate one, because obviously many mental illnesses are organic in origin and are not easily controlled or improved. It is for this reason that, in my experience, those with mental illness face special obstacles in integrating the mental dimension with all the others. At the same time, the more we are able to improve our overall health (spiritual, physical, and relational), even if we suffer from mental illness, the healthier we become in all the other dimensions.

In talking about the integration of all of these dimensions, it is easy to misunderstand and think that I am suggesting that we can achieve some kind of interior and exterior dimensional utopia. We cannot achieve a perfect harmony of mind, body, spirit, and relationships. Only God can do it for us, and even at that, God often refuses to create this kind of perfect harmony. We can only do what we can do. In fact, there are times when God leads us into a state of disintegration in order to bring about greater health in a particular dimension, especially the spiritual dimension. I have suggested that we need to integrate all of these dimensions, but there are times when disease or turmoil in one dimension actually leads to a deepening and healing in one of the other dimensions.

For example, Paul was a man of great spiritual, mental, and relational health, but he was not in great physical health. He tells us that he had some sort of physical infirmity, a thorn from Satan, that forced him to surrender himself to God (2 Cor. 12:6–12). His physical weakness became a vehicle that allowed God's power to flow more strongly through him. This suggests that sometimes we need to experience trauma and pain in one dimension in order to be given greater health in the other dimensions.

The key in all of this is that we are called to abandon ourselves to God and to live lives that seek greater integration of the different dimensions of our lives. To foster this abandonment, we may encounter periods of spiritual, mental, physical, and relational suffering. It is when we abandon ourselves to God and let God integrate our dimensions that true healing begins to occur in our lives. Ultimately, walking the narrow, healing path is not just a path intended to bring greater healing to ourselves. It is a path we walk to bring greater health, wholeness, and holiness to others and the world. Every action of the Christian life is designed to bring wholeness and holiness into the world. Mission isn't just about converting others or bringing medical care to others. It is about increasing the spiritual, mental, physical, and relational health of others. Emphasizing morality is not just a way of trying to constrict people's lives. It is an attempt to ground lives in a moral foundation that brings about greater spiritual, mental, physical, and relational health. The emphases on loving others, grounding our lives in the Scriptures and traditions of our faith, creating communities of faith, caring for the poor, giving, and all the rest ultimately are meant to bring a sense of healing, wholeness, and holiness to every part of life.

To Be a Healer of Others

Since healing is not just intended to focus on ourselves, how do we become healers in our lives? How do we become a healing presence to others?

The first thing we need to do is to realize that *ultimately all healing is by the power of God—by the power of Christ and the Holy Spirit—and not our own power.* When true healing occurs, it is from God. This is a crucial point because so many think that it is by the strength of their own ability to pray or have faith that true healing occurs. Conversely, they think that when healing is not apparent, it is because of the weakness of their own prayers or faith. If we are to be healing presences for others, it will never be via our own ability or will. It will only be by the power of God. God is the healer.

The second thing that we need to do to become healers is *to open our spirits, minds, bodies, and relationships to God's grace so that God's grace can flow through us to others.* We are called to be conduits of God's grace. This is the ultimate freedom God gives us—to choose whether or not we will let God's grace flow through us into the world around us. The more we choose to allow God's grace to flow through us, the more our lives can become healing to others. The more we choose to inhibit God's grace from flowing through our lives, the less we become a healing presence. In fact, the more we inhibit God's grace, the more we become destructive presences to others.

Agnes Sanford says about the choice to become conduits of God's grace, "We must learn that God is not an unreasonable and impulsive sovereign who breaks His own laws at will. As soon as we learn that God does things *through* us (not *for* us), the matter becomes as simple as breathing, as inevitable as sunrise."[13] This is a crucial point if we are to walk the healing path. In fact, it is a crucial part of walking all parts of the narrow path. We must learn that in everything God is sovereign, but also that our role is always to become conduits through whom God's grace, power, and love flow through. In fact, the purpose of walking the narrow path is to learn how to become open conduits so that the journey along our own paths increasingly allows God's love and grace to flow through us to transform the world and us. Our only true abilities as Christians arise in direct relationship to our ability to be open conduits for God. For instance, my abilities in preaching, writing, and pastoring are directly related to my willingness to be a conduit for God to work through me. I have noticed that the more open I become to God, the better I become at all of these. Things seem to flow naturally and effortlessly. When I take them back from God and claim them as my own, they become more difficult. The more they are by virtue of my own efforts, the more they become labored and hard. The more I let them become God's efforts, the easier and more natural they become. This is true of any part of the Christian life. Whether we are involved in ministries of social justice, mission, administering, preaching, teaching, evangelizing, caring, counseling, serving, singing, playing music, organizing, or healing, our only true abilities come as gifts from God. It is our willingness to allow God's power and grace to flow through us that increases these gifts and makes them stronger. The extent to which we are unwilling to let God's grace flow through us is the extent to which these gifts remain undeveloped, underdeveloped, or slow to develop.

So, in terms of healing, how do we become open conduits allowing God's grace and power to flow through us?

1. *We must believe and expect that God can and will heal.* This may seem like such a basic statement, but the truth is that most Christians don't really believe in God's willingness and ability to heal. The more mainstream we are as Christians, it seems, the less we believe. Evangelicals and especially Pentecostals tend to have a much stronger belief in God's willingness and ability to break into the world. Mainstream Christians tend to conceive of God as a distant God who is impotent. This is not the God of Scripture, nor is it the God Jesus revealed. The God Jesus revealed is God who is active in the world, and

who chooses to work through us to fill the world with God's grace, even though God also chooses at times to work directly. In regard to God's working through us, Jesus said, "Truly I tell you, whatever you bind on earth will be bound in heaven, and whatever you loose on earth will be loosed in heaven" (Matt. 18:18). One of the things Jesus was telling his followers and us is that it is the extent to which we allow God's grace to flow through us into the world that makes all the difference. If we believe and expect God to heal, that power will be loosed in this world. If we don't, it will remain bound in heaven.

2. *We must always seek God's guidance and will in determining whom and what to pray for.* There is a tendency among those new to healing prayer to believe that God wants what we want and that all it takes to be successful is an openness to God. I suspect this is why so many healing pastors and televangelists get caught in a variety of scandals. The moment the success of their ministries hinges on the consistency of their ability to deliver healing is the moment that they no longer become conduits of God's grace. Eventually, they quit relying on God and seeking to know God's will. Their livelihoods depend on providing a healing each and every time, and so they start manufacturing false healings in order to maintain the illusion that they can produce healing time after time.

When it comes to healing prayer and being a healing presence, we need to always begin by asking God whether or not we are to pray for that particular person. Francis MacNutt, one of the best-known writers in the area of healing, says,

> There are multitudes of sick people. Some of them are not ready to be healed, even when they ask for prayer; for others who will be healed I am simply not the right person to pray for them. I cannot presume that I am supposed to pray for every sick person I meet. . . . The first discernment we need is whether or not we are meant to pray for this person at this time.[14]

In addition to seeking God's will in terms of *who* we will pray for, we need to seek God's will in terms of *what* we should pray for. We should ask the person what she or he wants us to pray for, but we also have to ask God what God wants us to pray for. To truly be God's conduits, we have to focus our prayers on the right place. As MacNutt says, "we should also be alert to the promptings of the Spirit who may enlighten us, especially when we don't know what to pray for. It is not healthy to be unduly problem-oriented and symptom-centered. If we are truly united to Jesus Christ and his Spirit . . . we can rely upon their positive inspirations about what to pray for."[15] The ability to sense whom and what to pray for requires that we attain a certain level of spiritual sensitivity and trust that the gentle nudgings we faintly feel are right. So, if we gently sense that we are not to pray for a particular person at this time, or that we are to pray for something other or deeper than what the person has asked for, we need the confidence to trust and act according to this will.

3. *We need to live prayerful lives.* It is not enough just to pray on occasion. We must learn to turn our whole lives into prayer. Living prayerful lives means to become open conduits for God moment by moment. To be prayerful means to turn our whole lives into prayer. It not only means setting aside regular times for prayer, but also beginning a process by which every moment of life becomes prayer. This can be as simple as just carrying on a conversation with God in every part of our day. It means inviting God into our work, our parenting, our leisure, and everything else. Personally, I talk to God all day long. No matter what I am doing, I include God as part of it. That doesn't just mean I pray when I am in trouble or need help. I constantly thank God for the little epiphanies and moments of surprise I experience during the day. I ask God to bless what I am doing. I share with God moments I spend with my children by talking to God while I play with my children. I try to make God a part of everything I do. This is how we live prayerful lives. We make our lives full of prayer.

4. *We need to be very specific when we offer prayers of healing for others and ourselves.* We need to focus our prayers. Too many people are shy about what they pray for. They do not pray for specific healing, but instead pray in general or for God's will. Usually they do this to hedge their bets. In other words, they worry that their prayers won't work, so they pray in a way that lets God off the hook just in case the prayer doesn't work. By not praying for a specific healing, they give themselves a built-in excuse for why they weren't healed. They say that they weren't healed because it must not have been God's will. We do have to seek God's will, but we also must have the confidence to pray specifically.

We saw how important specific prayers were for Rita Klaus. Rita was reluctant to pray specifically. In fact, Rita had to be prompted by God to actually pray for physical healing because she kept making her prayers too general. While it is important to seek God's will, there does come a time when we need to have the courage to be specific.

5. *We need to persevere in our prayers of healing.* This is one of the most ignored parts of the healing path. We are not just to pray specifically, but we are to pray constantly. Paul says that we are to "pray without ceasing" (1 Thess. 5:17). Jesus says directly (Luke 11:5–8) and in parables (Luke 18:1–8) that we should not go to God just once, but over and over again. Unfortunately, many Christians pray once, twice, three times, and then conclude that prayer doesn't work. Part of prayerfulness is perseverance. I am not sure why God operates this way, but apparently God wants us to come to God over and

over. My theory is that our perseverance opens our blocked conduits for God and allows God's grace to continually increase as it flows through us.

6. *We need to thank God.* So many people take God for granted. They come to God in bad times, and then walk away in good times. Agnes Sanford asks,

> How many Christians down through the ages have failed to receive the answers to their prayers by taking this last step—the step of giving thanks! God is standing before us with the answer in His hands. But unless we reach out our hands and take it by giving thanks for it, we are not apt to receive it. For while love is the wiring that connects our souls with His, faith is the switch that turns on the power.[16]

Our thankfulness is a key component of our faith. In fact, many spiritual masters of prayer insist that when we pray for anything we need to give thanks right away in the confidence that God has already answered our prayers. Our gratitude actually increases our faith. This is clearly shown in the story of the ten lepers (Luke 17:11–19). The ten lepers call out to Jesus, asking him to heal them. He heals all of them, but only one returns to Jesus, thanking and praising God in a loud voice. And Jesus says to him, "Get up and go on your way; your faith has made you well" (v. 19). Thankfulness and gratitude connects us even more strongly to God and continues that process of opening us up so that we can be conduits for God's grace.

7. *We need to accept the ways God heals.* We discussed this earlier, but when it comes to healing, what God wants and what we want are not always the same thing. God seeks a deeper healing than we usually do. God has a view of our whole lives and all eternity. God's wisdom is always infinitely deeper and more expansive than we can possibly fathom. When it comes to healing prayer for others or ourselves, we need to trust God by accepting whatever God does. As Francis MacNutt says, "If we really believe that God makes himself responsible for the results of our prayer, we can do our part, which is to pray, and then leave the results to him."[17]

Why Are Some Not Healed?

One of the biggest struggles for all who attempt to walk the narrow, healing path is the question, "What about those I've prayed for but were never healed?" This is a difficult question to answer because it assumes we can know the mind of God. How can we possibly assume we can begin to know the whys and wherefores of God? At the most, we live about eighty to ninety years. God is eternal, which is not the same thing as saying that God lives forever. To say that something or someone lasts forever is to say that that thing or person will last as long as time and space lasts. God exists outside the realm of time and space. How then do we, who are trapped in a time- and space-bound life, understand God, who transcends time and space? At the same time, this does not mean that we can never understand why God doesn't heal in all cases. I can offer some possible answers, but ultimately the answers lie in God, not in any explanations a human can offer. The following are some possibilities for why prayers for healing sometimes seem to go unanswered.

First, it may simply be due to the fact that *we are not meant to be completely healthy throughout life*. God created a world in which disease, accidents, disasters, catastrophes, and death abound. This is the natural way of things. To assume that somehow being a Christian allows us to defy the nature of life is naive. While God's vision for life may be wholeness, it is still a vision in the midst of a world that contains disease and death. In fact, while God's vision is one of healing, we often mistake this for being cured. Being cured means to be absent of all illness or disease. To be whole means to be holy and healthy despite illness and disease. Healing allows us to transcend our disease. Thus, Paul was given a thorn in the flesh (2 Cor. 12:7)—an illness or trauma—yet in giving it over to God he was made whole. He still had the infirmity, but it became a part of the process of God making him holy and whole. Without it, pride may have caused him to be free of all physical illness but fragmented and unholy in his relationships, mind, and spirit. In effect, there are times when we can be unhealthy physically, mentally, or even relationally, but still whole and healthy because we have surrendered ourselves to God.

Second, our lack of healing may be due to the fact that *we are not very open to God's healing*. The simple fact is that not very many people believe in the power of God to heal. We've learned to be skeptical. Those of us born and raised in a twentieth-century, Western context live in a very scientific, technological culture that prizes skepticism. How do we put that aside when it comes to healing, especially when the medical profession bases its work in scientific skepticism? Yet to be open to healing does not mean to be a naive fool. We have to believe, but at the same time we have to be open to even the possibility that we will not be healed. The dividing line is that we cannot let skepticism be our faith. Christian faith is always rooted in hope. To be open to God's healing we have to believe that God can and will heal, and then hope for that healing. Otherwise, the conduits will be closed and no healing will be possible.

Third, *our illness is intended to be transforming and redemptive*. As with Paul, not all physical illnesses should be healed. Some actually can transform us. In fact, often the deepest faith is formed in the throes of unhealed illness because those are the times we are most likely to confront the shallowness of our faith. When we are seriously ill, maimed, or hurt, we are put into a situation in which we have to decide whether or not to truly trust God. For so many people, it is in their illnesses and suffering that they find God. I've discovered this many times in talking to those Christians I know who always seem to have the deepest faith. Again and again they have told me that it was in the midst of illness, depression, unemployment, divorce, or in the grieving of death that they turned their lives over to God.

This is the theme of transformative suffering that we find expressed throughout the Bible. In fact, it is a paradox that arises over and over again throughout Scripture: *in the desert our faith blooms*. (Incidentally, this is a paradox that I did not explore in my book, *Paradoxes for Living*, but it is as powerful as any in Scripture.) This is a paradox demonstrated by every major figure in the Bible. Abraham comes to know God deeply as he wanders through the desert. Joseph is sold into slavery in the desert, and afterwards experiences a personal desert as a slave and then a prisoner in Egypt. It is in the depths of these experiences that he discovers God most profoundly. Moses finds God and faith after he flees into the desert, and then leads the Israelites through a forty-year trek through the desert as they form the strong and resilient faith necessary to enter the Promised Land. David lives in the desert for years as he tries to elude the murderous King Saul. Elijah flees to the desert from Jezebel and Ahab, and there learns to hear God in the silence. Jesus is led by the Holy Spirit into the desert before he embarks on his ministry. Finally, after having a conversion experience on the road to Damascus, Paul is led into the desert (Arabia) for three years. In fact, the only people in the Bible who were asked to form their faith in a garden couldn't. Adam and Eve tried, but they failed and were exiled into the desert wilderness.

In Scripture, there is a definite connection between suffering and the formation of a deep faith. In most of the biblical cases, it is actually God who leads us into the desert. The desert is a place that transforms us and redeems us. Unfortunately, we modern people fail to see the value of suffering and struggling. We live in a culture that idolizes pleasure, happiness, instant gratification, and ease. We don't realize that times of suffering are often the times in which our faith deepens. Suffering actually can be good for the soul because when we are in the midst of the desert—in the midst of suffering and desolation—we are left with a choice: are we going to trust God to lead us out of the desert, or are we going to try to retrace our steps to recapture what we had? If we choose the former, we end up with deeper, richer lives. If we choose the latter, we end up with more shallow lives built upon sand.

Finally, we may not experience healing because *God heals from the soul outward*. Simply put, healing may be taking place, but its beginnings may not be where we expect. Most often, God works at the deepest levels and then slowly moves to the surface. This is what happened in Rita Klaus's case. Her healing began with a spiritual healing. With this came a healing of her relationships with her family and friends. A few years later came the forgiveness of sins, which led to a healing of the soul, mind, and emotions. Eventually, a few years later, she experienced physical healing. We often depend on tangible evidence to determine if our prayers for healing are working. The fact is, our prayers may be working, but they may be working at such a deep level it can take years to detect. True healing is a lifelong process of becoming whole and holy. When it happens, it takes place in God's time, not ours.

To Walk the Narrow, Healing Path

Having looked at the connection between faith and healing, let's examine what it means to walk the narrow, healing path. To begin with, it means seeking *healing*, *wholeness*, and *holiness* for self, others, and the world instead of *cure*. Too often people only want God to cure them and then leave the rest alone. In other words, we want God to completely remove all affliction so that we don't have to suffer. To truly seek healing, wholeness, and holiness may require going through pain and suffering. It may require giving up cherished possessions, relationships, and beliefs in order to seek God's way, will, and work.

To walk the healing path also means to care for our relationships, bodies, minds, and spirits in a way that deepens our souls. It means to live integrated lives that try to keep everything in balance, and through this to be open to God as God's Spirit flows through our lives.

It also means to be grounded in community—in the body of Christ. True Christian healing is for building up of the body, and the body promotes healing in its members. The ability to heal others is a gift given to us from the Spirit to promote unity in the body of Christ (1 Cor. 12:4–31). Healing is also something that the body of Christ brings to its members, as they pray for one another and uphold one another (Jas. 5:13–16).

Walking the narrow, healing path means trusting in God completely, no matter what happens, whether or not we experience healing. We all have expectations of how God should work. True healing comes when we give up those expectations and let God be in charge. Part of that means surrendering everything, even the need to have God heal us. When we are truly open to God's healing powers, we are able to go to God and say, "I am yours to do with me as you will. You know I want healing, but God, even if you don't heal me I will find a way to serve you in my illness, deformity, or suffering."

Finally, walking the healing path means simply keeping our relationship with God at the center of our lives. Ultimately, we are called to do only one thing in life: to love God with all our minds, hearts, souls, and strength (Luke 10:27). Everything else flows out of that. If God is not at our center, then no healing can take place. When we place God at the center, though, everything becomes possible.

Questions for Reflection

1. How comfortable are you with the connection between faith and healing? To what extent do you think there is a connection?
2. How strong is your skepticism and rationality, and to what extent do you think it has kept you from accepting God's healing power?
3. What gets in the way of your praying for healing for youself or for others?
4. How have you experienced healing of the spirit, mind, body, or relationships as an individual or part of a church or community?

Key Learnings

- True healing takes place when we form a deep and trusting faith that opens us to God's healing power.
- To be saved means to be healed physically, mentally, and spiritually so that we become holy and whole.
- The healing path is one that entails commitment to a Christian community, abandonment to God, persistent and open prayer, and acceptance of how God acts.
- We embody God's healing power when we let God be the healer and we become open conduits for God's healing to work *through* us.

Chapter 6

Walking the Servant Path

*W*hen I was in seminary during the 1980s, the great emphasis on social justice, which had captured the hearts of so many Western Christians, was beginning to wane. Today, many still have a passion for social justice in religious and political arenas, but other concerns have surged to the forefront of church and denominational attention—issues such as evangelism, morality, and salvation. Throughout the twentieth century, an emphasis on social justice and love (as opposed to a focus on personal morality) steadily grew in power and influence. The social justice movement was inspired, among other biblical passages, by Jesus' command to love others as we love ourselves (Luke 10:27), and by Jesus' description in Matthew 25:31–40 of how we would be judged by God in the end: "Truly, I tell you, just as you did it to one of the least of these who are members of my family, you did it to me."

Slowly, many Christians began to realize that they had been focusing too much on their own morality and welfare at the expense of others. They had been ignoring the poor, the oppressed, the hungry, the hurting, and so many others whose lives had been torn apart by uncaring governments, economies, institutions, systems, and Christians. These Christians may have been impeccable in their own personal morality, but they were deficient in their sense of social morality—of loving others as they loved themselves. So, they increased their emphasis on caring for these people. This led to religious ministries such as Mother Teresa's work among the poor, Martin Luther King Jr.'s work for civil rights, and Gandhi's work for Indian independence. It also led, in part, to the rise of social welfare, the Marshall Plan to rebuild Europe after World War II, and an awareness of the need to work for civil rights for minorities. Despite the terrible wars of the twentieth century, it was also a century that saw a worldwide increase in people caring more for and about one another.

Still, despite this emphasis by my seminary professors on love and compassion, I struggled with the whole idea of social justice. I didn't struggle with it because I disagreed with it. In fact, the concern for justice was central to my theological and religious beliefs. My problem was that I was always confused about what to do to respond to all the world's great problems. Going to Africa or the inner city to work among the poor scared me. Besides, what skills did I have to offer? While I cared deeply about women's rights, I was and still remain male. Often we men are not welcomed among women who have been victims of male violence, hatred, or indifference. While I cared deeply about minority rights, I was and still remain a white, Anglo-Saxon Protestant (a WASP). Often we WASPy types are not particularly welcomed among the minorities fighting for equality. I wanted to help others who were oppressed, but I didn't know how to do this, especially if I had aspirations to be a leader in whatever field I chose.

What I did have was a passion for helping others through counseling. Unfortunately, among so many of my fellow seminarians, working as a counselor was not considered a true vocation of justice, at least not on par with working for the poor, the hungry, and the oppressed. What was I to do? For a long time I just felt guilty. It was a deep guilt that I rarely shared with anyone. I felt guilty for wanting to be a counselor and for not wanting to work among all these oppressed people. At the same time, I saw my work as ministry to people who were oppressed in a different way. They were people who grew up in middle- to upper-class families, but were oppressed by childhoods spent in broken, abusive, and/or alcoholic homes, whose parents offered little structure and guidance, and who had little or no psychological and spiritual guidance.

In addition to counseling, I was deeply interested in the field of spiritual formation. I was developing a passion for prayer, the spiritual disciplines, examining my heart and myself, and helping others along the spiritual journey. Again, other Christians have not always embraced my interest in spirituality, especially those devoted to social justice issues. Many consider spirituality to be self-indulgent and overly self-focused. In contrast, they see working for social justice as gloriously other-focused. What was I supposed to do? I felt called to be a counselor, not a protester. I felt called to be a spiritual director, not a soup-kitchen worker. I felt called to teach others and to lead them to a deeper spiritual life, not to greater economic, social, and civil rights, although my hope is that leading people to a greater spiritual depth will also lead them to form a deeper compassion for others. I still passionately supported all these things that I didn't feel called to do, but I didn't know what to do about them. So, I felt a deep guilt. How could I reconcile my desire to live in obedience to Matthew 25 with working as a pastor, counselor, and spiritual director?

It was in learning about the life of George Müller that I discovered the path to reconciling these two desires: to work on behalf of the poor and oppressed while working as a counselor and pastor. George Müller was an incredible man who managed to integrate the deep spiritual life with a life devoted to the poor and oppressed.

The Life of George Müller

George Müller was born in Prussia in 1805, the son of a tax collector.[1] Looking at his childhood, one would not have suspected that this young boy would grow to become one of the nineteenth century's spiritual giants. His childhood and adolescence were spent mainly seeing what he could get away with, such as stealing from his father, an accountant and tax collector. His father sent him to a religious school, hoping it would straighten him out and prepare him to become a pastor, but Müller continued to rebel. The only things he excelled at were chasing women, drinking, gambling, and manipulating others. At times he tried to change his life, knowing in his heart that he was on a self-destructive course, but soon he would slip back into his old ways. This pattern of drinking and partying continued after he graduated from school and began attending college. He seemed to be destined for a life of self-destruction.

It was in a bar one night during his third year at the university that the seeds of his redemption were sown. As he sat in a bar drinking, in walked a man named Beta. Müller had known Beta back in high school, but they had never been great friends. Now, however, they struck up a friendship as drinking buddies, and began spending much time together over the ensuing months. One day, Beta told Müller about some new friends he had made. He said, "For some weeks I have been attending a meeting on Saturday evenings at the home of a Christian. . . . They read the Bible, they sing, they pray, and someone normally reads a sermon."[2]

Attending a Christian meeting wasn't the kind of thing that would normally pique George Müller's interest, but Beta kept talking about how wonderful these meetings were. Müller was willing to try anything once, even though he was skeptical, so he decided to join Beta at the next meeting. What he didn't realize was that God was about to extend an invitation for Müller to join God by walking the servant path.

At the meeting, his new friends read Scripture, sang, and prayed. Müller was deeply affected. He had never really seen someone pray deeply before, and he was caught by a contrast: "I could not pray as well, though I am much more learned than this man."[3] From that moment, Müller was caught by the power of Christianity, for he was seeing the Christian faith through new eyes. It wasn't the dry, dead faith he had seen in church, but an alive, vibrant faith that transformed lives. This transformed Müller's life. He would no longer live a life devoted to self-indulgence. He now would serve Christ.

Over time, Müller immersed himself more and more in the Bible, and eventually decided that God was calling him to be a missionary and, after that, a preacher in England. After serving there for several years, he made another decision that would change his life and put an indelible stamp on his future ministry. Müller decided to surrender completely to God, and to rely completely on God for his welfare. He decided that he would no longer take a salary for his preaching. Instead, he would rely completely on God to help him and his family financially. He had already been moving in this direction for some time. Ever since he had become a Christian, he had been struck by the passage in Matthew 7:7: "Ask, and it will be given you; search, and you will find; knock, and the door will be opened for you." Was this true? How do we find out if God will really give, reveal, and open the door if we ask, seek, and knock? He had been experimenting for years on giving more and more of his life to God. It seemed that whenever he had trusted in God completely, God had always come through. When he needed money to finish his university education, some wealthy American students had approached him to be their tutor. They paid enough money for Müller to finish his education. He had also experienced God's providence in his work as a missionary and in his ministry as a pastor. Now, he was ready to extend this experiment to all of his life.

George Müller's life became a great experiment of faith. For years following his decision to rely completely on God, he never received a salary. Instead, he continually went to God in prayer, and in the end money always came in. Sometimes Müller and his family would be on the verge of missing a meal or losing everything, but God came through every time, even if it sometimes seemed that God provided only at the last moment. His life was not easy by any stretch of the imagination. Müller lost a fifteen-month-old child to pneumonia. He suffered financial strains quite often, but whenever he had to have the money, something came through. He learned that when he relied on God, especially in difficult times, God always provided.

As time passed, Müller felt called to care for the many orphans he saw on the streets of Bristol, England. This was the time of Charles Dickens' *Oliver Twist*, when only the children of the wealthy were able to go to orphanages upon their parents' death. The rest either went to workhouses or lived on the streets. People didn't care much about children in those days. As time passed, he couldn't get the faces of these children out of his head.

Müller felt God calling him to start an orphanage, but to do so in a way that radically relied on God and God's grace. This would be an orphanage of God for God's children. So, as he began to put his plans to paper, he sensed the need to set up certain guidelines that were grounded in faith. First, the orphanage would never ask directly for money. Instead, they would rely on God in prayer to provide money. If, at any time, the children missed a meal or could not have the things Müller felt they needed, he would close up shop and stop the experiment in reliance on God. He also was pretty stringent in his demands for the children: each boy would have three suits; each girl five dresses; each child would have her or his own bed and cubby, two pairs of shoes, three meals a day, fresh air, and work; and all would be taught to read and write, which was a radical concept in those days. In fact, he was often criticized for giving education to lower-class children. Today, we might not see this as being all that much, but you have to remember that in those days few cared about orphaned children, their condition, or whether they lived or died. Müller wrote in his journal his feelings and thoughts about this orphanage:

> I certainly did from my heart desire to be used by God to benefit the bodies of poor children, bereaved of both parents, and see, in other respects, with the help of God, to do them good for this life—I also particularly longed to be used by God in getting the dear orphans trained up in the fear of God— but still, the first and primary object of the work was that God might be magnified by the fact, that the orphans under my care are provided, with all they need, only by *prayer and faith*, without anyone being asked by me or my fellow-laborers, whereby it may be seen, that God is FAITHFUL STILL, and HEARS PRAYERS STILL.[4]

In 1836, he started his orphanage with just a few orphans living in a small house in Bristol in a working-class neighborhood. By early May, though, he had nearly thirty girls, and from there the orphanage kept growing as he added young boys. When they outgrew this house, they bought another, and then another. Soon, they moved to a large tract of land in the country and started constructing new homes. And then they built more. All along, they never asked for money, but coincidences (or providences) kept happening that allowed them to continually grow. When the price of land was too high, the seller generously dropped the price into their range. People Müller didn't know came from nowhere to give him money, usually on a whim. Almost always what they gave was right on the button for what was needed—no more, no less.

This is not to say that the whole process was easy. In fact, it often was a struggle. There were times, especially the years 1838 through 1846, when they barely managed to scrape by. During those years, there were times when, after breakfast, they had no money for lunch, and had to spend the morning praying for God to provide. Each time, God came through. Sometimes it was in the morning mail when several pounds would be included in a letter. Sometimes it was even more miraculous. One time, they finished breakfast with no money for lunch. As they prayed, they heard a knock at the front door of the main house. It was the town baker. For some reason, he felt the need to bake bread for the whole orphanage that morning. A little while later another knock came on the door. It was a milkman. His cart had broken down at the end of the driveway, and he couldn't fix the wheel unless he unloaded his cart. By the time he would have finished fixing the wheel, everything would have spoiled. Could the orphanage use his milk and butter? Things like this seemed to happen all the time to Müller and his orphanage.

By the time he died in 1898, the orphanage (which still exists today and has a record of all of the events described here) had 2,050 residents on a campus of 25 acres. There were many times when they had no money, but God always provided in the end. They never asked for money, but over the course of his life, Müller raised over $3 million simply through prayer. Today, this would be in the neighborhood of $50 million to $80 million. Before he died, Müller became one of the most popular lecturers in the world, speaking to churches and gatherings worldwide. It's amazing that so many have forgotten this man. It is easy to doubt him, except for the fact that he and others meticulously recorded all of his feats, and they are on public record in England.

Lessons on Servanthood

George Müller's life seems so fantastic and miraculous—so different from ours. What lessons could we possibly learn from his life? It is easy to dismiss Müller, to doubt the veracity of his story, and to be skeptical about his and others' claims. If we dismiss Müller, though, we miss some extremely important lessons about walking the servant path, and we miss an opportunity to discover for ourselves how wonderful God really is.

It seems to me that when we talk about being God's servants, we tend to make two mistakes. This is true for us on personal levels, as well as on congregational and denominational levels. The first mistake is seeing all the problems around us and believing that *we can't* do anything about them. The second is seeing all the problems around us and believing that *we can* do something about them.

The problem with believing that *we can't do anything* is that we succumb to the false belief that we are insignificant and helpless. What can one person, one church, one denomination do? We can do much more than we think, especially when we are focused, united, and partners with God. The problem with the belief that *we can do something* is that in reality we cannot do much without God. If God is not working in and through us, all our work, ministry, and mission is for naught. Müller never saw himself as being too insignificant to help the orphans. At the same time, he never saw his ministry as his own. In his mind, it was clearly God's ministry being done through him. So he didn't get overwhelmed but instead focused on doing what God was calling him to do right then and there. He considered everything to be God's work, and all of his successes to be God's successes accomplished through him. He let God be the master, while he was the servant. God would decide what to do, God would provide the resources, God would provide the children to be cared for, and God would receive the glory for the work. Müller didn't believe that God's providence was only available for him and his ministry. He believed that all work in life should serve God, and that if we relied on God, God would provide for us no matter what our work. He believed that the principles of relying on God were just as valid for business as for mission.

So often we get the focus and priorities of our service to God mixed up. We think that we should decide what has to be done, how it should be done, and what should be accomplished. When it is all done, then we also think that we should receive the bulk of the glory (with a few thanks to God when we have the time). This is why so many in ministry and mission become overwhelmed and eventually burn out. This is why so many in ministry and mission never really succeed (as God would measure success) and get embroiled in scandals. We don't realize that what we are doing is God's work, not ours, and that if we do our work in faith, then God will take care of the results. We have to become like George Müller: always faithful, always believing God will provide, and always loving others.

The servant path that Müller sets for us is one that unfolds in the tension between two extremes: prayerfulness and busyness. Too many Christians fail to keep these in balance. Either they devote themselves to a life of prayer and never reach out to others in act or deed, or they are a constant hub of activity and never ask in prayer if this is what God really wants. We are called to keep prayer and action in balance, much like Müller did. He was a prayerful servant who was actively prayerful and prayerfully active. He grounded himself in God's call through prayer and Scripture, and so his work bore fruits of the Spirit. His life and service have so much to teach us. The following are at least four lessons we can learn:

1. God is calling on us to *surrender* in radical faith to God in whatever we do.
2. God is calling on us to continually *listen* for God's special call for us—to continually ask, seek, and knock.
3. God is calling on us to *act* on our call in faith, hope, and love.
4. God is calling on us to *trust* in God and to let God be responsible for the results of our work.

This is how we walk the servant path. First, we are called to *surrender* to God in radical faith. This may be the most difficult thing of all for us to do. We humans are not the surrendering kind. Most of us have learned that to be successful in any venture, we need to be in control; or if we aren't in control, then we need to align ourselves with someone who is, a leader who will show us the way. Whether we seek to be a leader or a follower in God's service, we still have to surrender everything to God. If we don't, our work, our ministry will never be God's. It will remain our own.

Surrendering ourselves to God is foundational to walking the servant path. We will talk more about this later, but for now suffice it to say that surrendering in faith creates the conditions that allow God's grace and providence to begin flowing through our ministry. When we surrender ourselves to God, we are saying to God, in effect, "Lord, my life is yours. Lead me in your ways. There are times I will try to take my life back from you, but be patient with me and show me how to surrender. I give you my life, my will, and my work so that everything I do will flow with your love and grace."

This is what George Müller did. It is also what Jesus did. His life was a life of constant surrender. He surrendered to the Spirit when he was led into the wilderness after his baptism (Matt. 4:1–11). He relied completely on the Spirit for everything so that he could learn to will the Father's will. When he was facing his arrest and death on the cross, everything within him screamed to walk away and save his own life, but in the end he said, "Father, if you are willing, remove this cup from me; yet, not my will but yours be done" (Luke 22:42). To walk the servant path begins with surrender.

Next, walking the servant path requires that we continually *listen* for God's special call for us. We don't usually hear God's call because the noise of the world drowns it out. God is constantly whispering to us to serve God. God is constantly calling on us to love others, to care for them, and to serve them. But we are too busy. Our lives are filled with the sound of radios, televisions, and voices on the telephone. We are distracted by the many demands that scramble for our attention. Discovering how to serve God requires listening— constant listening. God is all around, speaking to us if we listen.

God is calling you right now to make God's kingdom real in the world. God is calling us to serve God right now in what we are doing. To hear God, though, we have to come to discover for ourselves how much God is part of this world. We have to listen. As Dallas Willard, a teacher and writer in the ways of discipleship and service, says,

> Jesus' good news about the kingdom can be an effective guide for our lives only if we share his view of the world in which we live. To his eyes this is a God-bathed and God-permeated world. It is a world filled with a glorious reality, where every component is within the range of God's direct knowledge and control—though he obviously permits some of it, for good reasons, to be for a while otherwise than as he wishes. It is a world that is inconceivably beautiful and good because of God and because God is always in it. It is a world in which God is continually at play and over which he constantly rejoices. Until our thoughts of God have found every visible thing and event glorious with his presence, the word of Jesus has not yet fully seized us.[5]

Third, God is calling on us to *act* on our call in faith, hope, and love. It is not enough to surrender and listen. The Christian life is a life of service in which we take our faith and turn it into action. In fact, there is no way to truly surrender ourselves and listen for God without acting, because faith always seeks to respond to God's love. The deeper our faith grows, the more it creates a yearning in us to serve. As Müller's faith grew, he yearned more and more to serve. In some ways, we can measure our faith by the strength of our desire to serve. That doesn't necessarily mean that how we serve is a measure of our faith, only our desire to serve. To some people, how we respond to God in service may not seem all that important. If it is a response to God, though, no matter what it is, it is important to God. It is the desire to serve that matters the most, not how we serve. This is where the listening comes in. We have to listen for how God wants us to serve, and then do it.

Finally, we are called on to *trust* God to be responsible for the results. Too many of us make the mistake of thinking our ministry is ours. It isn't. My ministry as a pastor is not my ministry. It is God's. My ministry as a writer, teacher, and spiritual director is God's, not mine. I have discovered that the more we give the results of what we are doing to God, the more God takes what we are doing and multiplies it. The key is remembering that everything we are doing is for God, and that success or failure on a human level is not what is important. I learned this lesson very clearly one day after preaching a sermon in which I told the story of George Müller. A member of our church told me that after the sermon, she was walking up the aisle of the church and overheard one woman say to another, "That was the *worst* sermon I have ever heard." Five minutes later, she overheard another conversation in which one woman said to another, "That was the *best* sermon I have ever heard." I learned from this experience that my words in preaching really don't mean all that much. One person heard God through my words. One didn't. The words were the same. In the end, God did with my sermon whatever God wanted. I learned that my sermons are God's sermons, and God can choose to touch whomever God wants. All that matters is that I serve as I'm supposed to serve, trust God, and let God take care of the results.

Responding to Our Call

The reality is that as Christians we may be called to live moral and ethical lives, but even more than that we are called to live lives of love and justice. Throughout Scripture, God's message is very clear. We are called to serve. We hear this in Micah 6:8, where the prophet says, "He has told you, O mortal, what is good; and what does the LORD require of you but to do justice, and to love kindness, and to walk humbly with your God?" In John 13:1–35, Jesus demonstrates how we are to live and serve God. He tells his disciples that they are to be servants of one another and all people, just as he is a servant to them. He says to them, "I give you a new commandment, that you love one another. Just as I have loved you, you also should love one another. By this everyone will know that you are my disciples, if you have love for one another" (John 13:34–35). Finally, he also told them in Matthew 25:31–46 what it takes to be a servant and to live in God's kingdom. We discussed this earlier. We are to care for the poor, the hungry, the naked, the imprisoned, the thirsty, the sick, and the stranger. This list of people we are to care for is not limited just to those cited. By implication it is a call to care for anyone who is rejected, maligned, and mistreated by the world because of their ethnicity, orientation, gender, illness, and the like. This would include minorities, women, homosexuals, immigrants, drug and alcohol abusers, and so many more. Wherever and whenever a person is treated unjustly, we are called to bring God's love.

Our calling is deeper than just a call to love. While love lies at the center of our calling, there is much more to our call. Jesus says, "I am the vine, you are the branches. Those who abide in me and I in them bear much fruit, because apart from me you can do nothing" (John 15:5). At the center of surrendering to, listening to, acting for, and trusting in God lies a call from God. Our calling is our connection with the vine—with Christ.

What we learn from George Müller is that we need to root our ministries and mission in God's specific calling for us—a calling that is discerned through prayer, faith, and action. Discovering our calling begins with prayerfully asking how God is calling us to serve. This does not mean that we should look around asking what we *should* do. It means asking God what God is calling us to do. For each of us the answer will be different.

For example, I know a woman who was struggling with the question of what God was calling her to do in her life. She was a teacher who loved working with her students. For a long time it seemed that teaching children and teens was her calling. Yet in recent years she had been struggling. The work had become draining, not inspiring. It was becoming increasingly more difficult to prepare for her classes. She would procrastinate, leaving her work until the last minute. We talked about whether this was really what God was calling her to do. I suggested that when we respond to God's calling, it usually feels right and is inspiring, even if it is tremendously difficult. If we feel burdened by our personal ministries and vocations (our calling) instead of inspired and hope-filled, then it may be that we are no longer serving God as God is calling us to serve.

As we talked about this, she began to shiver. My office was warm, but her whole body shook. She had never considered the possibility of not working, of not serving God through her teaching. As we spoke more, she began to talk about how, at her core, she had this feeling that she was being called to be a mother, a wife, and to serve more in her church. How would she say this to her husband? How would she tell her coworkers that she was no longer going to work? How would she tell her friends? Throughout her whole life she had been taught that to be a worthwhile woman she had to be working in a career. It was okay not to work when her children were infants and toddlers, but now that they were older, what would people think of her? We spent time talking about the importance of doing what God was calling her to do, not what her friends, coworkers, and even her husband were calling her to do. Of course, we also had to explore the financial ramifications. Would this put a hardship on her family? It didn't seem so. She knew that in the end her husband would be supportive because he loved her, but it would still be difficult to tell others. Finally, after much prayer and reflection, she decided that God was calling her to something else. She didn't quite know what it was, but she knew that staying on the present course would slowly drain her life. Following God's call, even if it meant doing something everyone else thought was foolish, was the right thing for her to do. She was about to enter a time of exploring her call. It wasn't clear, but the focus was now on serving God in the way she felt called to, instead of serving God in a way she felt she had to.

Clearly defining what our calling is remains one of the most difficult things to do as a Christian and a human being. What is a calling? It is hard to define this biblically because of the fact that being called by God is assumed more than it is defined. For example, Adam and Eve had an original calling, and in many ways their original sin was ignoring that call. A calling is what we were created to be and to do. It is our particular purpose in life that is a unique expression of God's great purpose for all of life. Adam and Eve, according to the biblical story, were created to tend to the Garden of Eden and to live in communion with God. They failed to follow their calling when they sought the knowledge of good and evil that only God could have. Abraham was called to have faith in God and to be the father of a great nation. Similarly, Moses was called by God out of the burning bush to lead the Israelites to the Promised Land; the prophet Samuel was called by God in the night; David was called by God through the prophet Samuel; all of the prophets were called by God in various ways; the disciples were called by Jesus; and Paul was called by Jesus. Whether it is directly or through one of God's servants, a calling is God's calling out to us, telling us what God wants us to do with our lives. It is God calling to us to serve God in our own unique and particular way.

So, what is our calling? A name often used for calling is "vocation." To Roman Catholics, a vocation often means a religious calling to become a priest, a monk, a nun, a brother, or a sister in a society or order. In more secular terms, a vocation is our career. The word "vocation" literally means "a calling." Both the Roman Catholic and secular ways of using the word are limited and somewhat inaccurate. A vocation may be to religious life, or it may be to a secular career, but even more a calling is a directive from God telling us to live a particular way, to be a particular way, and to serve God in a particular life mission. Each person has a particular call that is unique to her or him. Nobody can tell us what our true calling is because it is something that we can only sense for ourselves in dialogue with God. All that matters is that we are true to our own calling. As Paul says to Timothy,

> but join with me in suffering for the gospel, relying on the power of God, who saved us and called us with a holy calling, not according to our works but according to his own purpose and grace. (2 Tim. 1:8–9)

God endows us with a calling from the moment of our conception. Our calling is not just spiritual. It is genetic. From the moment we are conceived, our calling is initially formed in our actual DNA, for through our DNA we are endowed with particular physical and cognitive abilities, aptitudes, and temperaments. Our families also shape our calling as they teach, guide, and form us. Our culture, friends, teachers, pastors, associates, and acquaintances all help form our calling. God works through all of them to form who we are and how we will respond to our calling.

Everything about me genetically, socially, and historically has gone into my own particular calling. For example, I was given a certain genetic ability on an intellectual level, but this was also aided by the fact that I came from a family who valued education. College wasn't hoped for; it was expected. Graduate school was valued. I also was endowed with certain athletic abilities. My family valued sports, so I was especially active in sports, and this shaped me. Familial factors such as my parents' divorce when I was two and their subsequent remarriages sparked my interest in understanding family dynamics. My own loneliness at fifteen led me to want to be a counselor. My struggle to deal with the spiritual issues brought up by the adolescents I was counseling when I was in my twenties led me to eventually go to seminary. The fact that the seminary provided me with a strong theological foundation, but not a particularly strong spiritual one, led me to eventually do graduate work in a Roman Catholic university studying spiritual formation. My struggle to integrate the mystical traditions of Christian spirituality with my own life led me to dig deeper into understanding the mystics. The need to integrate what I had learned with my own Presbyterian tradition led me to ask questions few others I knew were asking. My work as a pastor and a spiritual director with laity has led me to want to make the wonderful but complex things I was learning understandable to laity. All of this and so much more led me to respond to a call to write this book. Writing these pages is part of my calling, or more accurately, part of my response to God's call for me.

The difficulty with understanding our calling is that we can never truly understand our calling. While we can articulate our call by applying it concretely to particular situations, we can never really "know" our calling. In other words, I can say that it is my calling to be a pastor, a spiritual director, a teacher, and a writer, but that is not the whole of my call. Our calling is deep and pervasive. We sense it deeply in our cores, but we cannot always describe it to others. The woman I mentioned before had been a teacher, and at one point teaching may have been the right response to her call, but her life and situation had changed. Teaching in that particular school with those particular children was no longer the proper response to her call. Her calling was now leading her to something else. She was now being called to be a mother and a wife, just as she was being called to take time to let the new articulation of her call—a new understanding of how to respond to her call—unfold before her.

As I said before, discerning our call not only is important for us as individuals, but is also important for congregations, denominations, and even organizations and businesses. For example, each congregation has its own calling, and it is part of the task of the congregation not only to ask what its calling is, but to constantly appraise whether what members are doing is part of that calling. Churches that struggle generally don't ask what their calling is. Instead, they try to preserve their past, imitate other churches, or do nothing as they languish in inactivity. All of this can similarly be applied to denominations. As they stop being true to their calling, they begin to die. When they become true to their callings, they tend to grow, perhaps not numerically but spiritually (although I believe the two often, though not always, go hand in hand). The same theory can be applied to organizations and businesses.

So, what is a calling? It is God's voice lying at our deepest core, responding to God's voice in the world around us as God invites us to meet the needs of the world. The needs may be great, such as the need to fight racism, or small, such as the need to care for a sick neighbor. In effect, our calling is God's voice crying from within, responding to God's voice that is crying from without. What we do in response to that particular cry from within will always be shaped by what we hear from and find in the world around us. We can see this in George Müller's life. From the earliest part of his life his father had been shaping him for a life in ministry. He was endowed with a keen and rational mind. He also was endowed with a natural ability to trust and to put his life on the line. The troubles and imprisonments of his youth taught him that the worst of life wasn't the worst that could happen. His calling constantly told him that his life of partying and self-indulgence was wrong, and so he kept searching for the life that was right. He responded to his call when he met his Christian friends and began reading Scripture and praying. He also responded to his call when he looked around at the orphans of England and felt the desire to do something. He responded to God's yearning call from within, pleading with him to respond to the poverty of the orphans he saw on the street.

For all of these reasons we can say that Müller's calling was particular to him. If we are to follow the course of George Müller, and indeed all of the mystics, by walking the narrow path, it requires that we ask what God is calling us to do to respond to the needs of present-day life. We are not called to start an orphanage in nineteenth-century England. We are called to respond to our own particular, unique callings in our own particular, unique situation.

Each one of us has a calling, and to be a servant we must begin in prayer by asking God what our calling is. Then, we need to do our best to articulate that calling as well as we can in response to the world's cries. Sometimes we will be clear about what we are to do. Sometimes it will take us years or a lifetime to gain clarity. The key is that before we can serve as servants, we must ask whether this mission, that ministry, this vocation, or that practice is true to our calling. But then we must act pragmatically to live that calling in concrete ways. As the apostle Paul says,

I therefore, the prisoner in the Lord, beg you to lead a life worthy of the calling to which you have been called, with all humility and gentleness, with patience, bearing one another in love, making every effort to maintain the unity of the Spirit in the bond of peace. (Eph. 4:1–3)

A final thing we need to do is to realize that our particular calling is not just ours alone. It is part of God's calling for the whole human race and the universe. Ultimately, we need to ask not just what God's call is for us, but also how we can adjust what we do to fit with God's call for everything. We are called to be servants who serve God by continually asking God how we are to serve in particular and in general. We are not called to be servants who respond to what we *think* we *ought* to do. We are to ask, seek, and knock, and to let God answer, find, and open the door for us.

But What If God Calls Me to Go to Calcutta?

In my work as a spiritual director, the issue of calling is one that comes up often, especially in my work with laity. Most of the pastors I work with know that they are called to be pastors, but many of the laity I work with aren't so clear about their call. They ask, "Is it possible that I'm just called to be a mother or a parent? Is my work my calling? Is the stuff I do in church my calling?" All of these are profound questions that I cannot answer. They can only be answered as each person searches his or her own heart and life. At the same time, a great question was posed to me by a woman who was struggling with her call, especially her calling to be a mother and a wife, but also to join the church. She had given up a career as a military lawyer and as a litigant in order to devote herself to her husband and her two boys, one of whom was disabled. She was fairly clear about this calling to be a wife and mother, but she also struggled with deepening her faith and taking seriously the idea that she was called by God to respond to the world's needs. As we talked about her calling, she asked me a very poignant and piercing question: "But what if God calls me to go to Calcutta? I don't think I could ask my family to do that. What if I listen to my call, and God calls me to go somewhere I don't want to go?"

I have to admit that this is a hard question to answer simply. At the same time, there is one important criterion for any kind of true calling. It can't only come from outside of us, but it also has to resonate with us at our core. So many of us worry about what will happen if we respond to God's call. I have to admit that I was that way at one point. I sensed that God was calling me into ministry, which was not something I wanted to do. Why would I want to enter a career where I get paid little, lose much of my privacy, get criticized on a regular basis, work lousy hours, get no weekends off, and for which I would receive few tangible rewards? I used to say that God dragged me into ministry kicking and screaming. At the same time, I became a pastor because I knew in my heart that this was the only thing I could do. Nothing else seemed right.

Mother Teresa understood this. She was one of those people who *was* called to Calcutta. Do you know what Mother Teresa did before she became Mother Teresa of Calcutta? She worked as a teacher in a Catholic school for wealthy and privileged children in India. She had no training or experience working with the poor. What could she possibly do to help the poor? During the 1940s and 1950s many of the great social experts went to Calcutta, trying to figure out what to do to alleviate the poverty. All came away, shaking their heads, saying that they couldn't do anything. Sister Teresa, as she was known at the time, said that she didn't know what to do either, but she was being called by God to do something. So she stayed and responded to God's call. She had no skills. She had no experience. But she trusted in God to provide. She began her mission by leaving her convent and just walking the streets of Calcutta. Often she would gather children on a corner and begin teaching using a stick to draw letters in the dirt. From there her ministry and mission grew exponentially. Even at her death, many questioned what she had really accomplished. There was still crippling poverty in Calcutta. Malnutrition, disease, and hunger were rampant. What difference did she make? Mother Teresa was fond of saying that God had not called her to save Calcutta. God had only called her to care for the poor. She let God take care of Calcutta. She took care of what she could take care of and left the rest for God. God only asks us to take care of the things that are in our calling. God is not calling us to change the whole world. Still she managed to care for hundreds of thousands during her life.

Whatever we are being called to do, in order for it to be valid, it must make some sort of internal sense. At the same time, we also need to be willing to surrender to God and let God lead the way by revealing to us what we are to do. If our calling is to be a mother, then we need to rely on God to show us how to do this. God will train us through articles, books, friends, family, television, radio, church, conversations, and insights. God will use everything to make us the best parents we can be, as long as we are willing to devote what we do to God. The same is true if we are to make our work a ministry. If we are working as a lawyer, a doctor, a businessperson, a teacher, or anything else, and if we surrender to God and devote our work to God, God will train us to make a difference in the world through what we do, produce, give, or teach. It won't always be grand, but it will be important because it is important to God.

God is not going to call us to Calcutta without giving us a heart for Calcutta. God is not going to call us to Calcutta without training us and providing for us along the way. To follow God's calling, we have to let go of our fear and just surrender to God. God will give us a heart for our ministry and mission, and God will provide for us along the way.

The Path to Consonance

The work of Adrian van Kaam is extremely helpful in guiding us to determine whether a potential vocation, ministry, or mission is truly what God wants. He says that in appraising whether or not to respond to a great need in the world or in our lives, we should ask four basic questions: Is my potential service to God *congenial with my calling*? Will it be *compassionate* to those around me? It is *compatible* with my situation? Do I have the *competence*?[6] When asking these questions, we need to remember that they don't only apply to a religious mission or ministry. Anything we do that is devoted to God can be part of our walk on the servant path. Everything we do, from our work to our volunteering, has the potential to be a ministry. These questions help us to clarify how God wants us to serve.

We have already devoted enough time to the issue of *calling*. Suffice it to say that we need to get a sense in our cores, our hearts, and our guts whether a particular course of action is "right" for us. After we've reflected on the question of call, the next question we need to ask is to what extent our ministry or mission is truly *compassionate to others*. This can be an easy or hard question to answer, depending on the circumstance. If we are engaging in a ministry of care to prisoners, giving food to the hungry, medicine to the ill, and love to the lonely, the issues may seem fairly clear. Most of us, though, feel a calling to ministries and vocations that are less defined and/or religious. We need to ask whether a potential course of action or personal ministry is truly compassionate and caring for those with whom we are seeking to work.

The issue of compassion is a big one because it has to do with whether what we are doing is actually best for others. For instance, one of the hot-button issues in Christianity today has to do with how heterosexual Christians are to reach with compassion to homosexuals. What is truly compassionate in our work with and on behalf of them? If we disagree with their lifestyle, is it compassionate to simply love and accept them and say nothing about their lifestyle? Is it compassionate to expect them to adhere to certain sexual standards, whether that be celibacy or monogamous commitment in their homosexual relationships? Is it compassionate to push them to engage in therapies designed to change their orientation? Is it compassionate to shun them and to ignore them if we don't approve of their lifestyles? Is it compassionate to deny them leadership roles in our churches unless they change their orientation or lifestyle? I won't pretend to know the answers. In fact, answering these questions is incredibly difficult because they force us to ask what lies at the center of our beliefs. At the same time, unless we ask what is the most compassionate course, we are not truly seeking God's path. As Christians, the question of compassion *has* to lie at the center of our response.

All of these questions are difficult to answer, or at least they should be because they strike right to the core of what compassion is. Compassion isn't just caring for someone. It literally means sharing the suffering of another. When we have compassion for another, we literally suffer with that person as she or he struggles with specific issues or conditions. For instance, in dealing with the question of how to respond to the call to care for homosexuals, we can't just make a blanket statement about what they should or shouldn't do in their lives. We have to try to understand life from their perspective and experience. It's not enough to say that they should change to meet our expectations, or that we should change our expectations to meet them. We have to actually spend time with people who are homosexual, while simultaneously spending time in prayer, asking how God wants us to respond to them.

Many Christians opt out of this important struggle. They may say, "Scripture says homosexuality is a sin, and so we need to call them into a more moral life." Others may say, "We are called to love them and not judge them, so who am I to tell them what to do?" It seems to me that neither may be particularly compassionate. To really grapple with how we should personally respond to the crying need of homosexuals in our world, we need to ask whether what we sense we are called to do is truly compassionate. Does it truly share the suffering of so many who have had their lives destroyed by human hate, ignorance, and indifference? This goes beyond the question of what Scripture really says. We need to be guided by Scripture, but we also need to understand what we read in Scripture in light of God's love and the Spirit's guidance. The question of compassion is a deep question, and not one to be taken lightly.

We also have to ask whether what we sense we are called to do is *compatible with our situation*. For example, if I feel called to move to Ghana, Africa, is this compatible with my situation? Is it appropriate to move my family there? What if they don't feel the same call as me? Is it financially feasible? Is it physically feasible? What if I suffer from some sort of chronic illness that requires medical attention and care that can only be found in a developed country? Will my family's or my own life be threatened? This does not mean that we should avoid dangerous situations if God is calling us to engage in them. Reflecting back on Martin Luther King Jr.'s life, we know that he was called to be the leader of the civil rights movement, but it was obvious that it was compatible with his situation. Despite the dangers, he was a father and a pastor living in the dangers of prejudice. To do nothing meant to continue to be crushed by the hate of racism. Neither he nor his family could escape these dangers, so to fight the dangers was compatible.

It is for this same reason that Mahatma Gandhi often told British supporters of Indian independence to pray for the Indian people and to offer financial support, but that the fight for independence was for the Indian people alone. Their calling was to support Gandhi and the Indian people with prayer and money, which was compatible with their situation. It was not compatible for Gandhi's British supporters to be involved in *satyagraha*, which was Gandhi's term for their method of fighting the British, a method that sought "the vindication of truth not by infliction of suffering on the opponent but on one's self."[7] It wasn't compatible because they were not Indian, and this was a struggle for *Indian* independence.

This does not mean that for a situation to be compatible it must directly affect our lives and put us in danger. It only means that we need to assess carefully the extent to which our service will fit the situation. For our work, ministry, or mission to be compatible, we should ask whether or not it fits our situation and the crying need of the world around us. We may sense that something is our calling and that what we plan to do is compassionate, but if it is not compatible with our situation, then it will fail. To be involved in God's ministry, we need to ensure that we are being true to our calling, compassionate to others, and compatible with our situation.

Finally, we must ask whether or not we *have the competence* to engage in this ministry, or at least ask whether we can gain the competence. Basically, this is a question of skills. Do I have the necessary skills to do this work in service of God? For example, if I want to start a ministry to those recovering from divorce, do I have the necessary organizational skills? Do I have the necessary sensitivity and understanding to care for those struggling through divorce? Do I have the basic ability to inspire confidence and trust in others? If I don't have these skills, can I get them?

Asking the question of competence is a tricky question, and one that prevents many people from engaging in ministries and missions to which they are called. They conclude that they don't have the skills necessary, and so never seek the ministry or mission. A crucial component is asking whether the process of being trained in those skills is part of our calling, is compassionate to others, and is compatible with our situation. For instance, if I feel called to be a spiritual director, what would it take to get the necessary training? Is it compatible with my family's and my own situation? What hardships would I have to undergo financially, and is my sense of calling so strong that it seems to be worthwhile to pursue it? The question of competence is a question of whether and if we can gain the competence. A lack of skills should not be a deterrent, but if we cannot learn the skills, we must ask whether God can provide the skills. This is what happened with Mother Teresa when she went to Calcutta. She didn't have the skills, but she trusted in God. In George Müller's case, he had been developing his skills his whole life, so when he was called to start the orphanage, he already had the necessary faith and organizational and pragmatic skills for his mission. In some cases we may already have the competence to respond to the world's crying needs in a particular way. In other cases we may need to acquire skills. The key question is whether we have the competence and, if we don't, whether we can acquire it.

Van Kaam says that if we satisfactorily answer the questions of congeniality to our calling, compassion, compatibility, and competence, then it will lead us to a sense of consonance about our ministry and mission. This does not mean that everything will always work out perfectly. We may suffer, struggle, and encounter darkness in our ministry and mission. Yet even in the midst of this, we will feel a general sense of harmony with God that we are doing the right thing. It is this sense of consonance that keeps so many people working for God even in the midst of the most dangerous and heartrending situations. It is what allows people to work against oppressive governments even as it threatens their lives. It is what allows people to work among the poor even though the violence of their situation may imperil their lives. It is what allows people to work in seemingly hopeless situations against all the odds. They know it is their calling, they know they are being compassionate, they know they are being compatible with their situation, they know they have the skills, and it leads them to have a sense of consonance in their hearts that they are doing the right thing. When any part of the four Cs is missing, it can lead to a sense of dissonance—a sense of discontinuity that nags at people, telling them that they are not truly serving God.

One last thing must be said about the issue of congeniality to our calling, compassion, compatibility, and competence. When we act in these four, it is an act of *faith*. The problem is that *fear* always stalks those who are called to act in faith. To follow our call and respond with compassion, compatibility, and competence to the crying needs of the world can require us to face a tremendous amount of risk. Fear preys on this, leading us to follow a counterfeit set of criteria. For instance, when we become afraid we do not ask whether something is our *calling*, but we look at others and *compare* ourselves to them. We act in a comparative way, imitating what they do because it seems

safe, even if what they do isn't right for us. Instead of asking whether this possible ministry is *compassionate*, we act in way that is *competitive* with others. We do something not because it is loving, but because in our competition
with others we have to prove ourselves through our ministry. In fact, it ceases
to matter whether our ministry or mission is caring toward others because all
we care about is receiving accolades for what we do. Instead of asking
whether what we are doing is *compatible* with our situation, we act in a way
that *conforms* to the expectations of others. So, we may engage in a ministry,
mission, or work that looks just like everyone else's. There is no uniqueness
to what we do. Finally, instead of asking whether we have the *competence* to
carry out this work, we become *controlling* and *coercive*, forcing the situation
to hide our lack of skill and understanding.

The more we let fear and the guidelines of fear dominate our work and ministry, the more what we do will fail. The more we let faith and openness to
God's will guide us, the more God will work through us in ways that are loving, healing, and transforming.

Faith, Hope, and Love

To truly walk the servant path requires also that we allow three qualities to
be formed in us: faith, hope, and love. Without these three, whatever we do
will fail.

Faith: To begin with, we have to have faith in God. We spoke about this
before, but it is important to discuss this again in greater detail. Having faith
means surrendering to God and trusting that God will show us the way and
how to do what we are to do. Too many people think the point of their mission or ministry is to be perfect in what they are doing. In fact, seeking perfection destroys many ministries and missions. We cannot be perfect, nor are
we expected to be perfect. What matters is that we seek what God wants and
act in faith. We have to see God as a partner in our work. In fact, we have to
take a step further. We have to see our ministry and mission not as our work,
but as the work God accomplishes through us.

One of the great missionaries of the twentieth century was a man named
Frank Laubach, and he demonstrated how important faith is to our ministry
and mission. It isn't so much his work that made him great, although that in
itself was great. He spent much of his adult life in the Philippines, teaching
reading to thousands and bringing faith to millions. He also wrote fifty books.
These, though, are not the important things. What is important is the life of
faith he lived. He made a decision in his forties to live a life of radical faith,

letting God inspire and support his mission. He wanted his work to be God's work flowing through him. So, he gave his ministry to God in faith:

> I feel simply carried along each hour, doing my part in a plan which is far beyond myself. This sense of cooperation with God in little things is what so astonishes me, for I never have felt it this way before. I need something, and turn around to find it waiting for me. I must work, to be sure, but there is God working along with me. God takes care of all the rest. My part is to live this hour in continuous inner conversation with God and in perfect responsiveness to his will, to make this hour gloriously rich. This seems to be all I need to think about.[8]

Others have experienced the same kind of connection between faith, ministry, and mission that Frank Laubach did. For example, the same kind of faith and practice has been instrumental in the work of Henry Blackaby, a Canadian Southern Baptist. Being a Southern Baptist, his focus in mission often has been on starting new churches. He has learned how to make a surrendering faith a part of his work in his ministry. He says that each time the churches or organizations he was a part of tried to start churches by their own efforts they would fail, but each time they did it in reliance on God, they would succeed. Time after time, they would fail whenever they relied on a typical business model for starting churches. They would do all the surveys and population studies, but nothing would happen. Either they would not be able to find people interested in joining, or they couldn't find a pastor to start a church. Then they would go back to praying, and suddenly someone or something would show up. Blackaby consistently says that when we rely on God, things happen:

> You need to believe that [God] will enable and equip you to do everything He asks of you. Don't try to second-guess Him. Just let Him be God. Turn to Him for the needed power, insight, skill, and resources. He will provide you with all you need.[9]

Ultimately, what you will notice is that God seems to work equally with all Christians of faith, regardless of their theology or denomination. God seems to work with Roman Catholics, Protestants, liberals, conservatives, moderates, fundamentalists, Pentecostals, evangelicals, and anyone else who relies on God in faith. What seems to matter most is whether we have faith, not what our theology or denomination is. Unfortunately, so many works of ministry fail because they rely too much on human effort. They do not follow the advice of Proverbs 3:5–6: "Trust in the LORD with all your heart, and do not rely on your own insight. In all your ways acknowledge him, and he will make straight your paths."

It is not just in the religious sphere that God works through our faith, although we may think so because much of the writing about serving God, including my own, uses religious examples. There is a growing movement today to find ways of integrating spirituality into the workplace and, in effect, find a way to rely on God in the process of doing business. For example, ServiceMaster, a Fortune 500 company that generates over $6 billion in business from brands such as Terminex, ChemLawn, TruGreen, and Merry Maids, is committed to serving God in its everyday work.[10] This company sees service to God as essential to what it is doing, and outside its headquarters is a statue of Jesus washing the feet of his disciples. It is not a perfect company by any means, but it is a company that sees serving God, not making money, as part of its calling. Employees try to find a way to act with faith in God in everything they do.

In essence, we have to trust God in our service to God, whether it is in church mission or our careers. We have to be responsible for our work, but we also have to let God be responsible for God's work. We have to do what we can and let God take care of the results.

Hope: Beyond faith, we also have to have hope. We have to believe and have hope that God will find a way to make our ministry or mission work. If we lose hope, we lose God. Hope is more than just wishing. It is believing. When we hope, we look ahead believing that God will make things work, even if all seems hopeless. The very nature of God is to make things that seem hopeless hopeful—to make the impossible possible. The moment we begin to think that all is lost or that God cannot or will not work, it is almost as if we close a door on God's Spirit. I can't prove this, but I am convinced that even though God has the power to work whether or not we let God work, God generally does not work in our lives without our invitation.

How do we generate hope? The best way is to form a thankful and appreciative faith. We need to look around us with thankful and appreciative eyes, seeing possibility and God in everything. No matter how down things seem to get, we look for possibilities. If our ministry or mission (or even our life) does not seem to be working, we must either look for ways it may be working that we've missed or look for ways to modify it. If it isn't working, perhaps we should consider that God may be telling us to slow down, to simplify, to be clearer in our goals, to spend more time in prayer, or to give more of the work to God. Ultimately we have to approach our ministries with a sense of hope that is rooted in prayer and thankfulness. The apostle Paul says, "Rejoice always, pray without ceasing, give thanks in all circumstances; for this is the will of God in Christ Jesus for you" (1 Thess. 5:16–18).

Love: This may seem obvious, but many people forget the primacy of love when they are trying to serve God. Without love for God, others, and ourselves, nothing we do can come to any real good. Love is the key to everything when it comes to serving God. So much of the Bible says this. In his first letter to the Corinthians, Paul says that we can have every kind of spiritual gift available, but if that gift is not supported by love, then it is nothing (1 Cor. 13). In the first letter of John, the author tells us that love is everything. If we say we love God and do not love others, then we do not really love (1 John 4:20). He also says that God *is* love (4:16). Ultimately, everything we do must be grounded in love. As Jesus says, "You shall love the Lord your God with all your heart, and with all your soul, and with all your mind. . . . You shall love your neighbor as yourself" (Matt. 22:37, 39). In effect, it is only because of our love for God that we can truly love others and ourselves.

The key for being a servant of God is that we have to root everything we are doing not only in our calling, but in our love for God and God's love for us. Everything must emanate from love. Without this love, nothing is possible. We cannot truly be God's servants if we do not love all. So many Christians proclaim that they hate the sin but love the sinner. In fact, many of them hate the sin and are indifferent to the sinner. They really don't love at all, especially not as God calls us to love.

It is a difficult thing to tell if we are truly grounded in love, but if there is a question on the servant path, the answer is always to err on the side of love. Unfortunately, many choose to be like the Pharisees and the Sadducees, erring on the side of purity, standards, and law. I remember hearing a nun who was involved in a mission to the poor who was asked about her work among drug addicts, thieves, and criminals. She was asked how she could work among these immoral people. She responded by saying something to the effect of, "God didn't ask me to judge them, God only asked me to love them. I let God take care of the judging. I just know that God calls me to love." Some may quibble that she is allowing these people to wallow in their immorality, but when in doubt she errs on the side of love. This is what God calls us to do. In my reading of the Bible, I don't remember any incidents in which Jesus criticized any who were erring on the side of love. In contrast, he constantly criticized those who erred on the side of purity. He continually and consistently criticized the Pharisees and the Sadducees for making the law more important than people. Jesus was very clear: his ministry was one of love, and his love purified those around him. The law was made for humans; humans were not made for the law (Mark 2:27). It is for all these reasons that we need to be so careful about engaging in any ministry that may lead to judging others. We are called to love first and foremost.

Conflict on the Servant Path

One of the most frustrating and confusing aspects of walking the servant path is trying to decide what actually is and isn't the right path to walk. Another way of saying this is that it is always a struggle determining what is the right way of reaching out to the world's needs, especially when it comes to reaching out to people who are seen as sinners, in ministries that spark controversy, and in missions that cause conflict. We live in an age of controversy and conflict over whose ministry or mission is right. This is especially true when it comes to dealing with hot-button issues, such as homosexuality, abortion, evangelism, salvation, and the ordination of women. How these issues are played out in actual ministries and missions says quite a bit about how well we are walking the narrow servant path.

The basic problem with all of these issues is that the people who gain the most attention from the public are usually the ones with the loudest voices and the greatest zeal. Unfortunately, they are also the ones who tend to be the most extreme. Often they have strayed from the narrow servant path and are serving in ministries that are more about power, ego, and satisfaction of selfish desires than they are about being God's servants. These are the people who stand on the ridges to our right and our left, screaming at us that their way is God's way. This is a constant problem for those of us who seek to walk the narrow servant path. The debates and discussions over these controversial issues are always defined by those with the loudest voices and the most zeal, but this does not necessarily mean that they are right. In fact, often their zeal and loudness obscure the fact that they are no longer seeking God's voice and will. Instead, they are seeking to serve their own agendas, egos, and sins, while proclaiming themselves to be on the righteous path.

The people on the extremes may cite Scripture, the Ten Commandments, and the law, but so did the Pharisees, the Sadducees, the scribes, and the priests. They may base their acts on the traditions of their faith, but again, so did the Pharisees, Sadducees, chief priests, and Romans. There are always Christians who will loudly, confidently, and stridently proclaim that their perspectives, beliefs, and ministries are best, but it is not the forcefulness of our voices that makes our actions right. It is God who makes them right, and the answers, ministries, and missions that God leads us to undertake sometimes defy easy and clear-cut paths. We are often called to act, even though we may not be sure that what we are doing is the right thing. We are called to act with humility, for the humble person is the one who serves God. The prideful person, even when she is prideful in her service to God, serves mainly herself.

As we stated in chapter 1, the more we sit on the ridges to the right or the left of the narrow path, the more we end up losing the path that God leads us to walk, especially in our work on behalf of God. The ridges represent the extreme, clear-cut, easy, and only partially right answers. The folks who walk on these ridges often take a small portion of God's path and proclaim it to be the whole path. So, for instance, they might say that converting the impoverished of Africa, South America, and Asia is all that matters, not the physical condition of the people. Or they might claim that taking care of their physical condition, and not their spiritual condition, is all that matters.

When we walk the narrow servant path through the obscured and twisting valleys of God's ministry, we are still fed by the streams that cascade down the hills from those extreme ridges. Those who stand on the ridges, offering us clear-cut answers, do provide some important answers. They just don't supply all the answers, no matter how much they may say that they do. The struggle we face is how to integrate the two seemingly opposite beliefs in our particular service so that we can discover God's unique call for us. The problem is that as soon as we walk the path that attempts to integrate both views, we climb onto a narrow path that is obscured. It requires time, a willingness to wallow in confusion and make mistakes, and a determination to seek God's way, not our own way. Now, some might want to label me as an individual who is afraid to take a stand. In fact, that has never been one of my shortcomings. In the past, I have often taken zealous stands that I realize now were not stands taken for God's way. They were stands taken so that I didn't have to think, or ask what God wanted, or seek the narrow path and say, "Right now I'm not sure what the right answer is."

One of the basic problems in Christianity today is that religious people of all denominations are trying mightily to determine who is right and who is wrong in all of these battles over theologies, spiritualities, creeds, beliefs, practices, and the like. In essence, all sides are engaging in battles over orthodoxy that cannot be won. Each side tries to carve out an orthodoxy, or "right teaching," but the problem is that the moment we become too rigidly immersed in an orthodox position, we lose God. Why? Because Christian religion is about discovering God's ways by wading through the paradoxes of Christian faith. Orthodoxy always exists in tension with paradox.

A paradox is something that seems to contradict itself, but when we immerse ourselves in a paradox we discover God's deeper truth.[11] In my own work with paradoxes, I have discovered that we Christians are called to paradoxy rather than orthodoxy. Everything about Christian faith calls us into paradoxes. The whole idea of a Trinitarian God who is one God and three persons is a paradox. The idea that God could become human, die, and resurrect God's self is a paradox. The idea that a man—that God—could be born of a virgin is a paradox. The idea that God's kingdom could come rushing in through failure is a paradox. In fact, so many of the biblical ideals and stories lead us into paradoxes: to be strong we have to be weak (2 Cor. 12:1–10); to be first we have to be last (Matt. 20:1–16); to gain we have to lose (Phil. 3:7–11); for our faith to bloom we must go into the desert (Exodus); to be mature we have to become like a child (Matt. 18:1–5); to find our way we have to lose our way (Exodus); to live we have to die (Rom. 6:5–8, 11); to be wise we must be fools (1 Cor. 3:18–20); to receive we have to give (2 Cor. 9:6–12, 15); and so many more. Christianity is a paradox, and it has always resisted orthodoxy. This is why, as a faith and a religion, Christianity never becomes static. It is always becoming paradoxically reborn. The narrow path is a paradoxical path.

In the modern church, we constantly fight over who is right and who is wrong, yet we never grasp that we may be both right and wrong at the same time. Both sides on any debate may be both right and wrong. How can this be? It is a paradox. The problem is that in our zeal to carve out clear and unambiguous positions, we fail to integrate the valid perspectives of our foes. Because we seek right over wrong, we never see other possibilities. So, we are called to particular ministries that seem to be polar opposites of other ministries to which God calls other people. They both may be right in ways that are paradoxical.

Let me give you a metaphor for this that might help you understand my point. I've experienced on a firsthand basis the paradox of God's calling. I am a Presbyterian pastor, and I am married to a Roman Catholic—and an active Roman Catholic at that. We both come from faith traditions that are convinced they are right, and that the other, while perhaps not "wrong," is certainly misguided. Our denominations refuse to recognize the other as being an equal. They recognize each other's baptisms, but little else. They do not accept each other's pastors or priests, they do not accept each other's Communion, and they do not accept each other's theological and traditional beliefs. As a pastor, so many laity are surprised that my wife, Diane, has not become a Presbyterian. It is the common custom when pastors marry outside their denomination for the spouse to convert. Some of Diane's family and friends are surprised that she would willingly marry a pastor of another denomination. This is not necessarily what good Irish Catholics, like my wife, do. All we can answer is that when we got married, we made a conscious decision that our marriage was about loving each other instead of converting each other. Bringing together these two faiths and practices in our marriage is hard at times, yet both of us recognize that we are doing something that our denominations cannot do. We are bringing our traditions together based on love, and in that love we begin to see God's face in each other's practice. We are walking a narrow path. Because of our marriage, I can now sit in a Roman Catholic worship service with Diane and experience God. I can read works by Roman Catholic theologians and writers and hear God. I can pray with Roman Catholics and experience God with them. And Diane can do the same when she encounters my tradition.

The same kind of integration is possible when bringing together people of opposite ministries and missions. As long as we both are ultimately trying to be grounded in God's love, we can slowly begin to see God's voice in one another's perspectives. It is in the encounter of genuine love that we begin to discover God's voice and hand in one another's work, even if someone's perspectives, beliefs, and actions seem to be polar opposites from our own. The problem is that we are seldom willing to come together in that love. This brings us back to the main point of this chapter. If we are truly to engage in God's work and ministry, we have to be willing to set aside our own desires, egos, and expectations in order to do what God is calling us to do. This requires that we constantly question our own positions, not so that we can be wishy-washy and indecisive, but so that we can be sure we are listening for and serving God instead of the false gods that we would create, given the opportunity. Ultimately, serving God requires that we seek communion with those with whom we disagree. It is in our communion with others that we discover true communion with God as God shapes and renews our visions, even through those whom we might regard as enemies.

The thing that we need to keep in mind through all of this is the metaphor for the Christian community that Paul taught us in 1 Corinthians 12:12–21, when he said, "Indeed, the body does not consist of one member but of many." To walk the narrow servant path means continually asking, "To what extent is this person part of the body with me? How can I work with this person to bring greater health to the body? How should I assess my own beliefs and work so that what I do serves the body of Christ?" To walk the servant path means to ask questions not only of calling, compassion, compatibility, and competence, but also communion. Where communion with others in Christ is missing, the body becomes divided and unable to truly do God's will.

To remain on the servant path, we have to realize that God is calling us to serve God in our own particular ways and in our own particular ministries. These ministries can range anywhere from serving in Calcutta to serving in our own homes. Not everyone is called to Calcutta, nor is everyone called to serve at home. We are all called to our own particular ministries. To walk the servant path means to look for where God is leading us, listen for where God is calling us, and respond in the unique ways in which only we can respond and serve.

Questions for Reflection

1. In what ways do you feel a conflict between the demands of your life and the call to care for others?
2. As you read about George Müller's life, what lessons did you learn about being God's servant?
3. What do you sense that you are called to do and be in your life? Try to define it as clearly as possible.
4. Take a look at how you serve God. To what extent are you being congenial to your calling, compassionate to others, and compatible with your situation, and to what extent are you acting with competence?
5. How have faith, hope, and love been a part of your service to God?

Key Learnings

- Walking the servant path requires surrendering to, listening with, acting for, and trusting in God.
- The servant path begins with our asking God what God is calling us to do in life, and then responding in faith to what we sense God's answer is.
- Our calling is God's voice crying from within as it resonates with God's voice that is crying from without, inviting us to care for God's creation.
- A sense of consonance comes when we sense that our work is congenial with our calling, compassionate toward others, and compatible with our situation, and that we have the competence to carry it out.

Chapter 7

Walking the Integrated Path

*O*ne of the most frustrating things about modern religious life is the constant battles being waged between the different and competing denominations, movements, traditions, beliefs, and practices in the Christian world today. We are constantly confronted by Christians who are convinced that they are right and we are wrong. We've discussed this issue in earlier chapters, but it deserves to be revisited. I figure that with two billion people worldwide claiming to be Christian, at least 80 percent probably believe that they are right and that everyone else is wrong (of course, I could be wrong, too). They see their theology, religious practices, and/or spirituality as being superior to all others, no matter what denomination, movement, or belief they subscribe to.

Whether we are talking about Roman Catholics, Protestants, charismatics, progressives, conservatives, evangelicals, moderates, Pentecostals, fundamentalists, orthodox, or any other group of Christians, there is always a large core of people who are completely convinced that they are right and all others are either wrong or misguided. No wonder we Christians have such a hard time coming together. We are told to ground our faith in love for the one Trinitarian God, and to love others as ourselves, but we don't. Instead, we keep searching for the "right" path, the "right" belief, the "right" spiritual practice, or the "right" church that will guarantee our salvation and inclusion among God's chosen. So we argue, fight, accuse, defend, and split in our conviction that we are "right" and that all others are wrong.

Each time we determine that we are on the absolute "right" path, one that all others should follow, we have assuredly strayed from the narrow path. We have strayed from the mystical path of God that is humble, faith-filled, and open to God's guidance. The entrance to this path is revealed in the words of Dorotheos of Gaza:

There are certain kinds of trees which never bear any fruit as long as their branches stay up straight, but if stones are hung on the branches to bend them down they begin to bear fruit. So it is with the soul. When it is humbled it begins to bear fruit, and the more fruit it bears the lowlier it becomes. So also the saints; the nearer they get to God, the more they see themselves as sinners.[1]

Dorotheos and so many of the mystics recognized that it is folly to search for the "right" path because it doesn't really exist in a clear, objective way. We only find it as we faithfully and humbly walk the path God sets for us. Unfortunately, as long as Christianity exists, people will probably compete over who is right and who is wrong, mainly because competing with others and needing to feel superior is a natural part of our humanity, and it is among the strongest evidence of human sin. So many of the mystics, however, have stressed that humility—instead of being in the "right" church, denomination, or movement—is the way to God.

It is not just among denominations, movements, and churches that the competition exists. The competitive spirit reigns within movements especially among three particular aspects of the Christian life: the roles of theology, spirituality, and religion. Within each particular denomination, for instance, are people who are attracted to theological thinking and reflecting, and they are convinced that it is mainly through proper theological grounding and thought that we find God's way. Other people think that too much theology can damage the soul by causing us to live only in our heads. Instead, they emphasize religious practice and participation as the path to wholeness and salvation. Finally, there are those who are attracted to the more spiritual aspects of faith, and mistakenly believe that the whole key to being on the "right" path lies in practicing the spiritual disciplines and having spiritual experiences.

The problem with adherents to each of these fields is that they fail to realize that the narrow path is an integrated path. For theological understanding, religious practice, and spiritual experience to lead us to God's path, they need each other. They need to be integrated in a way that allows each to complete the other. Unfortunately, in this day of fragmentation and specialization, it is difficult to integrate them. When we become focused mainly on one of these, we tend to diminish the importance of the others. They are like three strands of hair in a braid—if you use only one or two strands, the braid cannot be completed.

A good place to see the lack of integration and its impact on modern Christianity is in mainstream Protestant seminaries. Most of them are staffed primarily by professors and teachers who are experts in theology and biblical studies. Their focus is mainly theological. In other words, their focus is to teach students how to think theologically as they train for their future work in ministry, pastoral care, and worship leadership. Almost all seminaries offer classes in worship leadership, administration, and pastoral care, but the focus is on giving students a theological foundation for these endeavors. It is only in the past ten years that most seminaries have begun adding classes in spirituality, and it is in only a few that these classes in spirituality are core classes that a student must take. More often the classes are electives.

Most of these seminaries would defend their lack of focus on religion and spirituality by saying that they are theological institutions: their focus is supposed to be on theology. But there's a problem with this. They aren't just theological institutions. Seminaries are places where church leaders are trained. These students certainly must be theologically trained, but they also will end up working mainly in the religious sphere—in churches—and are expected to be spiritually deep people of prayer and faith. Why would theological thinking be emphasized the most for people who are expected to be deep spiritual people and leaders of religious life in churches?

The answer is that an emphasis on rational thinking has dominated all fields of study over the course of the past two hundred years, and this has affected seminaries as much as everything else. Theologians, who are the rational thinkers for the realm of faith, have dominated the training of clergy and church leaders, yet most of them are not trained in a way that allows them to see the inherent problems with relying purely on the rational approach. Is it any wonder that the mainstream church continues to decline? The primary training we give our church leaders is theological, yet their work is mainly religious and spiritual. So pastors and church leaders end up reflecting their training as they overemphasize theological thinking in the belief that all the challenges and problems they face are theological in nature and can be solved by theological answers.

What the trainers of church leaders do not see is that a healthy religious life and deep spirituality cannot come mainly from pure theological thinking and reflection. Still, among many church leaders the perception persists that theology is the "right" path. I remember once talking to a man who years ago had been the moderator (the main position of leadership) of the Presbyterian Church (U.S.A.). He told me that the whole problem in the modern church is that "we don't think theologically enough." In other words, if we just thought with enough theological clarity, everything would work out and our denomination would begin to grow again because we would be clearer about what God wants. The reality is that so many Christians in so many different denominations have spent their lives thinking theologically, and it still does not lead to clarity and growth. The people our modern churches try to attract are searching for answers that are not necessarily addressed by the abstract, rational, and intellectual realm of theology. They want concrete answers to such questions as "How do I save my rocky marriage? How do I raise my children so that they can avoid drugs and violence, not get pregnant at fifteen, and grow up to have meaningful lives? How do I deal with the constant pressures of my career, which seem to conflict with my family? How do I get over all of my past pains? How can I be healed of my illnesses and afflictions? How do I get God into my life so that my life isn't so miserable? How do I get God to answer my prayers?" The field of theology gives answers, but often not ones that are concrete and pragmatic. Theological explanations do offer many crucial answers, but to truly provide answers that can be applied to daily life they must be complemented by the perspectives that religion and spirituality offer.

At the same time, many devotees of the spiritual formation field (including myself) have mistakenly believed that if only we could all become steeped enough in prayer and the spiritual disciplines, we would all discover God leading us on the right path. This is not true, either. Prayer and practicing the spiritual disciplines are not enough. If we only follow the path of prayer and spirituality, it eventually leads us away from God's path. In the past, I have been guilty of chasing the "spirituality and spirituality alone" path in the hope of trying to find a more pure path. Those of us who have devoted our lives to prayer, discernment, the spiritual disciplines, and the reflective life tend to emphasize personal experience of God over everything else. Our weakness is that often we can generalize our own experiences, thinking that what is right for us is right for everyone. For example, many in the spirituality field are attracted to the contemplative life, which is a way of living that attempts to discover God through simplicity, solitude, and reflection. The problem is that not everyone has a temperament that is suitable to this kind of life, but those of us who are contemplative don't understand this. "Everyone has a natural, contemplative ability," we think. "They just don't use it."

I remember hearing two experts in spiritual formation speak to a conference of Christian educators several years ago. One of the speakers, a contemplative woman, was talking about a wonderful experience she had recently enjoyed during a thirty-day silent retreat. She extolled the virtues of silence and contemplative prayer. After she said this, the other speaker started to speak, paused, and then laughed, saying, "I'm such a talker, I think that if I went on anything more than a day's silence I would drive myself crazy." The audience burst out in laughter. Why? Because most of them did not have a contemplative temperament and were secretly thinking what the second speaker had just said out loud: "How could I possibly do something like that? Where would I find the time? What would my family think? What would I do with myself?" This does not mean that the first speaker was on the wrong path. Silent retreats can be a wonderful time of discovering God and God's path for us. The problem is simply that this silent, contemplative approach is not necessarily "right" for everyone. While silent retreats would benefit many people, not all people have the kind of introverted-contemplative temperament needed to truly benefit. To say that contemplative prayer is *the* way is just as much of a problem as saying that the answer to all of our problems is to think more theologically. The more appropriate question is whether God is calling me to go on a silent retreat, and how it will complement and strengthen my theological foundation and my religious practice.

Finally, many devoted to the religious sphere see this sphere as *the* "right" path. They see those who emphasize theological thinking as being elitist, over-intellectual snobs who live too much in their heads and are not rooted in the real world. They see those devoted to the spiritual life as being namby-pamby, wimpy, touchy-feely folks who are not rooted in the real world.

Those who are devoted to the religious life tend to emphasize church participation, worship, and service as the right paths. They often are deed oriented and see the "right" path as leading through our works. For example, I know one Roman Catholic laywoman who insists that giving to the church, participating in weekly mass, and receiving the sacraments is all that matters. It is not important for her to think theologically or to pray with any frequency. Again, what she pursues is an incomplete and false path. It has many elements of God's path, but over time it leads to a false summit unless it is complemented by the insights of theology and the wisdom of spirituality.

The problem is that those devoted to theological thinking, those devoted to spiritual seeking, and those devoted to religious acts all see their own particular paths as the right ones. What they don't realize is that they are making false idols of their fields, treating them as gods, and failing to see that only together can all three lead us to form a deep and loving relationship with God. The paths are sacred only to the extent to which they open us to God. As much as we would like to separate the three, they are each incomplete on their own. Theological thinking needs spiritual grounding and religious expression to reveal God and God's truth. The greatest theologians have always been people of prayer and religious commitment. Religion needs a theological foundation as well as a grounding in spiritual experience to teach us God's way. The greatest church leaders have always been people of prayer and theological thinking. Spirituality needs the structure of religion and the direction of theological understanding to help us come to know God in a personal way. The great mystics have always been strongly rooted in worship and the church, as well as in the theological teachings of the church.

The original Christians on the day of Pentecost intuitively and inherently understood the delicate balance and integration of theology, spirituality, and religion (Acts 2:1–47). On Pentecost, the disciples and followers of Jesus were gathered in Jerusalem, awaiting the gift of the Holy Spirit that Jesus had promised. Jesus had already given them a solid theological foundation. He had spent three years teaching them all the things they needed to know, although this still wasn't enough. If theology was enough to form a strong faith in his disciples, they wouldn't have scattered in fear when Jesus was arrested. In terms of their religious lives, they had been Jews all their lives, and the communal life of worship, practice, and service was already a strong part of their lives. They had already begun the process of forming a strong Christian religious community. Despite their theological training and religious grounding, they were still missing something. It wasn't until the Holy Spirit rushed into their lives that their spiritual core was ignited. It was only then that they fully understood everything that they needed to do. They became spiritually alive. Their theological beliefs, religious commitments, and spiritual lives all came together. There was no longer any conflict. Initially, there was no trace of the conflict that afflicts us today among those who seek salvation in theological knowledge, those who seek it in religious activity, and those who seek it in spiritual awareness. All three came together to show the disciples how to live with God in God's kingdom on this earth.

The Roots of the Conflict

How did we get this detachment between theology, religion, and spirituality? For the first three hundred years or so of Christianity, a dynamic connection existed between theology, religion, and spirituality. It may not have always been smooth or peaceful. Certainly, tensions among the three were apparent as the early Christians tried to understand the role of each, and often these tensions led to conflicts in the early Christian communities, such as the church in Corinth and those in Galatia. Still, there was a dynamic connection that allowed the Christian faith to spread quickly across the Roman Empire. This is something that the New Testament and the church fathers attest to. The teachings and traditions of the Christian religion were still being formed, and so there was more room for theological, religious, and spiritual exploration. The early Christians, as the Pentecost experience shows, were very much alive theologically, religiously, and spiritually. This all began to change around 325 A.D. As we discussed in earlier chapters, this is the year the Emperor Constantine called the great Council of Nicaea. A few years earlier Constantine had declared Christianity the faith of the empire, thus ending several hundred years of persecution of Christians. The Council of Nicaea was a meeting of the bishops and great Christian thinkers of the time. They gathered to set down the dogmatic beliefs and doctrines of the church, and to end once and for all the disagreements throughout Christianity on what was and wasn't truth. This was a great feat, and it was important for the formation of Christianity. But afterward it also had the effect of slowly making religion and the church more important than theology, and certainly more so than personal and communal spiritual experience.

Over the next twelve centuries, the church became more of an institution, and maintaining stability in the institution was a primary concern. This was especially true as civilization broke down when the Roman Empire fell apart. First, spiritual experience became less important as maintaining stability became increasingly important. Then, as literacy rates dropped and religious teaching decreased, theological understanding became less important. Following the practices of the church became the most important thing because that increased stability. Over the course of the Dark Ages, the laity of the church had less of a role in the church. Over time, the laity ceased to even be involved in the work of the church because they were considered too ordinary to understand the theological teachings and spiritual experiences of Christianity. These teachings and experiences were reserved for clergy and monks.

Europe entered a renaissance period during the thirteenth century as it emerged from the darkness of earlier centuries. With it came a greater interest in theological pursuits, especially through the work of Thomas Aquinas, who reacquainted Western Christians with the philosophies of Aristotle and applied them to traditional Christian theology. With this renaissance came a greater interest in personal spiritual experience.

The Reformation in the sixteenth century was a spiritual movement that tried to reintegrate theology, religion, and spirituality by recapturing the spirit and practice of the original Christian communities and churches. Reformers such as Martin Luther, Ulrich Zwingli, and John Calvin emphasized the need for laity to read the Bible for themselves, and so they translated it into languages other than Latin. They also emphasized the participation of laity in sacraments and allowed the laity to have leadership roles in the church. All of this was an attempt to bring theological foundations and spiritual experiences and gifts back into religious life. This led to a wonderful time of spiritual growth as over the next several centuries people like George Fox and John Wesley formed new ways for people to bring spiritual experience, passion, and zeal, as well as solid theological teaching, back into the practice of religion.

Over the past two hundred years, though, theology, religion, and spirituality have slowly become split again as churches have often emphasized theology and religion over spirituality. There would be movements, like the Great Awakenings of the eighteenth and nineteenth centuries, that would reintegrate the three for a time, but for the most part religion and theology have gained the upper hand in so many of our churches. Thus, adhering to the teachings, doctrines, and religious rituals of Christianity have become more important than forming a spiritual relationship with God and having the spiritual experiences that result from these relationships. Because of this disconnection between spirituality, theology, and religion, recently (over the past thirty years) there has been a new movement in American culture that has tried to emphasize spirituality and disconnect it from religion and theology. We typically call this the New Age movement, but it is much larger than that. It has become influential even in our churches as Christians try to break free of what they see as oppressive doctrines and restrictive religious systems.

The emphasis in this movement is to create a spirituality that is unfettered by religion and theology. They want pure spirituality, and to do so they try not to be bound by religious tradition or theology. They engage in what I call a "smorgasbord" or "brunch" spirituality. If you go to brunch on a Sunday afternoon, you'll get a sense of what I mean. At brunch, you rarely eat what's nourishing. Instead, you pick and choose among all sorts of goodies. If you are like me, you grab a beautiful Belgian waffle and smother it in syrup. You get a greasy omelet filled with all sorts of stuff. You eat danishes, cakes, croissants with jam. In the end, you are stuffed to the gills in a sort of sugar reverie that can make you feel ecstatic at the time but that later leads you to become sluggish and sleepy. This new spirituality movement is similar. It takes the salty bits of Christianity, the spice of Islam, the sugary taste of Buddhism, and then adds a dash of Taoism, a chunk of Native American belief, and mixes it all together into a mishmash faith that is self-focused and self-serving in a way in which none of the original traditions are. It may taste good, but it isn't very nourishing. It is spirituality without a solid theological and religious foundation, and it is just as much of a problem as theology and religion without spirituality. This same kind of spirituality has also begun to influence many within the Christian church as Christians seek a spirituality that isn't necessarily bound to the Christian religious tradition or theology.

While religion and theology have mostly remained partners in the modern church, a growing number of churches and Christians emphasize having the right theology over religious commitment and spiritual experience. For example, one pastor said to me and others in a group that over time he has trusted his experience less and his theological reading of Scripture more. I think he had experience and emotion confused, but the effect is the same. What mattered for him was theological clarity. For him, true religion and spirituality were all about having a "right" theology, which incidentally was his brand of evangelical theology. He believed that having a clear scriptural theology was what led us into a relationship with God through Christ. Unfortunately, if you take away spiritual experience, you also take away any connection with the Holy Spirit. Spirituality, by its very name, is meant to be a living connection with the Spirit. To distrust experience is to distrust the Holy Spirit.

Finally, we have Christians and churches that emphasize religion over theology and spirituality. All that matters is that we show up for church and take part in the sacraments. We are told to let the church take care of theological matters. All we need to do is to be obedient to the church and to blindly follow its theology and teaching. The laity are not really encouraged to think theologically for themselves, nor are they really expected to grow much spiritually. Spiritual growth is reserved for mystics and saints.

Ultimately, it is difficult to keep theology, religion, and spirituality in balance. Over the course of Christian history, true integration has been more the exception than the rule. Why is it so hard to keep them in balance? The reason is that each one appeals to a different dimension of life—the *intellectual*, the *expressive*, and the *experiential*. Depending on which dimension is most dominant in us, we will gravitate toward one or the other. For instance, theology appeals to those who are *intellectually inclined*. When those who are intellectually inclined dominate the church, then theology is emphasized the most. Religion is more *expression oriented*. It appeals to people who want to express themselves and their faith through rituals, singing, worship, church polity, and service to God in ministry and mission. When people who care mostly about these aspects of Christian faith dominate the church, then religious *expression* is emphasized the most. Spirituality is concerned mostly with matters of Christian experience, and it appeals mainly to those who want to tangibly experience God's presence and grace. When those who care mostly about spiritual experience dominate the church, then spirituality is emphasized the most.

It is very rare to find people oriented to each of these three dimensions sharing the power of a denomination, church, or movement. Instead, they tend to vie for power. When the power struggle becomes too intense, new denominations, movements, and churches form. Today, in the North American church, these three are rarely kept in balance. Instead, there is a split. Those who care about matters of theology tend to gravitate toward churches or movements that emphasize theological thinking. Those who care about expressing themselves and their faith tend to gravitate toward churches or movements that emphasize religious participation. Those who care about matters of the heart tend to gravitate toward churches or movements that seek to emphasize spiritual experience. Very few movements or churches keep all three in balance, and this is one of the reasons why there is such conflict within movements, denominations, and churches today.

Walking a Theological, Religious, and Spiritual Path

Religion, theology, and spirituality are all important aspects of forming an ever-deepening relationship with God. Each one has elements that are crucial to walking the narrow path with God. To diminish or reject one is to slowly diminish our ability to discern and discover God more deeply in our lives. For us to form deep lives, all three aspects must work together in our lives.

So, what should the relationship between Christian theology, religion, and spirituality be? In Ezekiel 37:1–6, the prophet Ezekiel gives us a great metaphor for this relationship. The Lord asked Ezekiel to prophesy to a valley full of bones, saying to them,

> O dry bones, hear the word of the LORD. Thus says the LORD God to these bones: I will cause breath to enter you, and you shall live. I will lay sinews on you, and will cause flesh to come upon you, and cover you with skin, and put breath in you, and you shall live; and you shall know that I am the LORD. (37:4–6)

Ezekiel does as God asks, and the bones come together and form sinews, muscles, and skin. And then breath (or spirit) comes into them and they come alive. You probably know this passage very well, although you know it better by the words of the old song: "Dem bones, dem bones, dem dry bones. Dem bones, dem bones, dem dry bones. Dem bones, dem bones, dem dry bones. Now hear the word of the Lord: The foot bone is connected to the ankle bone. The ankle bone is connected to the shin bone. The shin bone is connected to the knee bone. . . ."

Theology is the bone, the skeletal structure on which religion and spiritual experiences are built. Religion is the muscle, the sinews, and all the rest that we need to pragmatically express our faith in God. Spirituality is the breath of God that gives this body life and enables us to experience God. How do the three work together?

Theology

Without the bones of theology, religion and spirituality become a formless life that can do little other than exist. They become a formless body that cannot truly worship or serve God. They can breathe but have no real life to live. Unfortunately, this is what so many want today, both inside and outside the church. They have grown tired of the intellectualizations of theology, and so they seek a religion that is spiritually alive but requires little theological grounding. They create rituals and spiritual exercises that worship a God they can create in their own image. This is a major problem in Christianity today as people try to break away from its traditional theological grounding in an attempt to reinvigorate Christianity by exploring new beliefs. They create churches with lots of activity but no depth. They become like modern pop musicians, trying to create hits but offering little of substance to deepen the soul. This does not mean that we shouldn't explore new ways of understanding God and acting on our faith. It simply means that we need to be careful that we ground these explorations in a strong theology. It is not enough to do something because it will attract others. We have to ground our actions in a solid purpose that leads others and us to God.

So, what is theology? Theology deals with the ultimate questions about God, life, the universe, and us. It is the scientific part of Christian faith. It may seem odd to call theology a science unless you understand what true science is. We tend to think of science as the accumulation of knowledge through empirical means, but this is a narrow understanding of science. Science is simply the accumulation of knowledge (in Latin, *scientia*—"to know").[2] Like biologists, psychologists, and anthropologists, theologians are also scientists, for theology is the science of religion. They try to understand truth about God, the universe, humans, and life. They base their knowledge on rational and prayerful reflection of Scripture, tradition, and religious experience.

Theologians use the best methods and material at their disposal to try to discern eternal truths. The information gleaned from experiments provides the foundation for theories by biologists, chemists, astronomers, and other scientists; in a similar way, theologians glean their information from a disciplined study of scriptural and human experiences of God. They base their teachings on wisdom accumulated from both. In effect, theology is a kind of science that is grounded in an intellectual, rational, yet prayerful understanding of life's mysteries. It is the body of knowledge that deals with the divine, the supernatural, and the numinous. While we may complain about the lack of true objectivity in the material at theologians' disposal, how else does one go about measuring, testing, and ascertaining these things based on purely physical evidence? Theologians devote their lives to helping us understand the ultimate issues about life. Unfortunately, just as understanding the philosophical and psychological nature of thought is not all we need in order to think more clearly about how to handle a broken marriage, understanding the deep theological answers to life's mysteries and God is not all we need when it comes to learning how to pray, listen to God, and follow God's will. Theology is important, but there is more.

Religion

We may have the bones of theology and the life of spirituality, but without the body of religion to give them expression, we become immersed in a dry, brittle, intellectual theology and/or self-indulgent and self-serving spirituality. Our faith becomes nothing more than thinking about God and seeking personal experiences. There is no service to others or real worship of God. Eventually, our theology falls apart because there is nothing holding it together, and spirituality has no body to fill with Spirit. Bones and breath need muscle, sinews, and organs to maintain life. Otherwise, they become dry bones with wind blowing through them. Many people have a strong theology, and they develop their own personal spiritual practices, but they are not part of a religious body that gives form to what they do.

Again, forming a strong theology and personal spirituality without religious participation is a problem that afflicts many people who have left the church. They have strong opinions about God and how to reach God. They may experiment with Buddhist, Muslim, or Native American spiritual approaches, but their faith is all about experimentation and their own experiences. Slowly, their spirituality and theology become self-motivated and self-focused. The traditions of religion and churches teach us how to live life with and for others. What, then, is religion?

Religion is literally the body of traditions that connect us with the Divine—with God. The word "religion" literally means to "bind us" (the Latin word *ligare*) "back" (the Latin prefix *re*). Through the traditions of a religion, we are bound back to the originators of the faith. So when we practice the Christian faith, it binds us to the examples, teachings, and practices of the prophets and teachers of ancient Israel, as well as Jesus' disciples, apostles, followers, and even Jesus Christ himself. By reading Scriptures, participating in the sacraments, coming together to pray, listening to and learning lessons of the Christian faith, serving on committees, tithing, and serving in particular ministries and missions, we become bound to the traditions that lead us not only to know God, but also to serve God.

A religion is an institution, tradition, and community all rolled into one. A religion teaches us on a practical level how to express our faith in God: to pray, worship, understand Scripture, listen to God, and serve God and others. So, for example, while I am part of the overall Christian religious faith, I am also part of the Presbyterian religious tradition. My Presbyterian heritage binds me back to Christ through the Scottish and Swiss reformers of the sixteenth century. For better or worse, my Presbyterian faith has bound me to a religious practice that is grounded in a rational and intellectual understanding of Scripture. It is a tradition that emphasizes a personal and communal grounding in Scripture alone, along with an emphasis on the equality of all in community, service to God in work with the poor and hungry, and a certain kind of diligence in my religious practice. This is very different from other Christian religious traditions. For example, the Roman Catholic religious tradition may be based on Scripture, but it is equally based on the edicts of its 1,500-year-old tradition. It is grounded in a hierarchical structure with a strong central authority. While it is also Christian, the actual practice and way of being a Roman Catholic is very different from the Presbyterian way.

The key thing that religions do is to ultimately provide us with religious communities that guide us on how to live day to day with God. They do this by immersing us in the traditions of the faith. Religions give us practical instructions on how to live lives that are open to the Divine. By teaching us disciplines of weekly worship, daily prayer, fasting, tithing, reading of Scripture, and so much more, they ground Christian theology in spirituality and daily religious activities.

An important part of religious participation is involvement in a church. Churches provide us with communities of practical faith that tangibly and pragmatically help us to express our faith. When we become involved in a church, for good or for bad, we become involved in communities where we have to learn how to serve God and one another. We become accountable to one another as together we try to worship, love, give, and serve. These communities also push us to become other-oriented and not just self-oriented. Churches are not perfect by any stretch of the imagination, mainly because so many have jettisoned spirituality, lost their grounding in solid theology, or both. Still, they are communities that are meant to encourage us as we form strong theological backbones and breathe the breath of the Spirit. When we reject religion, and especially churches, we usually end up forming a very self-focused and weak faith.

I see how self-focused and weak faith can be without religion all the time. Although I am a pastor in a church, the reality is that I have a love-hate relationship with religion. Perhaps it has to do with the fact that I am constantly confronted by people within the Christian religion who are spiritually dead and/or theologically weak. They tend to believe that binding others to their rigid beliefs, emphasizing only the customs of the past, enforcing the rules and regulations to the letter, and maintaining order are more important than forming a living faith, hope, and love.

Despite these pitfalls—these problems so many religious people have with forming a strong theological foundation and spiritual life—I also know that without the activities and expectations religious participation in a church brings, faith becomes brittle and weak. I see people for counseling all the time who have rejected religion. They will say that they are spiritual, but usually their spirituality is self-focused, not God-focused.

For example, one woman I saw, who had rejected the church years before, had a husband walk out on her, a sister die, and her mother die all in the space of two years. She told me that she was convinced that God was doing this to her to make her stronger—that she needed to be stronger. In other words, her divorce and these deaths were all about her. When I suggested that the deaths had nothing to do with her, that they had to do with the randomness of life, she vehemently disagreed: "No, no, it was to make me stronger. God knows that I need to be stronger, and this is God's way of making me stronger." No matter what I said, she wouldn't let go of this idea.

What difference would participation in a church and religion have made for her? In a church, we confront death all the time. Members die, and we have to face death honestly. But in the midst of these deaths, there is support, love, and a frank willingness to recognize with humility our own mortality and need to rely on God. People share stories of their own suffering and faith with one another, and help place our suffering in context. They help us understand more clearly, if not in our heads, then in our hearts, how God is active in our lives. During funerals and at other times, we read Scriptures that teach us about God's love, especially in the valleys of the shadows of death. We realize that it is not all about me, but about God and us together. Without religion, our theology and spirituality slowly become self-focused and limited as we confront the mysteries and suffering of life.

Spirituality

Without the breath of life that spirituality brings, theology and religion die. This has been the ongoing problem of religious life for so long. It is much easier to form a strong theological foundation and engage in religious activity than it is to let the breath of life—the Holy Spirit—into our lives. For so long, this has been my struggle with the modern Christian church. We create worship services that are dry, dull, and dead. We see signs in front of churches that say, "Come, Celebrate with Joy!" Then we walk inside, hoping for a positive experience, and see anything but joy. Instead, we find a dry and musty worship service, with the people going through the motions, praying, singing, and responding without life. We see churches and denominations teaching a theology that is dry, intellectual, and not grounded in experience, and they communicate this theology through religious rituals that have lost their meaning. For theology and religion to have life, they have to lead to an encounter with God, but this is a problem. So many Christians are scared to encounter God because an encountered God is not a safe God. This is God who is powerful, unpredictable, and who transforms our lives. So, we suck spirituality out of the church, labeling those who seek spiritual experience as delusional, caught up in a fad, self-focused, touchy-feely, and wimpy. We are suspicious of spirituality and prayer, and of those who cherish them.

What is spirituality? There are a lot of complicated definitions out there, but probably the best I know of is that spirituality is the life of love that we share with God and others. Christian spirituality is about loving God with all our minds, hearts, souls, and strength, and loving others as ourselves. The Christian spiritual life is focused on forming a relationship with God that allows us to live in God and God to live in us. The spiritual life is a life that leads us to become mystics. To be a mystic, which is the name given to those adept at the spiritual life, requires that we fall in love with God. As Evelyn Underhill says, a mystic is simply someone who has fallen in love with God.[3] The more we fall in love with God, the more we develop an unquenchable thirst for God. The more we fall in love with God, the more we want to live in intimacy with God so that God becomes a tangible presence, minute by minute. The irony is that the person who seeks to be alive spiritually is not necessarily focused on having personal spiritual experiences, although that is the desire of many who first become interested in Christian spirituality. Instead, she is focused on deepening her loving relationship with God, and this leads to personal spiritual experiences.

This love of God emerges from time spent in prayer, in service to God, and in self-examination that leads us to let go of our sin and give it to God. It comes from engaging in spiritual disciplines of prayer, confession, service, worship, contemplation, reflection, meditation, and spiritual direction, as well as from working on forming certain virtues, such as love, humility, faith, compassion, meekness, and so many more. Most of all, this spiritual love of God emerges from our becoming open to God, which leads to experiences of God. We become open to the purposes of God the Creator, the presence of God the Son, the power of God the Holy Spirit. As we experience these three, our love for God deepens and so does our spirituality.

You can see why theology and religion without spirituality become dry, dull, and dead. Without the love of God that spirituality nurtures, theology becomes nothing more than speculation about abstract realities. Religion becomes blind fidelity to a set of rituals devoid of passion. Unfortunately, as we said earlier, this is what so many people today experience in our churches. There is no expectation on Sunday morning that God will be encountered in worship and that love will be shared. The answer to this dilemma, despite what so many today think, does not necessarily lie in making the service more contemporary or upbeat. The answer lies in forming a service that actually attempts to connect people where they are with God. The music and style of worship is not as important as the spiritual focus on connecting people with God. The question is what we should do in order to help people discover and fall in love with God.

We can also see the effect of theology that is devoid of spiritual life as we listen to pastors preach theological sermons that have no vitality or pragmatic connection to our lives. These preachers may offer erudite tomes on Christ's sacrifice on the cross and the need for our salvation, but what difference do they make if they are not connected to our daily lives? So often, we are left sitting in the pew wondering, "So what if Jesus died for my sins? What does that have to do with the fact that I'm unemployed, my marriage is a mess, and it doesn't feel as though God cares about me?" Without the life of spirituality, theology becomes dry and boring, and we easily fall asleep or think about other things instead of focusing our thoughts on God.

Without the vitality and life of spirituality, religion and theology are nothing, just bones and a body—a cadaver. Spirituality is the integrating core that brings everything together. Unfortunately, in today's world of declining mainstream denominations and religious attendance, many church officials and theologians tend to emphasize dry worship and theology even more. "We just need better worship. We just need better theology," they think. Yet what we see is that people are spiritually hungry. You can see this just by looking at the best-seller lists. Books on everyday spirituality thrive. People buy them by the millions. In fact, the Christian inspiration, religion, and New Age sections are often the largest ones in the mega-bookstores that are popping up all over. Many of these books are written by people who have left Christian religion and theology behind. Pop culture is attending to this hunger because Christian denominations and churches have quit doing so. So many people want living springs of spiritual water, but there are none available in so much of modern Christianity; not because they have dried up, but because we refuse to emphasize and share these springs with others. Instead, we argue over who is more theologically and ritualistically right. Christian spirituality brings life to theology and religion by connecting both with God through love.

The whole point is that for us to discover, experience, and serve God, we need to let solid theological understanding be our bones, religious participation be our muscle and organs, and spirituality be our breath and life. Whenever we decide to jettison one or more, we diminish our lives. We become bones rattling in the wind; muscle and organs with no structure or life; or breath and life with no substance or foundation. To walk the narrow path means to keep the three in balance. The problem is that this is very hard to do, especially when we live busy, modern lives that treat religion, theology, and spirituality as leisure activities.

Walking the Integrated Path

How do we keep theology, religion, and spirituality in balance, especially in the midst of a culture that tells us to be spiritual but not religious or theological because they are suspect; in the midst of churches that tell us to be religious but not overly spiritual or theological—to leave that up to the experts; in the midst of people who value theological thinking, but seem to have no interest in religious participation or spiritual experience? This can be difficult, especially since most of us don't appreciate the importance of all three. We may see the value of one or two, but have a problem with the third.

Walking the narrow path means walking an integrated path. It means walking a path in which we take our spiritual relationship with God seriously, try to ground our relationship in a solid theology, and embody that relationship and theology in a life of religious worship, participation, and service. In the midst of this, a major problem arises. How do we keep the three in perfect balance?

The reality is that we can't keep theology, religion, and spirituality in perfect balance. We all have biases, abilities, and interests that cause us to emphasize one over the other. For example, not all people are going to be adept at theological thinking and study. One reason is that theology can be confusing, and few people have the time or energy to devote themselves to the long periods of study necessary to become adept in Christian theology. Another reason is that to study Christian theology means possibly changing our beliefs and stretching ourselves, and many do not want to be stretched. Still, it's not as though people today have no theological understanding of life and the world. In fact, almost everyone has a basic theology, although some people's theological understanding is more sophisticated and deeper than others. Atheists have a theology of God's absence. Agnostics have a theology that can best be described as "Let's wait and see." Those of us who are Christian also have a basic theology that is both in sync with and opposed to our basic denominational theologies. Each one of us has beliefs about everything. Our personal theologies are a mixture of Christian, denominational, folk, and pop theologies, as well as our own personally constructed beliefs. Growing theologically means being willing to stretch our beliefs, but most of us would rather maintain what we have because it makes us feel safe and secure. We don't want to go through the turmoil that comes when we are stretched to think about things we would rather not consider.

We also struggle to keep religion, theology, and spirituality in balance because not all of us are comfortable with religious participation, especially when the churches we attend seem so dead. We live in a time of individualization, and being part of a religious community can be difficult when we have a distrust of institutions and the people who inhabit them. It is so much easier to just go it alone than it is to share our spiritual journeys with others.

It can also be difficult to keep the three in balance if we don't feel much of a spiritual hunger. So many in today's world have a tremendous spiritual hunger, but there are those who don't. They just don't have much passion for God. They want to be with God when they die. They want God to care for them when they get in trouble, but they don't have much zeal for God in daily life. In fact, many would like God to leave them alone unless they get into trouble, at which point they desperately beg for God's attention. These people tend to either push religion, theology, and spirituality away, or remain happy with religious participation that entails little thought or passion.

How do we walk this narrow path in the midst of these problems? I think the answer is to go back to the lives of the mystics—to those people who walked this narrow path and managed to integrate theology, religion, and spirituality. What lessons can we learn from them?

While there are many things that we can learn from the mystics regarding how to walk the integrated path—the path that integrates religion, theology, and spirituality—there are several things that are most prominent.

1. *Grounding life in prayer and devotion to God*: If nothing else, the mystics of Christian faith have always grounded their lives in prayer and devotion to God. Their spiritual relationship with God has always come before religious participation and theological understanding. Everything emanates from the love of God above all else. The mystic Thomas à Kempis was a Roman Catholic priest and monastic who lived during the late fourteenth and early fifteenth centuries. His classic book, *The Imitation of Christ*, has influenced a

tremendous number of Christians throughout the centuries, including me. His faith and writings were clearly grounded in prayer and devotion to God, and he reminds us that this is *the* most important thing in the life of faith:

> What good does it do, then, to debate about the Trinity, if by lack of humility you are displeasing to the Trinity? In truth, lofty words do not make a person holy and just, but a virtuous life makes one dear to God. I would much rather feel profound sorrow for my sins than be able to define the theological term for it. If you knew the whole Bible by heart and the sayings of all the philosophers, what good would it all be without God's love and grace? Vanity of vanities and all is vanity, except to love God and serve only him. This is the highest wisdom: to see the world as it truly is, fallen and fleeting; to love the world not for its own sake, but for God's; and to direct all your effort toward achieving the kingdom of heaven.[4]

Thomas was very clear that everything begins with love of God. The problem is that we all too often begin with everything *but* a love of God. So many other things motivate us. For example, many are religiously motivated by the need to feel righteous, justified, and saved. True faith, though, lets go of worries about life after death—about whether or not we will make it into heaven—and focuses on loving God above all else in the present. Many Christians try to be perfect in their morality, but the true Christian just tries to love God and others, letting God take care of our souls and the judgment of our hearts. Many Christians try to figure everything out theologically, thinking that if they can just understand enough, they can figure out how to fit into God's kingdom. Unfortunately (or fortunately), the Christian life is not a matter of thinking the right things. For the mystics, it all comes down to the center of the gospel: "You shall love the Lord your God with all your heart, and with all your soul, and with all your strength, and with all your mind; and your neighbor as yourself" (Luke 10:27).

The key to falling in love with God lies in prayer. It is through prayer that we begin to form a personal relationship with God that leads to love. As we center ourselves in God through prayer, we find God at our center. When we pray for others, we begin to experience how God acts in their and our lives. When we offer our concerns and struggles to God in prayer, we discover how God loves us. Even during those times when God seems so distant in our prayer, our pursuit of God leads to a greater love. The more we pray, the more we fall in love with God.

The more we fall in love with God, the more our spirituality, theology, and religion flow out of that. Our theology becomes rooted in a theology of God's love. Our religion begins to serve God's love. Our spirituality breathes God's love. All begin to work together. This is the secret of the mystics. When we fall in love with God, everything else begins to come together, even if our spirituality is limited, our theology is flawed, and our religion is weak.

2. *Seeking answers to life's questions*: The mystics were seekers. They were questioners. Their lives were forged by their constant search for God and answers. This passionate seeking often emerged out of their personal frustrations, flaws, and failures in life. For example, Francis of Assisi was considered a failure by his family and friends. They considered him a dilettante and believed that his life would amount to nothing. He was a failure as a soldier and as a businessman in his father's business. He was aimless and self-indulgent. He was hardly the kind of person we would choose to inspire so many for centuries to come. In the midst of his failures, he had so many questions. During his military imprisonment, he began to ask some of these questions deep in his soul. Later, this desire to find answers led him to renounce wealth and the world, and to start a mission rebuilding churches and building community among the poor in the Italian countryside. He sought God and God's ways. He wanted to know the secret to living a life of love with God, and so he pursued it with a passion. In the process, he became a strong force for renewal in Christianity that still reverberates today.

Other mystics had similar paths. In chapter 6 we talked about George Müller and how his failure to find direction in his life led him to seek. His seeking led him on a quest to determine whether God really would care for us day to day. The answers he found led him to an incredible ministry on behalf of orphaned children in nineteenth-century England. Millard Fuller, who founded Habitat for Humanity, and whom we discussed in chapter 3, sought answers to the emptiness in his soul and his life. The erosion of his marriage led him to seek, and his seeking led him to found a tremendous organization on behalf of the poor worldwide.

So many of the great Christians and mystics of the past and present sought God with a passion after failing in their lives. The problem is that we become complacent in our lives, especially if we have failed or have been hurt. We have questions, but we don't seek. Instead, we settle for easy answers that can actually lead us away from God. Our failure to seek leads to a failure to find God. So, it becomes much easier for our spirituality, theology, and religion to become disconnected from one another.

How do we seek? We seek simply by asking God to show us God's way. We don't have to become a monk or a minister to do this. We can seek no matter what our life condition is. We seek by reading, we seek by joining with others in community, we seek by praying, we seek by worshiping, we seek by serving, and we seek simply by asking God to lead us to God's truth. This has been my experience over and over throughout the years. I remember praying to God to lead me to God's truth twenty-five years ago when I was in college. Interestingly enough, God didn't lead me right away to the church. That came five years later. God led me to study the human sciences, psychology, and Eastern philosophies. It was after discovering God's voice in them that God led me into the Christian realm. In an age when so many Christians try to proclaim God's voice in Scripture but not in anything else, I have found so many answers to my own questions through Christian Scripture and worship, but also in literature, music, television, film, philosophy, theology, the insights of other faiths, the guidance of other people, and in my own heart. The more I have sought, the more I have found (Matt. 7:7).

3. *Making a commitment to serve God in all of life*: Again, the mystical life is not a life spent only in prayer and seeking. It is a life of service. The mystics all were grounded in love, and their love needed to be expressed in their service. Mother Teresa served the poor in Calcutta. George Müller served orphans in England. Francis of Assisi served the poor in Italy and around the Mediterranean. Brother Lawrence humbly served others in his community by working in the kitchen. Frank Laubach served by teaching reading to the poor in the Philippines.

The particular service is not as important as the actual act of serving. As Thomas à Kempis has said, "Without love good works are worthless, but with love they become wholly rewarding no matter how small and insignificant they may seem. Indeed, God places more importance on the reason you work than on how much work you actually do."[5] We make a mistake if we think that God cares most about what our work is. What matters is that we make a commitment to God to serve God throughout our lives, and that we follow through on this commitment. For example, I have made a commitment to serve God as a pastor, spiritual director, teacher, and writer, but no less than that is my commitment to serve God as a father, husband, and friend. It is not the ordination that makes a difference in my service, for being a father, husband, and friend is no less important in God's eyes. It is also not the quality of what I do that matters. There are many ways that I am probably a failure as a father, husband, friend, pastor, spiritual director, teacher, and writer, but what matters is that I commit what I do to God. The same is true for anyone. Whatever we do can be turned into service to God. Our careers, hobbies, play, and so much more can all serve God if we are willing to commit our lives and our service to God. If we can't see how what we are doing can serve God, then perhaps we should ask if we need to change what we are doing.

The key is making a commitment to God. This commitment to God opens our lives up to God. It brings everything together in a holy integration. The problem is that our self-will does not want to make this commitment. This leaves us paralyzed. We cannot find God because we cannot commit. We cannot commit because we have not found God. To bring everything into harmony we have to find a way to commit in surrender to God. Heinrich Arnold, who was a member of the Bruderhof movement (a latter-twentieth-century movement in the Anabaptist tradition that seeks to live in radical community), speaks eloquently of this commitment. He says,

> We have to give ourselves wholeheartedly to God, and if we fail, we must give ourselves again. We all need daily forgiveness for our sins and failures. But what matters is whether we want to be faithful—faithful to the end of our lives. This means surrendering everything—our self-will, our hopes for personal happiness, our private property, even our weaknesses—and believing in God and in Christ. That is all that is asked of anyone. Jesus does not expect perfection, but he wants us to give ourselves wholeheartedly.[6]

This commitment brings integration because it leads to our becoming spiritually alive, to a desire to live in religious community while rooting ourselves in the Christian traditions, and to ground ourselves more and more in a theology of love. Our commitment kindles a passion for God, and this leads us to always purify and perfect our service through prayer, worship, community, and study.

4. *Grounding our devotion, seeking, and service in community*: The thing that is clear about the Christian life is that it is a communal life. This is a stumbling block for many in modern North American and European culture. All of our social and cultural philosophies since the Age of Enlightenment of the eighteenth century have emphasized the individual. It is this great emphasis on the individual that led to the incredible insights and freedoms expressed in the American Declaration of Independence and the pursuant constitution. Until the eighteenth century, the rights of the individual were never taken all that seriously, unless you were a wealthy individual.

The problem is that this great emphasis on the individual in the midst of the communal has become a problem. Today, we all are individuals. We don't really know how to live in community all that well. Twenty-first-century film, music, literature, art, and the like constantly bombard us with messages about the need to be an individual. We are constantly told that we have to express ourselves and be ourselves. As a result, we don't respect or love one another all that much. There never was a golden age of perfect, loving community, but prior to the eighteenth century the bonds of towns, neighborhoods, and families tended to be much stronger (sometimes to a fault).

The Christian life is a communal life. While there is an individual component to it, the Christian life is a life spent with others. The problem is that this
community we are called into is a strange community. It is a community of
rejected and wounded people who tend to other wounded and rejected people
out of our own rejection and wounds. The great teaching about this comes in
the parable of the Good Samaritan (Luke 10:29–37). Jesus offers this parable
as an answer to the question, "And who is my neighbor?" Unfortunately, when
we read this well-known parable, we don't really hear it with the freshness
and power with which Jesus' followers heard it. Jesus tells us that a man lies
injured on the side of the road from Jerusalem to Jericho. A priest and a Levite
leave him and pass him by. It is only the Samaritan who stops to help him,
tend his wounds, and care for him.

When we hear this story, we tend to think "Priest—bad! Levite—bad!
Samaritan—good!" This is not how the original listeners heard it. They would
have heard "Priest—good! Levite—good! Samaritan—bad!" The priest and
the Levite were righteous people. To touch a possibly dead body would have
kept them from serving in their Temple duties for seven days. They would not
have been able to serve God. They were righteous people, and serving in the
Temple was a crucial ministry. So, they pass, believing that service in the Temple is more important than the man lying on the side of the road. The Samaritan, though, is a rejected man. The Samaritans were not Jews, but they
worshiped the Jewish God. They had their own rituals and temple. The Jews
of Jerusalem considered them to be heretics. They were rejected people. For
a rejected person to be the one who cared for the dying man was an incredible concept. Not only did he care for the man by pouring wine (a disinfectant)
and oil (a salve) into his wounds, and then bandaging them, he also took the
man to an inn and paid for his care. This placed the Samaritan in a precarious
position. He could have easily been accused of hurting this man, and of caring for him only to cover up his crime. Who would believe a Samaritan? This
rejected man was the only one who had compassion enough to realize that caring for this man—this child of God—was more important than anything else,
even service in God's temple.

Jesus' point is that the rejected are called by God to care for the rejected.
This is the foundation of Christian community. It is not when we are morally
righteous that we love and become part of God's community. It is when we
are rejected and wounded, for out of our rejection and woundedness we discover how to love with God's love. This is one of the most important points
about the mystics. Because they walked the narrow path, they were rejected
and wounded. For example, John of the Cross—whose great works written
five hundred years ago, *The Ascent of Mount Carmel* and *The Dark Night*, still

inspire many today—understood this rejection. He lived during the late 1500s in Spain, and his ideas were often met with hostility. Because of his beliefs, he was imprisoned unjustly several times over the course of two years—years where he suffered greatly. His rejection, imprisonment, and suffering led to his incredible insights and writings. When he emerged from his imprisonment, he became a leader in reforming the Carmelite order and reorienting it toward a deeper love of God.

As long as we try to remain strong and perfect, we walk the broken path. Nothing becomes integrated. True community comes when we allow ourselves to be weak and to care for others who are also weak. So many people in the past have said that religion is a crutch, and they are right. It is a crutch for those who are weak, flawed, hurt, and broken, and it helps us to heal. Religion, theology, and spirituality all help us to heal at our deepest levels. The problem is that all of us in life are wounded, hurt, and broken. No one escapes the hurts of life. There are those who pretend they are strong, trying mightily to do everything by themselves, but the ones who truly walk God's paths are those who recognize their weakness and join with others to devote themselves to God, seek God with a passion, and serve God together.

Walking the Path of Faithful Integration

The truth is that there is no path of perfect integration. There is only the path of faithful integration, and it will always be an uneven path. None of us has the ability or time to spend all of our lives in prayer, to spend all of our time in religious pursuits, and to know all there is to know theologically. This is not the point of walking this path. What, then, is the point?

The point of walking the integrated path is to live our lives in a way that is more balanced. It is meant to be a path in which we form a spiritual passion for God that flows into every part of our lives. It is meant to be a path in which we discover God's purpose, presence, and power through the service, sacraments, rituals, teachings, and traditions of religion. It is meant to be a path in which we ground ourselves in Christian teachings that keep us God-focused, not self-focused. We cannot be perfect in this integration, only increasingly better.

What really matters is that we try our best to bring all of these elements together in our lives so that they flow through every part of our lives. When we are theologically, religiously, and spiritually integrated, we find that all of our lives become a prayer; that everything we do in love becomes both religious service and sacrament; and that everything we do becomes naturally grounded in Christian theology—a theology of love. No one can teach us how to walk on the path; others can only point out when we have become unbalanced and stepped off the path.

Questions for Reflection

1. To which aspect of faith do you feel the most attracted: theology, religion, or spirituality? Why?
2. How well do you think you integrate theology, religion, and spirituality in your faith?
3. How has Christian theology guided you in your faith?
4. How has your participation in the Christian religion deepened your life?
5. How has the Christian spiritual tradition deepened your relationship with God?
6. How can you balance theology, religion, and spirituality more as you walk your narrow path?

Key Learnings

- The narrow path is one that integrates and maintains a balance between theological thinking, religious practice, and spiritual experience.
- The failure to maintain an integrating balance between theology, religion, and spirituality has led to the splitting of Christianity into a variety of different denominations and movements.
- Without the backbone of theology, religion and spirituality become formless and self-focused activities.
- Without the substance of religion, theology and spirituality are reduced to dry, brittle, intellectual, and/or self-indulgent concepts, ideas, and speculations.
- Without the breath of spirituality, theology and religion become lifeless activities and dead teachings.
- We integrate theology, religion, and spirituality when we steep our lives in prayer, seek answers to life's questions, make a commitment to serve God in all of life, and ground ourselves in community.

Chapter 8

Standing at the Narrow Crossroads

*F*or a while as a child, I was fascinated with the explorations of Meriwether Lewis and William Clark. Lewis and Clark were sent by President Thomas Jefferson to explore the Northwest of what would become the United States. At that time, the Northwest was a wild territory, unexplored by the European settlers and early colonists. It was filled with wonders seen by none but a few Native Americans. No one had ever charted the territory for others to follow.

Can you imagine what it must have been like for Lewis, Clark, and their entourage to set out on this journey? They didn't know what lay ahead, and so it was hard to prepare. How much food should they take? How many muskets and how much ammunition? What should they take to trade with the Native Americans they met along the way? How would they know whether they were traveling in the right direction? They believed they would eventually reach the Pacific Ocean, but what if they got lost? How would they find the right direction?

Lewis and Clark boldly set out, but in the process they had to summon all of their skills to follow the right path and hope for a bit of luck. They had to decide who should guide them and who shouldn't. They were fortunate to find Sacagawea, a Native American woman who guided them along the way. They followed in trust, but she could have just as easily led them to ruin. You can imagine that along the way they faced quite a few crossroads that determined whether or not they should keep going.

In many ways, each of us is like Lewis and Clark on our own unexplored journeys of life. We are like explorers, searching for the paths that God has set before us, desperately looking for signs of God along the way. We search for God's footprints, a broken branch suggesting that God had walked this way, or a marker left by God to reveal the way. Our journeys are further complicated by the fact that along the way we come across so many people who point us in one direction, zealously assuring us that it is God's way. Then we meet other sincere and zealous people who contradict them, saying that God's path lies in the other direction. It is very similar to Dorothy in *The Wizard of Oz*, when the Scarecrow gives her directions to the Emerald City. He tells her that she can go this way or that way, and that some people go both ways. Which way is it?

The experience of facing competing paths confuses most of us as we try to walk God's narrow path. We constantly come to spiritual, theological, and religious crossroads that paralyze us as we struggle to determine which way is the "right" way. I experienced this intensely when I was studying for my doctorate in spiritual formation. I was determined to learn all I could about the "right" spiritual path. As I began to read and study the different spiritual masters, I became more and more downhearted. Each one seemed to point in a different direction, and the direction they pointed toward often seemed to be at odds with those of others. It wasn't just the fact that they came from different denominational traditions. They were often at odds with those even in their own traditions. The struggle for me was that what they said was so radical.

For instance, among the first classic spiritual writings I read were those of Julian of Norwich. I was ready to learn from her the secrets of becoming a "spiritual" person. I was convinced that by reading Julian's work I would finally find the "right" path. Julian of Norwich, whom we discussed in chapter 2, was a fourteenth-century Benedictine nun. She lived in England during a time of intense poverty and disease in Europe. She sensed that the suffering all around her had spiritual significance, and so she sought to discover Christ in her own suffering. In prayer, she asked God for three things: to experience Christ's passion on the cross; to receive some sort of bodily sickness; and to receive three wounds of the soul. Halfway through her thirtieth year, God answered her prayers. She became deathly ill and lay in bed for three days and nights.[1] As she edged closer to the point of death, she had a transforming vision of Christ suffering on the cross. She experienced her suffering as Jesus' suffering. She experienced a sort of mystical union with Christ in her own suffering.

I became more dejected as I read of her experiences. "If I have to get deathly ill to become spiritual, forget it!" I thought. "I can't believe that the path to God means I have to be on the verge of death." This was only the beginning of my frustrations with reading the great spiritual masters of Christianity. My frustrations continued to mount as I delved deeper.

I then read the works of Thomas Merton, especially his autobiography, *The Seven Storey Mountain,* and his classic *New Seeds of Contemplation.* At the time, I didn't understand much of what I was reading in *New Seeds of Contemplation* because I had not had much experience in the contemplative tradition. What I did understand confused me, because it suggested that the way to God required sitting in countless hours of silent, agenda-less prayer. I became discouraged: "If I have to become a celibate monastic to become spiritual, I don't think I'll ever get there."

The struggle to find the "right" path continued as I studied more spiritual masters and mystics. Eberhard Arnold, a spiritual master in the Anabaptist tradition, spoke clearly of the need to live together in community and to struggle against the world's injustices. His spirituality was very activist, rational, and theological. Again, I read his works and wondered whether I had to live in a Bruderhof community—a religious commune—and learn the Bible by heart, all the while protesting war in order to become "spiritual."

Later, I read Catherine Marshall's *Beyond Ourselves*. She was a charismatic Presbyterian who was very focused on following Christ and becoming open to the Holy Spirit in day-to-day life. Her approach was to simply allow ourselves to become open to the Holy Spirit at our foundations, and to allow the Spirit to transform us. My thought was, "So, do I have to become evangelical and charismatic to become 'spiritual?'" Each path I encountered seemed so different from the other paths. How could they all be right?

In the meantime, my own personal prayer discipline involved using a prayer book. The book offered a very structured way of praying. Each time of prayer began with reading a written prayer, followed by a Scripture reading for the day; a passage to be read and reflected on from a great work of Christian spiritual writing; a time of praying for the world, the church, others, and myself; and finally the words to a hymn. The whole process took about thirty to forty-five minutes. It was of great help to me for several years because it deepened me spiritually, but recently I had begun to chafe. I started to hate the sight of that book. Why was I having such a hard time with it? I talked about my struggles with people of prayer whom I respected, and they just said that I was going through a period of dryness and to stick with it. "What if I have to stay in this period of dryness for the rest of my life to become spiritual?" I thought. The book was doing nothing but frustrating me. How could I keep using it?

Eventually, I was given a great gift—a gift that helped me integrate all of these different paths. I told my spiritual director, whom I had been seeing for only a few months, about my struggle. With a puzzled look, she said, "Then why do you keep using the book?" "Because I'm supposed to," I replied. "Why? Who said you have to use that book?" "Well," I said, "isn't that the way it is? Aren't I supposed to follow a discipline?" "Yes, but why that particular one?" "I don't know. I suppose it's because I'm Presbyterian, and we're supposed to follow an order for everything."

She then calmly said to me, "Maybe your dryness is simply God calling you to explore a different form of prayer. Maybe God is inviting you to pray in a new and different way." As she said this, the sun's rays suddenly poured through the window onto her. It was as if God was giving a sign of approval to what she had said. I told her this, and she said, "This is one of the ways God smiles upon us. Don't take it as a coincidence; take it as God's speaking to you and inviting you to try another way of prayer."

Her gift to me was in helping me to see that there is no one "right" path of prayer or approach to God. This is not the same as saying that all paths are equal. Instead, it is a simple recognition that God doesn't call each of us to just one path. At different times in our lives, God calls on us to explore different Christian paths that lead to the same destination: God. Julian of Norwich's experience was a valid experience, and a potential pathway for us, but there are others. Thomas Merton's monastic path is a valid one for those called to it, but there are others. Eberhard Arnold's path is a path we need to explore and consider, and make part of our own, but there are others. Catherine Marshall's path is a path filled with the power of the Holy Spirit, but there are others. The point is not to find the perfect or right path, but to integrate elements from each of these pathways into our own so that we gain a greater depth of insight and experience than we could find on any one path. Unfortunately, we can get so caught up in finding the "right" path that we miss many right paths, and especially the right path *for us*.

Groping for the "Right" Path

One of the fastest ways to grow a church, denomination, or religion is to make it so exclusive and selective that only the people who are part of the church, denomination, or religion can be considered "saved" or on the right path. This is a secret that cult leaders inherently understand. It is hard for people outside a cult to understand a cult's power, but seen from the inside it is easy to appreciate. Cults, and specifically cult leaders, are extremely effective at setting up an opposition between the cult and the surrounding culture—at creating an "us versus them" situation. Whether we are talking about David Koresh, Jim Jones, the Rev. Sun Myung Moon, the Church of Scientology, Hare Krishnas, EST, or the Forum, we are talking about people and groups who attract others because what they offer is presented as the *only* way to happiness, bliss, and salvation. They offer their answers and solutions as God's only way for those mired in darkness and depression. They offer a panacea for people suffering with fragile and fragmented egos.

The drive of the ego to feel safe and secure is a powerful thing. We all go through life feeling insecure and fearful about the world around us. The world is dangerous. Threats abound. We can lose our jobs, health, marriages, families, memories, minds, and so many other things. For the most part it is never a question of *whether* we will lose these things over the course of our lives, but *when* we will lose them.

Our faith and religion are among the things that make us feel safe and secure. From a healthy spiritual perspective, faith and religion lead us to place our trust in God. They show us how to let God take care of our fears. This can be hard on our egos. Our egos want us to have control over our lives, not give them up to God. There are times when life seems so tenuous and tumultuous that we become desperate for signs that God can be trusted, that God can save us. Our egos, feeling powerless, look for ways to regain control. They look for anything that can restore a sense of control and rightness. This is what cults do. They create a system of belief that says we are saved and safe, and that others will perish—especially those who have hurt us. Cults make their members feel that they are doing something that will insulate them from the world's dangers, even while, ironically, cults actually expose them to mental, emotional, financial, and sexual dangers that are greater than those they faced outside the cult.

The same drive of the ego affects healthy religions, too. There is a need among most religious faiths, and especially among certain sects, to declare that their path is the true path. So many denominations and sects assert that they have the key to salvation. It begins with their assertion that "Christ is the only way," but it extends beyond that. While many, or even most, Christians believe that Christ is the only way, there are those who take this many steps further. They assert that while Christ is the only way, it is actually only their own practice of faith that they say leads to the "Christ who is the only way." They identify the path to discovering Christ as beginning and ending with their own practice: "Jesus is the only way, and we are the only way to Jesus." I would love to say that they are totally wrong, but there actually is some truth to their assertions. They may have found a particular path that is a true path to God, but the problem is that their path is not a complete path.

I have a theory about the problems that strike different denominations. Why is it that we all argue about our own approaches? Why do we assert the validity of our own, while denigrating those of others? One reason is that in many ways each approach devotes itself to a particular revelation from God. It is as though these particular Christians have found many interlocking pieces of a great spiritual and divine puzzle, and they are ecstatic about the picture revealed by their composite of puzzle pieces. The problem is that they do not own all the other pieces, yet they don't necessarily know that they do not have the other pieces. They own a large chunk of the puzzle, and perhaps a variety of unconnected pieces. So, they try to reconstruct the rest of the puzzle of God by generalizing what they have gleaned from their own pieces. It is like an archaeologist trying to reconstruct the Egyptian language from fragments of ancient hieroglyphics. They may be able to get part of the language, but they have to guess at the rest. It is an educated and well-reasoned guess, but a guess nonetheless. They don't have a Rosetta stone leading them to discover God's full truth, but they believe they do.

Each religious, theological, and spiritual approach to God reveals part of the mysterious puzzle of God. The problem is that we have such a hard time coming together to discern the whole puzzle. We don't know which parts of our puzzles are the original pieces and which are the reconstructed ones. So, we argue about whose puzzle is right and whose is wrong. There are Anglican pieces, Roman Catholic pieces, Methodist pieces, Lutheran pieces, Presbyterian pieces, evangelical pieces, pentecostal pieces, contemplative pieces, mainstream pieces, and a myriad of other pieces that have all been incorporated in their own systems. Our egos and the need to feel safe keep us from truly breaking apart our own reconstructed pictures in order to recapture the originally revealed pieces of God's puzzle that all of us have discovered.

I am not suggesting that we should scrap our denominations, our theologies, our traditions, or our spiritual approaches. In fact, I am suggesting the complete opposite. Discovering God's mysterious picture comes through maintaining our traditions, yet exposing them in the light of other traditions. On an individual level, it comes from our willingness to immerse ourselves in our denomination's spiritual practices, while simultaneously learning from others. Discovering God's path for us comes only when we are willing to grapple with the truth of our own traditions, while using the light of other traditions to reveal where our own is incomplete.

Coming to the Narrow Crossroads

Whenever we walk the narrow path, there is a point at which we will come to a crossroads where different perspectives and practices intersect. At this point, we become paralyzed because we don't know which way to go. Earlier I mentioned a scene from the film *The Wizard of Oz* in which Dorothy, embarking on her trip to the Emerald City, comes to a similar crossroads. She had not been told by the Munchkins that the Yellow Brick Road would require a choice. She hoped that she could simply follow it through to her destination. Wondering what to do, she says out loud, "Well, now which way do we go?" The Scarecrow, who is on a pole in the middle of a nearby cornfield, points to the right and says, "Pardon me. That way is a very nice way." Startled, Dorothy says, "Who said that?" The Scarecrow points to the left and says, "It's pleasant down that way, too." Finally, he crosses his arms, pointing both ways, and says, "Of course, people do go both ways!"[2] Dorothy is left in a conundrum. Which way should she go?

What Dorothy doesn't realize is that what her choice is doesn't matter so much as the fact that she *makes* a choice. Whichever way she chooses, it will lead to the Emerald City. Each road has different companions, dangers, and adventures. What really matters is simply that she chooses. With the Scarecrow in tow, she chooses, and her choice sends her on the path to psychological and spiritual growth as she confronts her fears, dreams, dangers, opportunities, and the deep lessons of life.

Many of us come to similar crossroads as we seek God, and when we do, we get paralyzed: "Which way is the right way to God? What happens if I go this way? What happens if I go that way?" The problem isn't what to choose. The problem is making a commitment. We spiritual people often don't want to make a commitment. This is true whether we are talking about making a commitment to a church, a denomination, a tradition, a spiritual practice, or a theological belief. We don't want to commit ourselves.

At the same time, there is a parallel problem. We can become so tied to a particular path—a particular church, denomination, tradition, spiritual practice, or theological belief—that we refuse to be open to the possibility that God can be revealed to us in other ways, too. The fact is that within certain parameters there are different approaches to God, and all have equal validity. Each has strengths and weaknesses. Not *all* approaches to God are valid, just as all roads don't lead to the Emerald City, but within a certain range exists a variety of approaches that are equally valid. The problem is that either we don't want to make a commitment to exploring one path or the other, or we refuse to explore the possibilities of those that lie beyond our chosen path. On the one hand, we need to choose our own paths and make a commitment to them, for they lead us to a deeper faith and spiritual life. On the other hand, we have to be willing to explore other paths, too, for they infinitely broaden our spiritual lives. Exploring other paths helps us to discover other ways of knowing and experiencing God that don't come through the experiences found only on one path.

In effect, we have to be willing to make a commitment to a particular path, but also be willing to explore other paths. When we augment our own path with the insights, practices, and traditions of others, we end up forming a more balanced spiritual life as well as discovering God in more depth. The struggle is keeping the different paths in tension.

Choosing at the Crossroads

When we talk about the spiritual life, there are four basic ways Christians *seek God*. We Christians tend to see them as being in opposition to one another, especially if we are committed to one of them, but in reality they complement one another. The four different ways of seeking God intersect to form four general spiritual approaches or paths we walk to discover God in our lives. The four basic ways of seeking God are seeking God through our *intellect*, seeking God through our *senses*, seeking the *immanent* God embodied in the world, and seeking the *transcendent* God who transcends the world.[3] These four ways of seeking God reflect our personalities, interests, and upbringing. Are we more intellectual in our approach, or do we seek confirmation of God's presence through our emotions and passions—through our senses? Do we seek the immanent God embodied in Scripture, others, ourselves, nature, art, film, literature, and the like, or do we believe that we can discover God more authentically by emptying ourselves of passion, intellect, and agendas?

Each way of seeking God has its own strengths and weaknesses. While each one connects us to God in one way, each one also inhibits our discovery of God in other ways. For instance, there are some Christians whose spirituality is so grounded in Scripture that they cannot discern and appreciate God who transcends Scripture. Some Christians want to feel God so much in their senses and passions that they do not see the value of pursuing God through rational, intellectual reflection. Most Western Christians are so tied to seeking the immanent God who is incarnated and embodied in the stuff of life and creation—of the world—that they have no appreciation for the need to become empty and purged of all intellect, senses, and even belief to discover the transcendent God who lies beyond our perceptions.

Each way of seeking God has the ability both to free and to imprison us, depending on how attached to them we are in our devotion and practice. All of us lie somewhere along a continuum between the different poles. In addition, the two poles intersect and complement one another to form basic approaches or paths to God—to form basic ways through which we try to serve and experience God. Our chosen path to God will determine the extent to which we believe a particular way of practicing our faith is genuine or not. For instance, is reading Scripture intellectually and rationally the only way we can experience God? Can we experience God by sitting in silence while letting go of all thought and emotion? Our approach to God determines what our answers will be.

In the following discussion, we will examine how the four different ways of *seeking God* intersect to form four basic *paths to God*. While each of us has our own way of approaching God, and we each try to walk our own particular path no matter what denomination we belong to, for discussion purposes it is easier to discuss them as denominational paths. It is important, though, to understand that just because we are a part of a particular denomination does not mean that we can only walk the path that is typical of our denomination. Also, it does not mean that each denomination exclusively seeks and approaches God in one particular way. Instead, this is a discussion of the basic and general ways people and denominations seek to walk on their journey to God. Figure 6 contains a diagram of these paths.

Each of us tends to seek God in one of four ways: (1) seeking the immanent God through our intellect—*the mindful path*, (2) seeking the immanent God through our senses—*the passionate path*, (3) seeking the transcendent

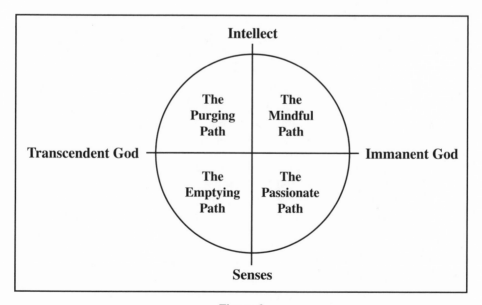

Figure 6

God by letting go of our senses—*the emptying path*, or (4) seeking the transcendent God by letting go of intellect—*the purging path*.

Walking the Mindful Path

What does it mean to seek the immanent God embodied in the world? It means to seek God as God is revealed in and through the people, things, and events of the world. It seeks God as God is experienced and known through things like Scripture, music, art, nature, our imaginations, others, and our own hearts. To say that we seek God with our intellects simply points out that many of us are most comfortable seeking and experiencing God primarily by thinking about God. We don't seek a tangible experience of God as much as we seek insights about God, the world, and our role in it. We want to understand, know, and see in our minds who and what God is, and what God is doing. It frustrates us when we can't figure God out, and we get such spiritual highs from insights that help us understand God—from those "Aha!" moments of clarity and understanding that come through intellectual theological reflection. Intellectually seeking the immanent God as God is embodied in the world is walking the mindful path.

As a Presbyterian I have been steeped in a spiritual approach that cherishes the mindful path. The Presbyterian tradition is one that emphasizes the search for God through rational, theological reflection on life and especially Scripture. In fact, Presbyterians are suspicious of spiritual experiences that don't have a rational, scriptural explanation. The Presbyterian Church, being part of the Reformed tradition (along with denominations such as the United Church of Christ, Disciples of Christ, and the Reformed Church), is rooted in the Swiss reform movement of the sixteenth century. It is especially rooted in the writings of John Calvin. By looking at Calvin's spiritual approach, we can see how it is still reflected in modern Presbyterianism and the Reformed movement. Calvin was very much a thinker who rooted everything in understanding and knowing Scripture. For instance, Calvin says that

> If true religion is to shine on us we must grasp the necessity of beginning with teaching from above and that it is impossible for anyone to gain an atom of sound doctrine without being a disciple of Scripture. We take the first step towards true knowledge when we reverently take hold of the testimony God has graciously given about himself.[4]

The key words in listening to Calvin are "Scripture" and "knowledge." For Calvin, spiritual growth comes mainly from knowing Scripture.

Following Calvin's guidance, we Presbyterians are very intellect- and Scripture-oriented. We are taught to seek God mostly with our intellects, and we do it mostly by reading and studying Scripture. This doesn't mean that all members of the Presbyterian Church do this. In fact, they don't, which is a constant source of angst among Presbyterian pastors and teachers. We complain that our folks are biblically illiterate and do not think theologically enough. We place a strong emphasis on theology, which can be considered an intellectual reflection on Scripture. Most of our arguments as Presbyterians center around the need to determine who has the proper theological position and scriptural interpretation.

We Presbyterians are not alone in our intellectual/scriptural/theological approach. We are joined by Baptists and Methodists. While those in the Southern Baptist tradition, which is much more conservative and fundamentalist, may seem to be miles away from Presbyterians, Methodists, Disciples of Christ, and other Christians from the Reformed tradition, they still seek God by attempting to cognitively know and learn Scripture. The result is that they emphasize coming to know God through proper doctrine and orthodox teaching, the point of which is to teach us how to read Scripture correctly in order to live correctly.

Methodists also tend to approach God through mental intellect and Scripture. John Wesley, the founder of the Methodist movement, was extremely scriptural in his approach. His "method" incorporated reason, Scripture, tradition, and experience, but his tradition was rooted in the scriptural emphasis of the sixteenth-century Protestant Reformation. For Wesley, experience could incorporate other ways of knowing God, but it still needed to be grounded in Scripture.

Not all Christians who seek God intellectually are so scriptural. Many Presbyterians, Baptists, Reformed, and Methodist Christians experience God in things other than Scripture. They seek and experience God in the created world through nature, art, literature, music, relationships, imagination, and their own hearts. While the theological and traditional emphasis may be on Scripture, on the experiential level many adherents of these traditions are also open to God as God is revealed throughout creation and the human world.

The inherent problem among those who are most committed to the mindful path is the problem of *rationalism*. In effect, as Christians become more rigid in seeking the immanent God embodied in the world, they can become convinced that God cannot be experienced beyond the mind. Everything about their faith must make rational, or at least systematic, sense. Thus, they emphasize the need for a systematic theology (which can be helpful, but can also be overly rigid and limiting), and/or they try to turn the Bible into a seamless document with no contradictions or possible flaws. In other words, they become biblical literalists. Ultimately, they chafe against the mystery of God by trying to create a more rigid, black-and-white spirituality and faith. The more rationalistic they become, the more they actually move away from encountering God. For instance, if they are biblical scholars, they may either reduce the Bible to a work of pure literature that they cannot accept as true because they consider it to be the writing of primitive people, or they literalistically exalt the Bible as a work of pure history that cannot be doubted or criticized, lest all of their theological beliefs come crumbling down. They cannot see the possibility of Scripture being both literature *and* history, while also transcending mere literature and history. They become trapped by their rational systems and approaches. When we become too rationalistic, we can even end up becoming agnostic or atheistic because we cannot accept the mystery of God.

Walking the Passionate Path

At the opposite end of the spectrum for those seeking the immanent God through their intellect lie those who seek the immanent God mainly through sensed experience—through their passions. They want to *feel* God deep in their souls. They want to be *stirred* by God's Spirit. They don't want a dispassionate spirituality. They want a spiritual experience of God that is tangible and real to their senses. The main group of Christians who approach God in this way tend to be Pentecostals and charismatics. What matters is whether they *feel* God's Spirit in their lives, not whether what they do, say, or think is intellectually and theologically correct. This does not mean that they don't care about theology and doctrine. They do, but theology and doctrine take a back seat to the need to *sense* God in the heart, mind, and body.

To see the difference between those seeking God through their senses and those seeking God through their intellect, all you have to do is participate in a pentecostal or charismatic worship service. Where Presbyterians, Methodists, and Baptists traditionally emphasize order in their services, Pentecostals and charismatics emphasize ardor. In many cases, there is little order to their services. They can last for hours, with people coming and going all the time. A sermon might be interrupted with someone cast to the ground as she or he speaks in tongues. Preaching is often very passionate and emotional. Rather than offering pure intellectual insight, the preacher may repeat himself or herself over and over again, with the focus on generating an emotional response from the congregation: "Amen! Yeah, Lord! You tell 'em! Praise the Lord! That's right!" A common question asked by a preacher might be, "Do you feeeeeel the Spirit in you? Do you feeeeeel Jesus touching your heart?" Healings, prophecies, speaking in tongues, swaying, praying with hands uplifted, crying, laughing, dancing, shouting, and the like are all hallmarks of worship that comes from walking the passionate path. Do all of these things in a Presbyterian, Baptist, or Methodist church, and you will get glares and stares from those who are determined that God can be experienced only through careful theological reflection and rational discourse. Conversely, if you tend to search for God from an intellectual perspective, you will struggle to understand those coming from a sensed perspective. Everything they do will come across as overly emotional, sentimental, and irrational. Meanwhile, Pentecostals and charismatics will look at you as dry, dull, lifeless, and uninspired by the Holy Spirit.

Still, Pentecostals and charismatics are very much advocates of seeking God in the world. They generally place Scripture at the center of their spiritual search. The main difference between them and those seeking the immanent God from an intellectual perspective is that their reading of Scripture will be much more devotional and emotional rather than rational and theological. While they may place Scripture at the center of their devotional life, they also will seek God through experiences that lead beyond Scripture. They want to experience God within themselves and others. They want to experience the Spirit at work in their actions, interactions, and prayers. They are very incarnational and embodied in their search for God. They want signs and miracles. The difference between them and more intellectual Christians is that they use more emotional, affective, tangible, and experiential criteria to validate their experience.

The inherent problem with this approach at its extreme is the problem of *pietism*. When Christians seek the immanent, embodied God in the world through their passions, emotions, and senses to an extreme degree, they can succumb to the lures of pietism. Pietism is the tendency to become *overly* personal and sentimental in our spiritual lives. All that matters is Sweet Jesus and me. If I feel something is of God, it must truly be of God because I feel it. This can lead to a very narcissistic and self-centered spirituality. While the passionate path is neither more nor less valid, at its extreme all that matters is what one feels. Whatever one feels and wants must be what Jesus feels and wants because Jesus is in one's heart and soul.

So, where do other Christians such as Anglicans, Lutherans, and Roman Catholics fit on this scale? For the most part, devotees of the Roman Catholic, Lutheran, and Anglican traditions tend to be somewhere between the two poles of seeking God through intellect and senses. Their approaches might be considered more of an intuitive approach (if you define intuition as the integration of intellect and senses) that straddles the mindful and passionate paths. In these denominations, the focus still tends to be on experiencing God in the world, but it is not necessarily as scripturally grounded. Of the three, the

Lutherans are probably the most aligned with the mindful path because of their emphasis on scriptural theology, but they also emphasize symbols and sacraments. Roman Catholics and Anglicans are even more focused on experiencing God in symbols and sacraments. This is why their churches are often filled with statues, art, stained glass, icons, and other symbols that express different experiences of God. For example, in their churches one might find crucifixes, stations of the cross, devotional candles, liturgical candles, colorful vestments and paraments, and artistic depictions of Jesus. In both denominations, the emphasis is on experiencing God both intellectually and via the senses through meditative reflection. In addition, the sacraments of weekly and daily Communion, along with bells and incense, are intended to help the worshiper experience God through taste, touch, sound, and smell.

Walking the Emptying Path

Most modern Western Christians have been predominantly formed in traditions that are oriented to seeking and discovering God as God is revealed in the stuff of the world. Most of us are raised to seek God as God is embodied in Scripture, nature, people, music, books, our own minds and hearts, and in some or all aspects of God's creation. This has not always been the case. There have been movements in Christianity that have sought not the immanent, embodied God, but the transcendent God.

Many Christians have felt limited by their experiences of God as God is revealed in the stuff of the universe. They have wanted to experience and discover the God who transcends this universe—to discover the God who lies beyond the sensed perceptions of sight, sound, smell, taste, and touch. This is God who cannot be rationally known, but is known by letting go of rational intellect. This is God who cannot be emotionally sensed, but is experienced by letting go of our attachment to sensing God in the world around us. This idea is foreign to most modern Christians because it means finding God by letting go, not taking on. Contemporary Western Christianity of the past five hundred years has tended to emphasize pursuing religious, theological, and spiritual knowledge, understanding, insight, and experience. It does not know what to do with practices and pursuits that emphasize letting go of knowledge, understanding, insight, and experience.

When it comes to those who seek the transcendent God from a sensed perspective, the closest most Christians come to this is those Christians who study Buddhist meditation. Buddhist meditation entails sitting in stillness to become open to the universe. This style of prayer and approach to God is similar to the Christian practice of *contemplative* prayer. Christian contemplation entails sitting in silent openness to the transcendent God. This practice is most associated with specific Roman Catholic orders such as the Cistercians (or Trappists), Carmelites, and other orders whose members take vows of silence and engage in a life of contemplative and other similar forms of prayer.

Contemplative prayer and openness are attempts to empty ourselves of all attachment to our senses, passions, and desires so that we can approach God in radical openness. We try to be open to God who is beyond everything. When we practice contemplative prayer, we try to let go of everything just to *be* with God—there is no agenda or desire, only openness. The world may swirl around us, but we let go of our attachment to it. We sense things, but we don't focus on these things. For instance, we may hear the clock tick, a car drive by, and the air-conditioning run, but we don't focus on those things. We may receive insights and think thoughts, but we let them pass by like clouds on a windy day. In many ways, it is like sitting in God's lap while letting go of all concern, intellect, or senses. The intent is stillness, which leads to a union with God. This union leads to our transformation as we begin to see the world through transcendent rather than worldly eyes.

This way of seeking God is sorely missing in our modern Christian life. Because we tend to seek the immanent God mainly through study, action, and experience, we rarely let ourselves be still and open enough to discover the God who lies beyond our ability to understand, sense, and experience. Engaging in contemplative stillness can bring a much-needed balance to lives lived in constant action and stimulation. It is for this reason that an increasing number of retreat centers and churches offer silent retreats and training in contemplative prayer. We Western Christians have explored God so much via the immanent, God-in-the-world road that we have failed to explore the lands discovered by traveling the transcendent, God-beyond-the-world road.

Of course, even those who do choose to seek the transcendent God, especially those who do so through a complete openness and letting go of their senses, can go overboard. The inherent problem at the extreme of this approach is something called *quietism*. This is not as much of a problem today as it was in the fifteenth through the seventeenth centuries. As the contemplative monastic movement began to grow, many monastics tried to live a life of prayer only. Quietism is the problem that occurs when people decide that it is enough simply to engage in a life of complete contemplation and reflection, without recognizing the need to be engaged in life. While we may be called to live lives of prayer, we are also called to live lives of engagement and action in the world. Probably the people most guilty of falling into the trap of quietism today are those engaged in transcendental meditation. While open meditation, the style taught in transcendental meditation, is not bad, the pursuit of a life spent in constant meditative prayer is misguided. Transcendental meditation emphasizes the release that comes through meditation, but not the responsibility to let meditation become a practice that prepares us to act in love and care in a ministry of compassion to the world.

For example, I remember watching an interview on a television talk show with a once-popular celebrity who talked about her experiences in transcendental meditation. She bragged that she had learned to meditate for ten hours a day. It is truly remarkable that she could do this, but the problem is that she had succumbed to the temptation of believing that hours spent in prayer were adequate in and of themselves. The problem with this and every other extreme form of seeking God is that it eventually turns the approach into a false idol. It ignores the need to be open to other forms of seeking and experiencing God, as well as serving God in the world. It becomes unbalanced, seeking an extreme that veers away from the narrow path. This is true of quietism, pietism, and rationalism. All tend to seek God in one exclusive way. Each approach to God is healthy as long is it maintains a sense of balance with an openness to other ways of seeking God.

Even among the most contemplative monastics, there is a recognition that contemplation must lead to action, even if that action is reduced to praying for the world. For many monastics, their action is limited to trying to build communities of love and faith that serve others through prayer, retreats, and other small but important ministries.

Walking the Purging Path

The purpose of walking the purging path is to become open to the transcendent God by purging ourselves and letting God purge us of ego, selfishness, and sinful intellect in order to be filled with God's thoughts and vision. Again, this is an approach that has not been very evident in modern Western Christianity. Probably the Christians most associated with this approach would be the Quakers. While they are a denomination that believes in intellectually reading and understanding Scripture, their main concern is with being open to the Holy Spirit through silence. This can be plainly seen through their style of worship. Especially in the form of Quaker worship practiced by Quakers in the Eastern United States, their worship does not include Scripture reading, preaching, singing, and oral communal praying. Instead, members sit in silence for an hour, waiting for the Spirit to inspire them to stand up and share their inspirations with others. There is no agenda other than being open to the voice of the Spirit. When a member feels so inspired, she or he stands and shares her or his inspiration.

Having visited Quaker meetings upon occasion, I have seen the power of this approach. While visiting a Quaker meeting north of Philadelphia on a cold February day, I experienced the power of the Spirit's fire to inspire an individual and a community through silence. The meetinghouse was old and furnished with worn wooden pews on a plain wooden floor. There were no symbols, pictures, or crosses, only bare walls. At the front of the meetinghouse was a paned window through which we could see the branches of a tree against a crystal blue sky. I sat with the community in silence, and on occasion someone would stand up and speak. I forgot most of what was said, except for the words of one woman. After about forty-five minutes, she stood up and said, "Looking out the window at the branches blowing in the wind reminds me of how the Holy Spirit works. We don't see the Spirit. All we see are the effects of the Spirit blowing in our lives." This gave me an appreciation of the Spirit I hadn't experienced before. It came about because she had let go of her intellect in order to be inspired by the Spirit.

Another way to walk the purging path is through confession and engaging in penitent rites. We focus on examining our hearts and ourselves in order to let God confess our sins and let God cleanse us. We become aware of how sinful our thoughts and hearts are, and so we consistently work to let go of our sins. This can include doing penance for our sins according to the guidance of a confessor. Ultimately, we are trying to purge ourselves of sin so that we can be clean and ready for God.

The inherent problem with the extreme of approaching the transcendent God by being purged arises when we become consumed with emptying ourselves of our sinful, limited, human thoughts. We become consumed with our own sinful intellects and how to rid ourselves of them so that we can dare to approach God. Most often, this obsession leads to something called *encratism*, an extreme pursuit of God through suffering. The idea that suffering is redemptive has been a part of Christian belief since the beginning, but some have taken it to an extreme so that they try to suffer in order to redeem themselves, purge themselves of sinful thoughts and impulses, and make themselves worthy of God. For example, they may kneel on uncooked rice while praying. They may wear rough clothing made of burlap, or wear a nail-studded cincture around their waists. During the bubonic plagues of the Middle Ages, it was not uncommon for groups of monastic flagellants to wander from town to town whipping and beating themselves along the way. They believed that the plagues were God's punishment for their sinful lives, and that by suffering and purging themselves of sinful intellect and action they could redeem a fallen humanity.

Few North American Christians fall into the trap of encratism today because we are so materialistic and seek our answers through acquisition of knowledge and experience. Still, the encratic approach remains a distinct problem whenever economic downturns, poverty, calamities, and/or disease afflicts a society, causing people to think that these are God's punishment for their sins.

Battles at the Crossroads

Why is it that we keep ending up with more and more denominations and sects, each pursuing and seeking God in different ways? Why can't we find one way to worship and follow God and finally bring all Christians together? The answer is that it is so difficult to be completely balanced in our spiritual lives. How do we seek God with our intellects and our senses at the same time? How do we seek the immanent God and the transcendent God at the same time? Perhaps only one person was ever able to do this completely, and that was Jesus. Even his followers struggled with this, and as the years have progressed, so have the divisions among Christians as we have tried over and over again to determine which is the "right" path.

Integration of the different approaches is difficult for individuals, but it is especially difficult for denominations and sects because they have a tremendous investment in their particular approaches and perspectives. To overcome differences means rethinking and rewriting creeds, forming new theological and spiritual perspectives, and probably struggling through a period of intense uncertainty about the validity of their tradition. In fact, each particular denominational approach was created in response and reaction to the overemphasis of the original denomination to another particular approach.

For instance, one reason the original reformers such as Martin Luther, John Calvin, Menno Simons, and Ulrich Zwingli emphasized intellectually knowing and understanding Scripture was the refusal of the Roman Catholic Church at the time to allow laity to read and understand Scripture. For centuries leading up to the fifteenth and sixteenth centuries, the Roman Catholic spiritual emphasis had been on the sacraments and worship. All that mattered was that one participated in the sacraments (which often meant clergy participating in the sacraments, since laity usually were not invited to participate). The emphasis was on seeking God through the senses, but the reformers wanted to seek God with their intellects, too.

The creation of the Reformed, Lutheran, Anabaptist, and Anglican denominations were all reactions to the Roman Catholic refusal to allow an intellectual exploration of the immanent God. Later, the Baptist, Methodist, and Quaker movements were reactions against the Protestant refusals to allow for people to seek God through other means. The evangelical awakenings of the eighteenth, nineteenth, and twentieth centuries were reactions against the established churches' refusal to allow for a more sensed experience of God that was rooted in Scripture. Even later, the pentecostal movement was also a reaction against the established evangelical and fundamentalist refusal to allow for a more passionate experience of God. Each denomination and movement always seems to arise in response to and reaction against the refusal of a more dominant movement to allow for their approach and way of seeking God.

If you look at each particular denomination and sect of Christianity, you will discover that their guiding principles are always in stark contrast to another denomination or sect. The answer to why there are so many different denominations, sects, and churches is that each corresponds to a different way of seeking and approaching God.

The Roman Catholic Church has had a different way of dealing with the need for individuals to seek and explore God in a variety of ways. With the exception of the Reformation, when members left the Roman Catholic Church to begin their own movements and denominations, Roman Catholicism has always created room for those called to different ways of seeking and exploring God. In effect, they have always created societies or orders that allow for an alternative exploration.

For example, Francis of Assisi wanted to seek the immanent God from a more sensed perspective by living in nature and experiencing the immanent God through nature. The Franciscan order was created to allow for this. Ignatius of Loyola wanted to seek the immanent God embodied in our own hearts and minds in a more intellectual way (in a way similar to many of his contemporary Protestants, although I doubt he would have ever have admitted that), and so the Society of Jesus was created. The Cistercians wanted to experience the transcendent God through contemplative prayer, and so the Cistercian order was created. There are many people in the Roman Catholic Church who want to experience the immanent God from a more tangible, sensed perspective. So the Roman Catholic Church allows for charismatic expression in its worship, along with allowing for healing and praise Masses.

Which way is better, the Protestant or Roman Catholic? It all depends on your perspective. The Protestant way of splitting from the dominant denomination allows for a more intense experience, as those committed to a particular approach band together to form a new denomination based on their approach. The problem is that they lose a sense of unity with other Christians as they succumb to the temptation to be competitive with other Christians. Selfish and narcissistic motives can easily slip into their approach, leading them away from God and into their own ego-dominated realms.

Roman Catholics are much better at maintaining unity, but the price is individual experience. While those adhering to a particular Roman Catholic order, society, or movement have intense experiences, they are limited in their freedom to truly test the limits of their approach. They are limited in their ability to discover how deeply they can experience God from any one particular approach. For instance, no matter how intellectual their approach is, they must maintain fidelity to Roman Catholic orthodoxy or risk censure. No matter how much they may want to explore God through charismatic expressions, they must maintain fidelity to the basic liturgy of the Mass.

The point here is not to determine which way is right and which way is wrong. It is to point out that traversing the narrow crossroads means continuing to walk a very narrow path. It is very easy to step off the path and seek the path of least resistance, of adhering to a more common vision. The struggle is to allow ourselves to understand the inherent conflicts that arise at the crossroads without allowing them to push us off the path or kill our faith and spiritual passion. The struggle is to maintain a balance between the need to adhere to a tradition and the need to explore God in the way God is calling us to do.

Embracing the Narrow Crossroads

As stated earlier, all of us encounter a crossroads along our narrow paths, which forces us to choose which way we are going to seek God. Will it be intellectual, sensed, or intuitive (which is the integration of the two)? Will we seek the immanent God embodied in the world, or the transcendent God by emptying and purging ourselves? Each approach is valid as long as it is kept in perspective. Many Christians would like to seek an ideal of perfect balance between all of them, but that is not possible. Why? Because to try to maintain a perfect balance between all of them means to mine deeply the gold of none of them. The problem is that each approach has its own power and spiritual depth. For example, as one steeped in the Presbyterian tradition, I have experienced the deep spiritual power of discovering God through the powers of my intellect and Scripture. I know many Episcopalians who have been deeply formed by the power of religious symbols and sacraments that are so central to their tradition. I have met contemplative Roman Catholics and Quakers who have a deep, intuitive sense of God that comes through letting go of intellect and senses.

What we need to do is appreciate the importance of our own paths and traditions, yet also appreciate how they can be enhanced by our exposure to other

Christian paths. We should appreciate the fact that while our own particular paths can nourish us through deep experiences of God, they are also fraught with flaws. Each path provides spiritual nourishment, but at the same time each also contains many empty calories. When we eat exclusively at the table of one path, we cannot tell what is meat and what is fat. We take in both indiscriminately. Exposure to other Christian paths helps us see our own more clearly. The answer, then, is not to be a universalist, eating little nibbles from each path. If we refuse to eat mainly from our own path, we end up starving because we do not receive enough deep spiritual nourishment that comes from the depths of our own traditions. It is like eating only the crust of a pot pie. The true nourishment lies deep within.

The real problem is that no matter how nourishing our own traditions are, they can be lacking in vital, spiritual nutrients. There are times when we need to supplement the nourishment of our own traditions by sampling the flavors and nourishment of others. Too many Christians fear this. They think that by sampling other paths and traditions, they are invalidating their own. So, they turn their own traditions into false idols. To maintain the integrity of their insulated cocoons, they criticize other approaches, saying that somehow they are invalid, naive, or misguided. For example, some Christians would say that God can be found only in Scripture, and that any other experience of God is invalid. Therefore, these Christians may be deeply critical and suspicious of meditation. They may be critical of Christians who are more sacramental or liturgical in their focus. They cannot see the validity of any other approach, and so they criticize what they don't understand and haven't experienced.

Other Christians assert over and over that a contemplative approach is the best approach to God. Many people who have been trained in spiritual direction, which I have also been trained in, are guilty of this. We believe that the main way to discover God's voice is through silence and contemplation. We can be deeply critical of Christians who are attracted to theology and an intellectual understanding of God. We tend to push the idea that intellectualizations lead nowhere, and that we need to steep ourselves in experience only.

At the same time, there are charismatic and pentecostal Christians who claim that the only valid experience of God comes when we exhibit the gifts of the Holy Spirit, such as speaking in tongues or prophesying. They say that we cannot truly experience God unless we have been saved, and the only evidence of salvation is these outward manifestations of the Holy Spirit.

Again, the problem with all of these and so many more is that they have become competitive in their approach. Their competition arises out of fear—fear that those following other approaches are somehow right. So, they mask their fear by making their way of seeking God the only valid one, while denigrating and dismissing all others. We need to immerse ourselves in our traditions and approaches while recognizing that they may be filled with flaws. We do this by being open to other traditions while maintaining fidelity to our own.

By immersing ourselves in our own traditions while allowing for the incorporation of other practices, we allow ourselves to be more deeply nourished by our tradition. The more we practice our own approach, while also practicing elements of other approaches, the more we discover what is meat and what is fat in our tradition. For example, an intellectually oriented Christian who tends to seek God mostly in Scripture and theology can gain a wonderful sense of perspective by practicing contemplative prayer. She can discover God who lies beyond words, intellects, and concepts, and this deepens her understanding of God in words, intellects, and concepts. It allows her to sharpen her intellectual focus by understanding and appreciating on an intuitive level the mystery of God. A Christian who seeks God mainly through the senses may discover through intellectual, theological study how his senses may have fooled him and actually led him away from God.

The point of all this is that as we encounter the narrow crossroads, we must choose a path but at the same time be open to future exploration of other paths. We need to embrace the depth of the narrow crossroads.

As a pastor, I have come to appreciate this very much in our congregation. The church I serve is a Presbyterian congregation that is made up of approximately 15 to 20 percent lifelong Presbyterians. By my approximation, the rest of the congregation is made up of 25 percent former Roman Catholics, 20 percent former Methodists, 20 percent former Lutherans, with the rest coming from other Christian sects or no tradition at all. The result is that while we are rooted in a Presbyterian structure, we have a wonderful freedom to explore other ways of doing things. We share in the sacrament of Communion in a variety of ways, borrowing from different denominations. We use a variety of music, from classical to gospel to contemporary Christian. We fill our sanctuary with banners and symbols. My own preaching and praying style is a synthesis of traditional Presbyterian style mixed with a combination of evangelical and pentecostal styles. Although I am clear that my own path has primarily been the mindful path, I have become very comfortable with exploring God by exploring the passionate, emptying, and purging paths. So has the congregation I serve.

Ultimately, it is by embracing these narrow crossroads that we truly discover God's depth and breadth. We will never come to know, feel, or experience God completely, but we can chip away at the mystery of God to deepen and broaden our experience of God.

Having Coffee at the Narrow Crossroads Diner

I remember an episode of the television show *The Twilight Zone* that provided a wonderful metaphor for all I have been speaking about. In it, a delivery man is given a package to deliver to a particular town. Eventually, he comes to a crossroads that isn't on any map that he's been given. He pauses for a while, and decides to take the road on his right. Soon he ends up in a small town. Completely lost, he stops in a noisy diner, hoping that someone can help him. He sits down at the counter and asks the waiter for directions. The waiter responds by saying something along the lines of "Don't worry. Just sit here and have a cup of coffee. Everything will be all right." The delivery man gets agitated. "I can't stay for coffee. I have to make this delivery. Just give me directions." The waiter says, "Relax. You have time for coffee. You have all the time in the world. Just enjoy yourself."

Frustrated, the delivery man walks out of the diner and decides to find his own way to his destination. He drives out of town the opposite way he came in. Eventually, he finds himself at the same crossroads. "How did I get here?" he asks himself. "No matter, I'll just take the other road." Soon, he finds himself in the little town again. He goes back into the diner. "Hey buddy, how do I get out of here?" he asks the waiter. "Like I told you before, just sit, relax, and have a cup of coffee. It's good coffee. You have all the time in the world." "Arghhhhhhh!" thinks the man. He storms out and decides to try again. He takes another way out of town and finds himself back at the crossroads. Exasperated, he decides to return home the way he originally came in on the crossroads. Backtracking, he eventually finds himself back in the small town. Determined to get away from the town, he goes off again, and once again he finds himself back in the little town. No matter how hard or how many times he tries, he cannot escape the town.

Finally he goes back into the diner and sits down at the counter, saying to the waiter, "No matter what I do, I can't seem to find my way out of this town." The waiter responds by saying, "That's what I've been trying to tell you. Look around you. All of us have come here the same way. There is no way out. What we've found is that the only thing to do is to sit back, enjoy the coffee, and make friends."

There's a lesson here for us. The lesson isn't that the path to God is a trap, leaving us in a small town that we can't escape. The message is that over time we discover that all of these different paths lead to God, but ultimately the way we must take involves letting go of our need to know which way is right and which way is wrong. The way involves relaxing, enjoying the company of others who walk the paths with us, and simply trusting that God will take care of us whichever way we choose. As long as the way we choose is a positive spiritual path to God, we are on the right path. Exploring all the roads of the narrow crossroads only solidifies our ability to live in openness and peace in God's kingdom.

Questions for Reflection

1. What are some of the different approaches to faith that you have tried or have been attracted to? How were they different from others?
2. To what extent have you been open to learning from the wisdom of other Christian paths to God? To what extent have you been closed?
3. How do you typically seek and approach God according to the four paths offered in this chapter?
4. Reflect on the different paths and what makes you uncomfortable with each.
5. What can you do to explore and learn from other paths?

Key Learnings

- Walking the narrow path requires that we immerse ourselves in our own religious and denominational traditions, while simultaneously exposing them to the light of other traditions.
- Walking the narrow path entails making a commitment to a particular path, yet also having a willingness to explore other paths.
- The mindful, passionate, emptying, and purging paths can all lead us to experience God, but when we bring them together we discover God more fully.

Appendix A

An Introduction to Spiritual Reading

Whether you sense it or not, God is continually calling you to deepen your faith. Through the Holy Spirit, God constantly nudges you to open your heart to God's wisdom, love, and grace. In addition, God is constantly talking to you and telling you how you can live a deeper and better life. Unfortunately, life is so noisy that it is hard to distinguish God's voice from everything else. The practice of spiritual reading will help you discern God's voice more fully in your life.

Reading Spiritually

I invite you to engage in the discipline of spiritual reading while you read this book. Spiritual reading means making your reading part of your prayer life. Instead of reading each chapter quickly so that you can get what it says in a hurry, spiritual reading entails reading slowly, reflectively, and prayerfully. This helps you discover God's voice in the readings. Thus, it requires taking your time and listening carefully.

This is a disciplined approach that allows God's Spirit to form you through the reading. The following will help you get everything you can out of the reading. Please practice the following and turn it into a prayer discipline:

1. Set aside a certain time, in a quiet place free of distractions, at least three times a week for prayer and reading (usually twenty to thirty minutes), but more often if you can.
2. Begin by centering yourself in a minute or two of silence. To help you center, pray silently "Bless the Lord" as you inhale and "O my soul" as you exhale.
3. Ask God to guide you.

4. Read slowly, ready to grapple with the reading.
5. Take time to pause, reflect, and pray about what you've read.
6. If you don't understand or disagree with something, ask God to help you understand.
7. Take time afterward to write in a journal what you have grappled with, learned, or discovered.
8. Offer your concerns to God in prayer, close in silence, and thank God for guiding you.

A Discipline of Spiritual Reading

The following are other tips to help you grow spiritually through your readings:

1. *Read humbly.* Be open to what God has to say by putting aside your ego, biases, and expectations. Try to listen for what God is telling you instead of focusing on whether you agree or disagree with the author. Remember that we often resist at first the truths that God wants to reveal to us.
2. *Read and reread.* Spiritual reading often involves rereading, dwelling, reflecting, and praying so that we can discover deeper messages. Be willing to prayerfully keep going over the same material.
3. *Stress quality instead of quantity.* Don't read the material just to "get it done," but instead try to dwell on it so as to discover what it says for your life. Also, don't try to read too many pages at one sitting. Read enough to discover what God may have to teach you. If you read too much, you may not integrate everything you have read.
4. *Read spiritually.* When we read intellectually, we can become overly critical or analytical. When we read emotionally, we often accept only those ideas that "feel right." Be open intellectually, emotionally, but especially spiritually so that God can speak to your heart.
5. *Be patient and trusting.* Stay with the material even if you don't get any great ideas or insights. Trust that God is speaking through the words you are reading. Sometimes God speaks in very subtle ways. Patience gives subtle messages space to grow.
6. *Wait upon God to disclose God's mysteries.* God always works and speaks in mysterious ways because God inhabits the realm of the eternal. God is more patient and gentle than we are.
7. *Keep a journal.* The Spirit speaks to you once through your readings and again through your reflections.

May God's blessings be with you.

A Guide for Use in Small Groups

*T*he following is a guide to help you in the formation of a small group or adult education class. This guide should help you use this book in community as together you seek God's way:

- When forming a small group, you may get some interest by publicizing it in bulletins and newsletters, but the best way to form the group is by invitation. Think about who you know is spiritually hungry, who wants to deepen their faith, and who might benefit from a group, and then invite them to be a part of the group.
- Limit the size of the group to six to ten members. Anything larger makes personal sharing difficult, while anything smaller can be uncomfortable for those who are slow to share.
- For a class, the size can be a bit larger, but it is incumbent on the leader to ensure that everyone has an opportunity to share in the discussion. Also, the leader should respect the right of those who want to listen and not speak; do not force anyone to speak. Encourage members to be punctual so that you have as much time as possible for sharing and discussion.
- Limit the time of the group to ninety minutes. Anything longer can cause members to feel trapped; anything shorter may inhibit a full exploration of the material. Try to end on time as much as possible.
- Consider having the members sign a covenant of commitment at the end of the first session or beginning of the second session. This is a covenant that heightens the sense of relationship among the members, while also strengthening the level of commitment to and participation in the group. The more the group is expected to make a commitment, the more likely members are to form a cohesive group. The following is a sample covenant, which you may photocopy if you wish, or the members can sign the one in their books:

A Covenant of Commitment

A covenant is an agreement between people establishing a commitment between them. When we enter into a covenant like this one, we are making a commitment to God to do our best to serve God by following through with our part of the covenant. We trust that if we remain faithful to our part, God will be faithful to us and bless what we are doing. In the case of forming a group to spiritually read and discuss *Discovering the Narrow Path*, we are agreeing to make a commitment to do our reading, praying, and discussing in a way that will help us grow in Christ and live as the Spirit leads us to live.

As for me, I am establishing my covenant
with you and your descendants after you. . . .
This is the sign of the covenant that I make
between me and you and every living creature that is with you,
for all future generations:
I have set my bow in the clouds,
and it shall be a sign of the covenant between me and the earth.
—Genesis 9:12–13

• *I agree to be part of this spiritual reading group for the eight weeks it will take to read and discuss the book.*

• *I agree to do my best to read the book spiritually and reflectively, and to do so in a way that is balanced and intended to deepen my faith and relationship with Christ.*

• *I agree to make this a priority for my life, and to do my best to put aside all other commitments when they are in conflict with my commitment to this group. I also understand that I must be balanced in this, not neglecting my family, friends, or personal life for the sake of this reading group.*

• *I agree to participate in the group by offering the insights, struggles, and questions that have arisen in my spiritual reading and prayer.*

• *I agree to listen to others in a loving, accepting, and nonjudgmental way that seeks what God is saying to them, not what I necessarily think is "right."*

• *I agree to pray for the other members of this spiritual reading group and for my church on a regular basis.*

• *I agree to be honest with others; keep matters within this group confidential; affirm others and the church; and refrain from criticizing others, including members of the church and this group.*

Signed _____

Date _____

The following is a study guide for group leaders to use. I hope that it helps your group to discover God's grace and guidance.

Chapter 1: Discovering the Narrow Path

- Place an unlit candle in the middle of the room. Invite the members of the group to take time in silence to let go of their schedules, anxieties, and concerns so that they can receive God's light. Have a member of the group light the candle, and rest in silence for thirty seconds to a minute. The leader can end the time by saying, "Amen."
- Have all the members read the following prayer together:

Holy and eternal God, you call us to walk a narrow path—the path ordained by the Creator, revealed by Jesus Christ, and guided by the Holy Spirit—but we are afraid. It is so much easier to walk the paths set by those with loud voices, strong convictions, charismatic person-alities, and black-and-white answers. But their paths lead us away from you. The path you call us to walk is the path of faith and surrender that leads through valleys, swamps, bogs, mists, meadows, and forests. These are paths that reveal your depth and beauty, but they also require commitment, sacrifice, and trust. These paths lead to you, but they are confusing because they lack clarity and certainty. We want so much to walk paths that are clear-cut, straight, and certain—paths that we can clearly walk without ever having to ask you to show us the way. So, we gravitate toward these easier paths and walk away from you. Help us to form the courage to be companions with you along the narrow path. Help us to follow where you call. In Christ's name we pray. Amen.

- Go around the room and ask all members to share their overall impres-sion of the chapter and how it may or may not have touched them.
- Take time to discuss the following questions:

    1. What denomination or faith tradition did you grow up in, and how did it seem different from others?
    2. Each of us tends to believe that finding God depends upon walking a certain path. What have you believed is the "right" path in the past?
    3. What paths are we taught by our culture to trust in instead of the paths God sets for us?
    4. What gets in the way of our trusting God and making a commitment to follow God's path for us?
    5. What commitments, decisions, and plans do we have to make to let God be more in control of our lives as we walk God's path?
    6. What are the extremes of life—secular or religious—that you con-stantly face, and how can you resist them in order to walk God's path?

7. What is the narrow path you believe God is calling you to walk, and what can you do to walk it?

- Close in a "circle prayer." Clasp hands and form a circle. Have the leader begin by saying a prayer. When finished, she or he squeezes the hand of the next person. If that person wants to say a prayer, she or he does so. If not, this person squeezes the hand of the next in line. Continue this until it comes back to the leader. The leader can close by inviting all to share in saying the Lord's Prayer together.

Chapter 2: Walking the Mystical Path

- Light the candle placed in the middle of the room. Bring a portable audiocassette or CD player, along with an audiotape or CD of relaxing, meditative music. Do not use music that has sung words. Instead, make sure that the music is simple, easy to listen to the first time, and relaxing for the members. Talk to the members about how God not only speaks through words, but also through music. Ask them to sit in silence and to just give themselves over to the music. When the music is finished, let the members sit in silence for five to ten seconds, and then say, "Amen."
- Read the following prayer together:

Holy God, you call us to walk the mystical path—the path of falling deeply in love with you—but we struggle so much with this path. The truth is that we believe in you, worship you, try to be obedient to you, and we may even like you, but loving you can be hard for us. It is hard for us to love One whom we don't know very well, but we don't know you well because we do so little to get to know you. We are reluctant to pray, surrender ourselves to you, live in the present moment, and humbly give ourselves to you. And so we give ourselves few opportunities to discover how wonderful you are. Help us to fall in love with you so that we can discover how incredible you are, and how much you want to love and cherish us. In Christ's name we pray. Amen.

- Go around the room and ask all members to share their overall impression of the chapter and how it may or may not have touched them.
- Take time to discuss the following questions:

  1. Who are some of the mystics you have met in real life, and who have inspired and guided you along your faith journey?
  2. What do you think is at the center of the gospel, the words of Luke 10:27 or something else?
  3. Share with one another the passages of Scripture you cherish, and discuss how they can be practically applied and embodied in daily life.
  4. What are the particular mission fields in which you serve God daily?

5. How do we begin to love God above all else?
6. How do we become more humble in our daily walk with God?
7. How do we pragmatically become more detached spiritually?
8. What gets in the way of surrendering our lives to God, and how do we actually surrender ourselves?
9. How can you live more fully in the present moment?
10. What gets in the way of our spending time in solitude?

- Close in a circle prayer.

Chapter 3: Walking the Balanced Path

- Light the candle in the middle of the room. Invite the members of the group to sit in silence. Ask them to let go of their burdens, anxieties, and pressures to rest in Christ. Have them sit with their legs uncrossed and their hands in their laps. As they breathe in, have them silently think with their indrawn breath, "Bless the Lord," and with their outward breath, "O my soul." Suggest that when they get distracted, they should gently let go of their distractions and to return to saying with their breath, "Bless the Lord, O my soul." Do this for about two minutes. The leader can end the time by saying, "Amen."
- Have all the members read the following prayer together:

O God of all life, you call us to live lives of balance centered in you. Yet we live lives of imbalance that are centered in everything but you. Sometimes we are centered in the demanding voices of work, family, and friends. Other times we are centered in the shouting cries of the marketplace, calling on us to make false idols of acquisition and possessions. Still other times we are centered in our own selfish desires and needs, as we become oblivious to the crying needs of life around us. Help us to become people centered in you so that we can discover the life of balance and love you call on us to live. In Christ's name we pray. Amen.

- Take one to two minutes in silent prayer to share with God your sufferings, and ask God to turn them into joy.
- Go around the room and ask all members to share their overall impression of the chapter and how it may or may not have touched them.
- Take time to discuss the following questions:

1. What factors, both inner and outer, contribute to our stress and imbalance?
2. How do we begin to place God at our fulcrums?
3. What does looking at the balance in Jesus' life say to you about how to live your life?

4. What dimensions of the human life are the strongest in you, and how is this evident?
5. How have you experienced imbalance and dissonance between the different dimensions of your life?
6. What can we do to rebalance our lives?

- Close in a circle prayer.

Chapter 4: Walking the Trinitarian Path

- Light the candle in the middle of the room. Invite the members to take time to offer themselves to each person of the Trinity. Ask them also to take time with each person of the Trinity to ask how they can become more open to that person of the Trinity. Take approximately two minutes of silence for this.
- Have all the members read the following prayer together:

Holy God of Purpose, Presence, and Power, I confess that I have not always been open to you as you truly are. I have constantly tried to create you in my own image instead of forming a relationship with you as Creator, Son, and Holy Spirit. At times I have been too self-focused to seek your purpose and will for me. At other times I have been too afraid of you to seek your presence in my life. I also have been too doubting to believe that your power could actually flow into my life. So, I have minimized you in my life. Help me to form a relationship with you as you are in each person of the Trinity. Help me to know you, but more important to love you as Creator, Son, and Holy Spirit. In Christ's name we pray. Amen.

- Go around the room and ask all members to share their overall impression of the chapter and how it may or may not have touched them.
- Take time to discuss the following questions:

1. To what extent has belief in the Trinity been central to your faith?
2. To what extent has the Trinity confused you?
3. How comfortable are you with God the Creator/Father/Mother? With God in Jesus Christ? With God the Holy Spirit?
4. To what extent are you christocentric in your faith, and to what extent have you been christoencapsulated?
5. Discuss the different churches and people you know. How have they gravitated toward God the Creator, God the Son, or God the Holy Spirit?
6. How have you experienced God's purpose for you and the world, and how have you responded to live according to God's purpose?

7. How have you experienced God as a presence in your life?
8. How have you been inspired by and experienced God's power in your life?
9. How is your own denomination or church split in its understanding and experiences of the Trinity?

- Close in a circle prayer.

Chapter 5: Walking the Healing Path

- Light the candle in the middle of the room. Invite the members to take time in silent prayer to focus on the things that they want to be healed in their lives, and have them ask God specifically to heal them. Take approximately two minutes of silence for this.
- Have all the members read the following prayer together:

Eternal God, we have so many questions and doubts. We are so skeptical and distrusting. Despite the fact that Jesus came to heal, and through the Holy Spirit you offer the gift of healing to us today, still we are unsure. We lack the faith to pray for healing, and then to believe that you can and will heal. We also lack the wisdom to see how you heal. Help us to form a healing faith so that we not only can be open to your healing in our lives, but so that we can become healing presences to others. In Christ's name we pray. Amen.

- Go around the room and ask all members to share their overall impression of the chapter and how it may or may not have touched them.
- Take time to discuss the following questions:

1. Before you read the chapter, what were your thoughts and beliefs about the connection between faith and healing?
2. To what extent are you skeptical, and to what extent do you believe in God's ability to heal through prayer and faith?
3. Has your previous understanding of salvation included healing? How does the connection between healing and salvation change your understanding of what it means to be saved?
4. Discuss the different kinds of healing that members of the group have had, and how God may have been involved.
5. How have you seen the connection between personal healing and involvement in a church or religious community?
6. What do you think is the connection between abandonment to God and healing?
7. What can we do to become more open to God's healing, holiness, and wholeness?

- Close in a circle prayer.

Chapter 6: Walking the Servant Path

- Light the candle in the middle of the room. Ask the members to center themselves in prayer, and then offer a time of thanks. Ask the members of the group to reflect on how they serve God in their own way. Remind them that no form of service is too small or unimportant to God. Then, while remaining in prayer, ask them to offer thanks out loud to God for allowing them to serve in their own ministries. For instance, they may offer thanks such as "Thank you, God, for allowing me to serve as a mother to my children. Thank you, God, for allowing me to serve you as a friend to others. Thank you, God, for allowing me to serve you in helping others laugh."
- Have all the members read the following prayer together:

Holy God, you have called us to be your humble servants, but it is so hard for us to respond. We get so busy, distracted, and focused on other things that we forget to serve you throughout our lives. We forget that we can serve you in whatever we do, as long as we seek your purpose and dedicate what we do to you. We also forget to make you a partner in our service, thinking that we are responsible for everything, including the results. Help us to be people of your call, responding to you in faith, hope, and love so that we can spread your grace and kingdom throughout the world. In Christ's name we pray. Amen.

- Go around the room and ask all members to share their overall impression of the chapter and how it may or may not have touched them.
- Take time to discuss the following questions:

  1. What conflicts lie between the call of Matthew 25 ("When I was hungry . . .") and the way you live your lives?
  2. What was your reaction to the story of George Müller? What causes you to be skeptical? What leads you to believe?
  3. How can you apply the four lessons of Müller's life—surrender, listening, acting, and trusting—to your life?
  4. What gets in the way of our defining our call?
  5. Discuss your own personal callings, and how you respond to them. How can you tell what your callings are?
  6. Discuss the role that the questions of congeniality with our calling, compassion, compatibility, and competence have when it comes to serving God.
  7. How has fear made it difficult to follow our calling in faith?
  8. How do we walk the servant path in the midst of the hot-button issues that constantly arise in modern Christianity and culture?

- Close in a circle prayer.

Chapter 7: Walking the Integrated Path

- Light the candle in the middle of the room. Invite the members to take time to offer a personal and silent prayer to God in which they reflect on ways they try to save their own lives instead of letting God in their lives. Ask them to give these attempts at personal salvation over to God. Take approximately two minutes of silence for this.
- Have all the members read the following prayer together:

Gracious God, we want so much to take the easy way to you, yet the truth is that there is no easy way to you; for the way to you requires an integration of understanding, relationship, and deed. It requires that we be steeped in the teachings of Christ, the traditions and community of faith, and a loving relationship with you and others. It is hard to keep these in balance. Too often we would rather focus only on your teachings, on traditions, or on love. Help us to be integrated people who follow wherever you lead. In Christ's name we pray. Amen.

- Go around the room and ask all members to share their overall impression of the chapter and how it may or may not have touched them.
- Take time to discuss the following questions:
  1. Which aspect of faith do the members of the group feel most attracted to: theology, religion, or spirituality?
  2. Which aspect of the Christian life do they feel most uncomfortable with: theology, religion, or spirituality? Why?
  3. To what extent is your own church or denomination dominated by interest in intellectual theology, religious expression, or spiritual experience?
  4. Talk about what you think the perfect church would be like, and discuss the extent to which that church would keep theology, religion, and spirituality in balance.
  5. How can we keep theology, spirituality, and religion balanced in our own churches?
  6. To what extent have you grounded your life in prayer and devotion to God?
  7. To what extent do you seek answers to life's questions?
  8. To what extent have you made a commitment to God in all of your life?
  9. To what extent have you grounded your devotion, seeking, and commitment in a community of Christ?

- Close in a circle prayer.

Chapter 8: Standing at the Narrow Crossroads

- Light the candle in the middle of the room. Invite the members to take time to offer a personal and silent reflection on the paths that God may be calling them to walk, and to make a commitment to God to walk this path wherever it leads. Take approximately two minutes of silence for this.
- Have all the members read the following prayer together:

O Holy Creator, Christ, and Holy Spirit, there are so many potential paths before us, and we get so confused. Which way should we walk? Which one is right? Help us to have the faith and conviction to remain faithful to the paths we have been walking, while also having the wisdom to recognize new paths and the courage to explore them. The uncertainty of your call and path can paralyze us in fear and confusion. Help us to rely on you to lead us in your way. In Christ's name we pray. Amen.

- Go around the room and ask all members to share their overall impression of the chapter and how it may or may not have touched them.
- Take time to discuss the following questions:
  1. Discuss the different spiritual paths to God that you have experienced over the years.
  2. What have been some of the biggest arguments over the years regarding the right approach or beliefs about God and faith?
  3. How have you been encouraged or discouraged from exploring different Christian paths to God?
  4. To what extent are you comfortable walking the mindful path?
  5. How comfortable are you with walking the passionate path? What gets in the way?
  6. How comfortable are you with the emptying path—with stillness, solitude, and silence? What gets in the way?
  7. How comfortable are you with the purging path? What keeps you from exploring this path?
  8. What can you do, as a group or individually, to begin exploring other paths while remaining faithful to your own?

- Close in a circle prayer.

Notes

INTRODUCTION

1. Jeremy Rifkin, Commentary for *All Things Considered,* National Public Radio, July 14, 2000.

CHAPTER 1: DISCOVERING THE NARROW PATH

1. Edward Lohse, *The New Testament Environments*, trans. John E. Steely (Nashville: Abingdon Press, 1988), 74–77.

2. Ibid., 77–83.

3. Hannah Hurnard, *Hinds' Feet on High Places* (Wheaton, Ill: Living Books, 1975), 82.

4. Henry T. Blackaby and Claude V. King, *Experiencing God* (Nashville: Broadman and Holman Publishers, 1994), 50.

5. Robert Lane, *The Loss of Happiness in Market Democracies* (New Haven, Conn.: Yale University Press, 2000).

6. Soren Kierkegaard, "Concluding Unscientific Postscript to the 'Philosophical Fragments,'" *A Kierkegaard Anthology*, ed. Robert Bretall (Princeton, N.J.: Princeton University Press, 1946), 215.

CHAPTER 2: WALKING THE MYSTICAL PATH

1. Evelyn Underhill, *Life as Prayer and Other Writings of Evelyn Underhill,* ed. Lucy Menzies (Harrisburg, Pa.: Morehouse Publishing, 1991), 107.

2. Ibid., 109.

3. Catherine of Genoa, *Purgation and Purgatory, the Spiritual Dialogue,* trans. Serge Hughes (Ramsey, N.J.: Paulist Press, 1979), 1–43.

4. Athanasius, *The Life of Antony and the Letter to Marcellinus,* trans. Robert C. Gregg (Ramsey, N.J.: Paulist Press, 1980).

5. Catherine de Hueck Doherty, "Preface" for Catherine of Genoa, *Purgation and Purgatory,* xiii.

6. N. Graham Standish, *Forming Faith in a Hurricane* (Nashville: Upper Room Books, 1998), 47–63.

7. Thomas R. Kelly, *A Testament of Devotion* (San Francisco: HarperCollins, 1996), 35.

8. Anthony de Mello, *The Song of the Bird* (New York: Image Books, 1984), 94.

9. Thomas Merton, *New Seeds of Contemplation* (New York: New Directions Books, 1961), 203.

10. Jean-Pierre de Caussade, *The Sacrament of the Present Moment*, trans. Kitty Muggeridge (San Francisco: HarperSanFrancisco, 1982), 10.

11. C. S. Lewis, *The Screwtape Letters* (New York: Simon and Schuster, 1996), 61.

12. Thomas Merton, *Thoughts in Solitude* (New York: Farrar, Straus and Giroux, 1958), 85–86.

13. Dallas Willard, *The Divine Conspiracy* (San Francisco: HarperSanFrancisco, 2000), 61–62.

CHAPTER 3: WALKING THE BALANCED PATH

1. Sandra McElwaine, "Millard Fuller, the Millionaire and His Mission," in *Biography Magazine* (July 1998): 38–41, 114.

2. Ibid., 114.

3. Thomas Kelly, *A Testament of Devotion*, 90–91.

4. The material from this section is adapted from the work of Adrian van Kaam, yet rearticulated in the more common "spirit, mind, and body" language used by our culture. For more information on van Kaam's work, please see Adrian van Kaam, *Fundamental Formation: Formative Spirituality, Vol. I* (New York: Crossroad Publishing, 1989). For a shorter summary of these dimensions, please see N. Graham Standish, *Paradoxes for Living: Cultivating Faith in Confusing Times* (Louisville, Ky.: Westminster John Knox Press, 2001), 28–32.

CHAPTER 4: WALKING THE TRINITARIAN PATH

1. Catherine Mowry Lacugna, *God for Us: The Trinity and Christian Life* (San Francisco: HarperSanFrancisco, 1992), 31.

2. Jerry L. Van Marter, "PC(USA) Membership Decline Worsened in 1999" in *News Briefs: Presbyterian Church (U.S.A.)* (Louisville, Ky.: The Presbyterian Church [U.S.A.], May 19, 2000), 5–6.

3. Zeb Bradford Long and Douglas McMurry, *Receiving the Power: Preparing the Way for the Holy Spirit* (Grand Rapids, Mich.: Chosen Books, 1996), 117.

4. Harvey Cox, *Fire from Heaven: The Rise of Pentecostal Spirituality and the Reshaping of Religion in the Twenty-First Century* (Reading, Mass.: Addison-Wesley Publishing Co., 1995), 124.

5. Kenneth L. Woodward, "The Changing Face of the Church," *Newsweek* (April 16, 2001): 49.

6. Thomas Kelly, *A Testament of Devotion*, 3.

7. Zeb Bradford Long and Douglas McMurry, *Receiving the Power*, 100.

8. Frank Laubach and Brother Lawrence, *Practicing His Presence* (Sargent, Ga.: The SeedSowers, 1973), 5.

9. Henry Blackaby and Claude V. King, *Experiencing God*, 71.

CHAPTER 5: WALKING THE HEALING PATH

1. Rita Klaus, *Rita's Story* (Orleans, Mass.: Paraclete Press, 1993).

2. Ibid., 287–299.

3. Ibid., 291.

4. Ibid.

5. Ibid., 194.

6. Ibid., 303.

7. Agnes Sanford, *The Healing Light* (New York: Ballantine Books, 1983), 3.

8. John Wilkinson, *The Bible and Healing: A Medical and Theological Commentary* (Grand Rapids, Mich.: Wm. B. Eerdmans Publishing Co., 1998), 65.

9. Donald Gowan, "Salvation as Healing," in *Ex Auditu: An International Journal of Theological Interpretation of Scripture, vol. 5, 1989* (Allison Park, Penn.: Pickwick Publications, 1990), 1–19.

10. David B. Larson, Dale A. Matthews, and Constance P. Barry, *The Faith Factor: An Annotated Bibliography of Clinical Research on Spiritual Subjects,* vol. 1 (Rockville, Md.: National Institute for Healthcare Research, 1993).

11. N. Graham Standish, *Forming Faith in a Hurricane,* chapter 1.

12. Agnes Sanford, *The Healing Light*, 14.

13. Ibid., 4.

14. Francis MacNutt, *Healing* (Notre Dame, Ind.: Ave Maria Press, 1974), 196–97.

15. Ibid., 200.

16. Agnes Sanford, *The Healing Light*, 27–28.

17. Francis MacNutt, *Healing*, 123.

CHAPTER 6: WALKING THE SERVANT PATH

1. Roger Steer, *George Müller: Delighted in God!* (Wheaton, Ill.: Harold Shaw Publishers, 1981).

2. Ibid., 18.

3. Ibid., 19.

4. Ibid., 65.

5. Dallas Willard, *The Divine Conspiracy*, 61–62.

6. Adrian van Kaam and Susan A. Muto, *Formation Guide for Becoming Spiritually Mature* (Pittsburgh, Pa.: Epiphany Association, 1991), 89–91.

7. Louis Fischer, *The Life of Mahatma Gandhi* (New York: Harper & Row, 1983), 77.

8. Frank Laubach, *Practicing His Presence*, 5.

9. Henry Blackaby and Claude V. King, *Experiencing God*, 25.

10. Marc Gunther, "God and Business," in *Fortune* (July 9, 2001): 64.

11. N. Graham Standish, *Paradoxes for Living* (Louisville, Ky.: Westminster John Knox Press, 2001), 4.

CHAPTER 7: WALKING THE INTEGRATED PATH

1. Dorotheos of Gaza, *Discourses and Sayings*, trans. Eric P. Wheeler (Kalamazoo, Mich.: Cistercian Publications), 98.

2. For a more thorough discussion of science and how it applies to all fields of inquiry, including religion, please see Donald Polkinghorne, *Methodology for the Human Sciences: Systems of Inquiry* (Albany, N.Y.: State University of New York Press, 1983).

3. Evelyn Underhill, *Life as Prayer and Other Writings of Evelyn Underhill,* 109.

4. Thomas à Kempis, *The Imitation of Christ*, 30.

5. Ibid., 44.

6. Heinrich Arnold, *Discipleship: Living for Christ in the Daily Grind* (Farmington, Pa.: Plough Publishing House, 1994), 76.

CHAPTER 8: STANDING AT THE NARROW CROSSROADS

1. Julian of Norwich, *Showings,* trans. Edmund Colledge and James Walsh (Ramsey, N.J.: Paulist Press, 1978), 179–81.

2. *The Wizard of Oz* screenplay (New York: Smithmark Publishers, Inc., 1993), 64–65.

3. This schematic is inspired by and adapted from Urban Holmes's "Phenomenology of Prayer," in his book *A History of Christian Spirituality: An Analytical Introduction* (San Francisco: Harper & Row, 1980). It is not a straight, one-to-one adaptation, but instead has been built on Holmes's concept in order to explore different ways of seeking God. In Urban Holmes's work, the four poles have to do with styles of prayer and spirituality: the speculative, affective, kataphatic, and apophatic.

4. John Calvin, *The Institutes of Religion*, ed. Tony Lane and Hilary Osborne (Grand Rapids, Mich.: Baker Book House, 1987), 40.